Advanced
Integrated
RPG

Advanced
Integrated
RPG

Thomas Snyder

MC PRESS

MC Press Online, LP
Lewisville, TX 75077

To my family.

*It takes persistence and hard work to achieve our goals,
and it takes smiles and family to achieve success.
Success is achievable!*

Thank you, Cindy, Raven, Jade, Tommy, and Mia.

Acknowledgements

I am very honored to have had the opportunity to write this book. I want to thank my beautiful and talented wife Cindy and children Raven, Jade, Tommy, and Mia for believing in me and supporting me during the writing of this book. I also want to thank Cindy for creating all the amazing illustrations throughout the book. Thank You Guys! We Did It!

Along with the support of my family, I also needed to have an opportunity. Merrikay Lee and Victoria Mack at MC Press gave me this opportunity, and I am extremely appreciative! Victoria was my entry point into the online publishing world and has always inspired me and motivated me to do more. She introduced me to Merrikay, and I have gained nothing but respect for Merrikay as we worked together to present this book. I also got the privilege of working with Katie Tipton as my very talented copy editor to make this book look as good as it does.

I take great pride in the material that makes up this book. I have been given the opportunity to work on the IBM i platform in combination with open-source projects to provide the best in leading-edge technology. I want to express my thanks to all the people who believe in and have contributed to iText, POI, JavaMail, and all open-source projects. Software written by people who believe in their software, running on a platform that has been proven to provide results, with both having strong communities of innovators—these ideals make me honored to present the best of both worlds, working together.

The final ingredient is you . . . the RPG programmer, knowing that you are working on the best platform out there. The platform that is not all about the hype but provides the results. This book will show you how to enhance your existing RPG programs to provide portability and compatibility that can surpass other options. I hope you enjoy it.

Tom Snyder
December, 2009
http://www.2wolvesout.com

Contents

Introduction   **1**
Why Not Just Use Java?   2
Minimum Requirements   3
Standardization and Compliance   5
Breadth of Content   5
Naming Conventions   5
AIR Service Programs   6
Downloading the Source Code   8
Compiling the Examples   8

Chapter 1   Learning to Provide Modern Solutions   **11**
Providing Solutions to Meet Today's Industry Standards   11
Evolving Your RPG Development Skills   14
Integrating RPG with Java   15
Creating Electronic Documents   17
Distributing Electronic Documents Using E-mail   17

Chapter 2   The Integrated Language Environment   **19**
Converting Existing OPM Source Code to ILE   20
Compiling ILE Source Code into a *PGM Object   21
Modules   23
Procedures   23
Prototyping   23
Procedure Interface   25
Activation Groups   26
Service Programs   29
Putting the Concepts to Work   31
Compiler Directives   43

Chapter 3   Advanced ILE RPG   **47**
Free-Format RPG   48
Built-In Functions   56
APIs   67

Chapter 4   Introduction to Java   **77**
Java Classes   77
Java Methods   78
Java Objects   78
Java Packages   79
Import   81
Class Path   82
Static Methods   82
Main Method   83
Naming Conventions   83
Public and Private Access Control   83
Encapsulation and the JavaBeans Naming Standards   84
Inheritance and Polymorphism   88
Integrated Development Environment   100
JavaDoc   101
A Good Foundation   104

Chapter 5   Java and RPG   **105**
Determining the Current Version of Java   105
Java Invocation API   106
Accessing Java Objects from Within RPG   107
Accessing Java Methods from Within RPG   108
Java Object Constructors   109
The QSYSINC/QRPGLESRC,JNI File   110
Java Primitive Types   110
Referring to External Jar Files   111
The SVAIRJAVA Service Program   113
Installing External Jar Files on the IFS   113
Standard JVM Streams: STDIN, STDOUT, and STDERR   116
Starting and Destroying the JVM   118

JNI Service Program QJVAJNI   121
Thread-Safe RPG with THREAD(*SERIALIZE)   121
Garbage Collection   123
Hello World   126

Chapter 6   Java Native Interface   **129**
Advanced JNI   129
RPG Code Sample to Access Java Instance Variables   137
Arrays of Objects   144
Exception Handling   149
On to the Fun Stuff   153

Chapter 7   Excel Basics   **155**
Creating Excel Spreadsheets Using Apache POI   155
Installing POI   156
POI Version Compatibility   157
Common Code   158
Apache POI and Java JavaDocs   159
Constants   159
Excel Components   161
Hello World   174

Chapter 8   Excel Formatting and Properties   **177**
Fonts and Colors   178
Cell Styles   181
Font and Cell Style Constructors   183
AirExcel_setCellValue *Xxx* Revisited   188
Data Formatting   189
Date Formatting   196
Column Width and Text Wrap   199
Setting Print and Display Properties   203
Headers and Footers   207

Chapter 9   Excel Formulas and Charts   **217**
Formulas   217

The Java Iterator Class   222
Using Sheet Indexes   223
Working with Rows Within Sheets   224
Working with Cells Within Rows   226
Working with Cell Types and Values   227
Reading an Existing Spreadsheet   230
Charts, Graphs, and Images   235

Chapter 10   PDF Basics   **243**
Installing iText   243
Common Code   245
iText and Java JavaDocs   246
iText Components   246
Adding Elements to a Document   254
Saving the PDF File   254
Hello World   260
PDF Metadata   262

Chapter 11   PDF Formatting   **267**
Colors   268
Fonts   271
PDF Tables   274
Adding a New Page   279
Hyperlinks   279
Lists   286

Chapter 12   PDF Images and Bar Codes   **291**
Images with Borders   291
Images with Text Wrapping   297
Bar Codes   301

Chapter 13   Sending E-Mail   **315**
JavaMail   316
Common Code   318
JavaMail and JAF JavaDocs   319

Sending a Text E-Mail   319
Calling a Static Method Using JNI   338
MimeMessage   339

Chapter 14   JavaMail Formatting and Attachments   **345**
Sending an E-Mail with HTML Content   346
Sending an HTML E-Mail with Images in RPG   352
Sending an E-mail with Attachments   354
Sending an E-Mail with Embedded Images in Java   360
That's a Wrap   361

Appendix A   EBCDIC/ASCII/Hexadecimal Translation Table   **363**

Appendix B   Data Formats for Use with HSSFDataFormat   **367**

Appendix C   References and Resources   **369**
RPG   369
Java   370
POI   370
iText   371
JavaMail   371
Other Topics   372

Introduction

So, you are an RPG programmer and you know that your IBM i system is running solid, proven business logic written in tried-and-true programs that have been used for years with robust performance and reliability. Now, you are at a point where you want to update your reporting and distribution to support today's electronic document formats.

Over the course of this book, you will learn how to modernize your existing reporting and distribution systems by integrating RPG with Java and open source. Specifically, you'll learn how to generate Microsoft Excel spreadsheets and Adobe Portable Document Format (PDF) files to be distributed using e-mail. Along the way, you may learn a few things that enhance your RPG programming skills.

This modernization will enable your system to evolve with technology to provide industry-standard solutions using your existing software. That sounds good enough to pitch to your boss for discussion at the next budget meeting! And it should justify dedicating the time to play around with some of the examples in the book.

"Modernization" is a popular word these days in the IBM i community. When you do your initial research into possibilities, you may find yourself overwhelmed by both the number of options and the learning curves required to achieve this goal. You certainly will discover the enhancements to RPG programming syntax, including free formatting and new opcodes. You may look at these options and see that you can make your code *look* better, but this is only the first step on the road to the final goal.

Your motivation toward modernization might be driven by the demands of your users. In this case, you may be considering quick-fix solutions that are cost-prohibitive and require you to rely on third-party vendors. Or, perhaps you're looking at transitional solutions provided by IBM to extend your current capabilities to provide the required services.

When evaluating these options myself, I found that the standardization and openness of Java satisfied all my needs without imposing any dependencies on limited, specialized technologies or throwing money at exuberant costs. Of course, there is always the obstacle of the learning curve when using Java, but this book reduces that complexity for you by providing access to Java capabilities through RPG, using real-world examples that direct you to the solution.

With Java, you can also improve your collaboration efforts with other sections of your technology department by creating a better synergy between the business systems and Internet departments to share resources and greatly improve the quality of software for both groups. Organizations usually draw a distinct line between their RPG programmers and their object-oriented programmers, so this could be the first step toward "talking over the fence" to share information.

Once you start enhancing your existing RPG programs to replace a current greenbar report with an Excel spreadsheet or a PDF file and e-mail the output to users automatically, be prepared for a large demand to make these changes to the rest of your reporting system. After I introduced this change, converting greenbar reports became the main priority among my user community.

Why Not Just Use Java?

Many times while researching the information in this book, I ran into Java programmers who asked, "Why don't you just use Java?" But just because you want to implement a capability that Java has from RPG doesn't mean you want to rewrite the whole system.

Suppose you have an RPG program that is the seasoned result of years of development and has been tempered in the fires of production. Time goes by, objectives change, technologies evolve, and now you want to have your solid application provide that bottom-line report that is used by the higher executives.

Why not have your existing application provide those golden numbers to an electronic document and e-mail it, in a way that could not be outdone by any other software application on the planet and that involves no monetary investment and can be done without an extensively long project to rewrite the entire system? That is why you would not "just use Java." You would stay within budget, enhance the value of your software and staff, and provide timely results.

Minimum Requirements

This book does cover modern topics, so I need to make you aware of the minimum requirements. I have tried to make everything compatible with V5R1 of the IBM i operating system, but I am currently using V5R4, so I have relied on the documentation to determine whether features are backward-compatible. Therefore, you may or may not run across some topics that will run on releases earlier than V5R4. However, I have reviewed everything extensively, so I don't think you'll have many issues.

I'm not sure which Java Software Development Kit (SDK) was provided in versions earlier than V5R4, so you may want to check that first and order the PTF now for your version so you'll have it available once you're ready to start using it.

Requirements

As noted, I've made every attempt to support V5R1 or later, but V5R4 was the actual system used for development. You will also need:

- Java SDK 1.4.2 or later
- iText 2.1.4
- POI 3.0.2
- JavaMail 1.4.2

In addition, it is recommended that you install the System Openness Includes (**QSYSINC**) library. To do so, install licensed program 5722SS1, option 13.

Pre-V6R1 Support for Embedded SQL

In releases earlier than V6R1, nested **COPY** files are not supported in programs that use embedded SQL. So, in special cases that handle this situation, I have not included **COPY** files within **COPY** files. This concession does not fully take advantage of modular programming, but it does enable maximum reusability of the **COPY** files.

Downloading the Java Resources

When working with open-source technologies in Java, you need to download the Jar file for the project. These programs are always evolving, so I recommend that you download them right from the source. Just make sure whatever you download is compatible with the version of Java you're using.

You'll find detailed installation instructions in each relevant chapter, but here are the Web sites from which to download in case you want to get started:

iText
http://www.lowagie.com/iText

iText is a free Java PDF library by Bruno Lowagie and Paulo Soares.

POI
http://poi.apache.org

POI (which stands for Poor Obfuscation Implementation) is a Java API used to access Microsoft format files. This project was created by Andrew Oliver and was joined by Marc Johnson, Nicola Ken Barozzi, and Glen Stampoultzis. It is currently a Top Level Project within Apache.

JavaMail
http://java.sun.com/products/javamail

JavaMail is a Java API for using e-mail, provided by Sun Microsystems.

Standardization and Compliance

Throughout the book, you will see that I've made every effort to accommodate worst-case scenarios with maximum compliance and standardization. There may be times when things could be done in several different ways, but I will comply with conventions and standards beyond the capabilities of the language itself.

I believe that if you set things up in the beginning to accommodate the worst-case scenario, you can minimize the impact of changes in the future. This practice also sets a reusable standard that can be propagated throughout the development cycle, provides solid components for reuse, and sets a good example when code segments are reused.

Breadth of Content

The focus of the book is to evolve your current skill set to be able to implement the code in Chapter 5 and beyond. In the chapters leading up to that one, I will not be covering common topics that are likely known to most experienced RPG programmers. For example, when discussing the compiler directives in Chapter 2, I will cover options for embedded SQL and free-formatted text and the other options that support modular code. But I won't discuss the options to put **SPACE**s into the code or **EJECT** the page because although these features can be useful, they do not target the goal of this book. IBM's *ILE RPG Programmer's Guide* and *ILE RPG Language Reference* are good materials for more information about these topics.

Naming Conventions

I have established some standard naming conventions to be used throughout the book to help you easily identify the source of the provided functionality. Anything that is custom-built for this book will include the letters **AIR** for *Advanced Integrated RPG* — such as service program **SVAIRFUNC** or procedure **Air_openFiles**. For anything that references an open-source solution, I've tried to reuse the exact name of the Java resource. I made some exceptions to this rule for highly generic object names that would conflict with each other; these cases should be obvious to identify.

Here are the naming conventions:

- Source code references will conform to the standard naming convention used by RPG **/COPY** statements: **LIBRARY/SOURCE_FILE, SOURCE_MEMBER**.
- All source code files and libraries that are custom-built for this book will contain the letters **AIR**.
- RPG programs will *not* include an **RPG** prefix in the file name.
- CL program names will use the **CL** prefix.
- Service program names will have the **SV** prefix.
- The names of **COPY** files used for prototypes will use the **SP** prefix.
- The remaining letters of each file name will identify the functionality of the resulting module.

These naming conventions are not required if you are creating new code. They are only guidelines used within this book to help identify resources that are specific to the book. If you find references that don't follow these conventions, that would indicate that the resource is not provided by this book and most likely comes from IBM, iText, POI, or Sun Microsystems.

As you probably know, the numerous name changes to the system have not been accepted positively in the "AS/400" community. One of my biggest gripes is how frustrating the generic "i" name is whenever I try to search the Internet for information. (It's even more ridiculous than writing a book and then sharing its name with a classical element or the latest Apple technology!) Throughout the book, I will refer to the AS/400, iSeries, i5, and System i simply as "IBM i" systems.

AIR Service Programs

We'll be creating several service programs that provide focused capabilities to the programs we'll be building. Use of these service programs helps you to organize your code and makes it easy to find what you're looking for. Table I.1 lists the AIR service programs and their prototypes.

Table I.1: AIR service programs and prototypes

Service program	Prototype	Function
SVAIRFUNC	SPAIRFUNC	General
SVAIRJAVA	SPAIRJAVA	Java
SVAIREXCEL	SPAIREXCEL	Excel using POI
SVAIRPDF	SPAIRPDF	PDF files using iText
SVAIREMAIL	SPAIREMAIL	E-mail using JavaMail

- **SVAIRFUNC** — Service program **SVAIRFUNC** is the most general service program we'll create. This program will contain autonomous procedures and constants that are general enough to be used anywhere and for any purpose. **SVAIRFUNC** could potentially be bound to every single program you'll use. We'll add to its contents throughout the course of the book.

- **SVAIRJAVA** — Service program **SVAIRJAVA** is the Java service program used to provide basic Java functionality that is not tied to any particular open-source programs and can be used with the Java Virtual Machine (JVM). It will contain all the detailed capabilities needed to support Java on the lowest levels we'll deal with, such as starting and stopping the JVM and reclaiming resources. **SVAIRJAVA** is intended to be bound with any program that will use Java. We'll build it in *Chapters five and six.*

- **SVAIREXCEL** — Service program **SVAIREXCEL** is a specialized service program designed to support programs that will work with spreadsheets using the POI open-source project and Java. We'll build this service program in *Chapters seven, eight, and nine.*

- **SVAIRPDF** — Service program **SVAIRPDF** is a specialized service program designed to support programs that will work with PDF files using the iText open-source project and Java. We'll build this service program in *Chapter ten, eleven, and twelve.*

- **SVAIREMAIL** — Service program **SVAIREMAIL** is a specialized service program designed to support programs that will work with e-mail using the JavaMail open-source project and Java. We'll build this service program in *Chapters thirteen and fourteen.*

All of these service programs are custom programs that were created as resources for this book. The programs all follow the standard naming conventions established for the book, and each has an associated RPG source file that contains any related prototypes and constants that can be included into your source code with a **COPY** or **INCLUDE** statement. The names of the prototype files use the **SP** prefix instead of the **SV** prefix used for the service programs.

You can, and will, use these service programs in combination with each other to provide multiple capabilities to a single program. For example, if you had a program that you wanted to have create PDF files and e-mail them, you could bind **SVAIRFUNC** to provide the basic capabilities, bind **SVAIRJAVA** to support Java, bind **SVAIRPDF** to create the PDF files, and bind **SVAIREMAIL** to e-mail the PDF after it is created.

Downloading the Source Code

All the code used in this book is available for download from the book's page at the MC Press bookstore at *http://www.mc-store.com/5105.html*. On the book's page, click the **reviews, errata, downloads** icon to go to the book's forum.

To use the code as is, you'll want to create a library called **AIRLIB** and a source file called **AIRSRC** and then upload the source code members into **AIRLIB/AIRSRC**. Doing so will let you compile and execute the examples and use the service programs and prototypes to get started with the capabilities presented in the book. If you don't want to name your test library and source code in this manner, you'll need to change the **COPY** references in the source code to make sure you can compile it.

Compiling the Examples

When running the examples that use service programs, make sure the library in which the service programs reside is in your library list. This step is necessary so that the compiler can find the service programs during compilation. As an alternative, you could specify the library location at compile time.

Each compilable source code file will contain comments at the top of the source code member to instruct you on how to compile the program. For programs that don't require service programs, we'll use the **CRTBNDRPG** (Create Bound RPG Program) CL command. For programs that require modules to be bound to the program, we'll use a combination of the **CRTRPGMOD** (Create RPG Module) and **CRTPGM** (Create Program) commands.

Figure I.1 shows a sample of the comment code you'll normally find at the beginning of each compilable source member. The lowercase *x* characters represent variable values that will change depending on which source code member you're working with.

```
H THREAD(*SERIALIZE)
F*********************************************************************
F*   HOW TO COMPILE:
F*
F*   (1. CREATE THE MODULE)
F*   CRTRPGMOD MODULE(AIRLIB/AIRxx_xx) SRCFILE(AIRLIB/AIRSRC) +
F*             DBGVIEW(*ALL) INDENT('.')
F*
F*   (2. CREATE THE PROGRAM)
F*   CRTPGM PGM(AIRLIB/AIRxx_xx)
F*      BNDSRVPGM(SVAIRxxxxxx SVAIRxxxxx) ACTGRP(*NEW)
D*********************************************************************
D/DEFINE OS400_JVM_12
D/COPY QSYSINC/QRPGLESRC,JNI
D/COPY AIRLIB/AIRSRC,SPAIRJAVA
```

Figure I.1: Common compile comments found in the AIR RPG code

You can compile the programs any way you desire, but if you create the **AIRLIB** library and **AIRSRC** source code file and choose to use them for your testing, the steps given in the comments will successfully compile your programs.

1

Learning to Provide
Modern Solutions

Over the course of this book, you will learn to enhance your existing applications to modernize the output of the system. To do this, we'll take advantage of the modern capabilities of ILE RPG that you can incorporate into your existing code. The Integrated Language Environment (ILE) enables you to write code in a much more modular way, which means you can write code in small, reusable components that are better encapsulated and easier to maintain.

Providing Solutions to Meet Today's Industry Standards

When you look at your Original Program Model (OPM) programs and think about why these programs were developed, the goal was likely to provide comprehensive software that would withstand the test of time and produce solid, reliable results as the backbone for business-critical operations. If you were to focus solely on this aspect, you might not see the need to even bother using ILE. After all, you have a programming language that works, it has been around for a very long time, and it is easy to understand. So, let's consider some of the limitations of this way of programming and define the reasons why modernization of the code is necessary.

The first thing that comes to mind when discussing modernization is aesthetics. When you have a system that provides indisputable data that is necessary for business processes, you may consider the ability to create "modern" reports in Microsoft Excel or Adobe PDF form as being an unnecessary enhancement. After all, the data is being generated, the information is being audited, reporting is being performed, and the company is generating revenue. How important is it to make the reports look better? Well, there are other factors beyond appearance that you need to consider when evaluating the need for spreadsheets and PDF files.

Portability

Portability is a big one. To address this issue, your initial thought might be to generate ASCII text files. If you've been working with RPG for a few years, there's a good chance you've already tried this approach.

However, if you delimit the ASCII data using a special character, you must make the user aware of which delimiter you're using, and the user must process the data properly. This means you need specifications that identify the fields and how they should be separated. In the end, the data is likely to be imported into an Excel spreadsheet anyway.

When you provide an ASCII text file, you may have different formats for multiple records in the file. For example, you may have a header that displays a title and possibly user information that does not match the layout of the data, requiring you to identify when record formats change.

There is also the issue of delivering the file to the users. Will you use a data transfer that must be defined for each user to download the correct physical file member? Will you use File Transfer Protocol (FTP) and require a user name and password?

If you e-mail the text file, its carriage returns and line feeds might be altered during conversion through MIME format. Will you zip the file to avoid this issue, or will your e-mail application embed the text into the e-mail message and force the user to copy and paste the data from there? You could make the data available using a Web server, but if you're going to go that far, you might as well use HTML.

The bottom line is that unless you're dealing with another programmer or a power user, you will likely encounter users who resist using ASCII text files, especially given the other options available today.

PDF files are built specifically to overcome these issues. With PDF files, all that users need is a reader, and they can view any PDF file without any of the preceding concerns. PDF readers are typically free and work on most operating systems. In fact, one is probably already installed with your OS.

Even though PDFs are portable, they can be difficult to modify, which can be a good thing or a bad thing depending on your intentions.

Microsoft Excel files offer the same portability as PDF files. A free viewer available from Microsoft lets users view these files in read-only mode. And with the availability of several open-source options, you can easily create and change such files using software that is supported on most operating systems.

Usability and Standardization

Another reason to provide electronic documents is usability. When you furnish data in an Excel spreadsheet, users can easily search and sort the data, creating ad hoc reports and performing "what if" scenarios. They can also create graphical representations of the data using charts and graphs.

Last, Excel and PDF are two of the most commonly used types of data. Providing data in these standard formats makes the work of your users much easier to use and share with others.

Evolving Your RPG Development Skills

In the following chapters, we'll explore the evolution of RPG from OPM to ILE and discuss how to exploit the new capabilities of the IBM i platform. Our discussion is structured in a logical direction, first building on your existing RPG coding skills by explaining the new features available in ILE and the new concepts involved with scoping and modular coding practices.

We'll start by converting some sample OPM source to an ILE-compatible format and implementing the use of the ILE compilers. With ILE, there are some new concepts to cover that involve the binding of components and the differences between an OPM program and an ILE program. The primary objective of the book is to integrate RPG with Java, so we'll focus our efforts on capabilities that directly lead us to this goal.

Once we have the code in an ILE format, we'll begin to discuss procedures, service programs, and activation groups and why you may want to use them. For the purposes of this book, we'll look at how you can access Java objects and methods.

We'll discuss the definitions of objects and methods thoroughly in upcoming chapters. But on the simplest conceptual level, you can think of an object as being similar to a program that is called and put onto the call stack. It will be initiated to be contained in memory and will have variables initialized to specific values based on their data types.

Java methods are similar to the subroutines that are available to a mainline program. Each subroutine has a specified name and function designed to make the subroutine a reusable resource to the mainline program. Java methods are actually more like procedures because they have clearly defined parameters — one of the new ILE RPG capabilities we'll discuss. So, learning to use this new feature will also help you to understand Java methods when we get to that point.

Developing Reusable Code

In our journey toward understanding the use of Java classes and methods from RPG, we will make every effort to encapsulate the Java interface into reusable code. When we do this, I'll go into a detailed analysis of how to interface with the Java environment, and I'll provide some RPG-friendly code that you can use in the future. I call these pieces of code "RPG wrappers" because we'll be wrapping RPG code around the Java classes and methods.

You can make the RPG wrappers available to the program you're working with and then use pure RPG code to access the Java functionality. This technique not only makes the code easier for you to use in the future; you can also use it to perform all the exception handling, so you won't have to repeat the same code.

This approach also lends more stability to your code because as you reuse the code, it will be exposed to more applications that employ it in different scenarios, flushing out any problems. This, in turn, will cause you to make the necessary changes to the code, which will then become more stable for the application in question and all the others that use it. When you start the next project, you'll have some solid building blocks with which to begin.

Once you have proven, reusable code components, you also will be able to reduce development time for subsequent projects and lessen maintenance support time because you'll be using a smaller percentage of first-time code. So, you win all around with the use of reusable code.

Another benefit to wrapping Java classes and methods in RPG is that you can easily share the new Java capabilities with your fellow RPG programmers in a form that they will be able to use immediately.

Integrating RPG with Java

Enhancing your RPG development skills is a great side effect of the primary objective of this book, which is to exploit the capabilities of Java from within RPG. When we get to that point, we'll explore all the new concepts you need to understand about Java to get it to work properly. It would be nice if you could just plug in a Java method, as you can an application programming interface (API). But there are other things you need to think about when dealing with the Java Virtual Machine, such as starting and stopping it. And because two totally different environments are communicating with each other, you need to take some extra measures to handle some of the ugliness of reclaiming memory resources.

Some of these topics may sound unappealing to you, and I agree. But fortunately, both IBM and Sun Microsystems have provided some useful code segments for dealing with these types of matters. So, what we'll do is create some handy procedures that will take care of most of these details for us, and we'll have to do minimal coding to support these issues.

It took me quite a while to get through all these issues when I first started. There were little pieces of information all over the place, and I had to discover the solutions as I stumbled through one frustrating setback after another. I hope to provide you with a much smoother transition into the world of Java than I had.

I don't mean to sound discouraging. If anything, I intend just the opposite. My goal is to help you to easily overcome those obstacles and get you into production mode relatively quickly. As with the introduction of any new programming language, you will have to go through the growing pains of the initial learning curve. But a practical programming guide dramatically accelerates your ability to provide results quickly. And here we are!

This book introduces you to the Java components necessary to provide the results you're looking for. It is not intended to teach you Java, but it does introduce you to Java and how to use specific parts of open-source technology to provide the product of your hard work, which in this case will be Excel spreadsheets and PDF files that you can distribute using e-mail from RPG.

Creating Electronic Documents

This is where the fun stuff starts to happen. You will learn a new skill in a real-world environment that will actually produce tangible results that are clearly visible to your users. Most of the time, new programming skills give you a greater knowledge base and better mechanics for your code development. But the latter sections of this book will give you the capability to hand over to your users a shiny new product that you know they will totally enjoy! This, in turn, will add much value to your software in the eyes of your users.

If your objective is to provide reports that can be sorted, graphed, charted, and manipulated, you can convert your greenbar reports into an Excel spreadsheet. We'll do this using the Horrible Spreadsheet Format (HSSF) capability of the POI open-source project.

If your intention is to provide documents that can be distributed easily to users and customers in a portable format that anyone on any operating system can use, you may want to convert your greenbar reports, billing invoices, or labels and bar codes to the PDF format. We'll use the iText open-source project to provide these capabilities.

We'll accomplish these objectives by first defining the technical terms and concepts of the components that make up an electronic document and relating them to the Java classes and methods available in POI and iText. Then, we'll convert the methods and parameters into an RPG-friendly format and build wrappers for them. After that, you can start using them from within RPG. Sounds simple enough!

Distributing Electronic Documents Using E-mail

Once you have a program that generates electronic documents, you'll need to decide how you're going to get the end results to your users. My first step was to put the electronic documents onto a publicly accessible network drive. This solution was okay when I first got started with a few users. But my user base quickly grew, and certain reports needed to be visible only to specific users, and it just got out of control from there. Users were starting to archive their reports on the network drive and calling the IT support line about files they were seeking. As the number of files grew, the amount of time required to perform backups grew as well, requiring more administration than I had bargained for.

So, I soon decided to accommodate these requirements using an automated e-mail system. This approach allowed the distribution lists to be changed to send only to particular users, gave users the option to save or delete the files, and did not require users to have a network drive mapped. It also made it possible to easily send the reports to customers who didn't have access to the network.

When evaluating the options to provide my IBM i system with e-mail capability, I found JavaMail to be the most self-contained and flexible solution. Using JavaMail, we will build an e-mail client that simply creates the e-mail and relays it through your current e-mail server — no additional servers or configuration required. We'll start with a simple text e-mail, specifying the to, from, and subject, and then advance to formatted e-mails containing HTML and attachments. You can even embed the images right into the e-mail, if desired.

Using JavaMail for your e-mail client frees you from being tied to the operating system. Once you understand the JavaMail API and you start using Java, you'll be able to easily rewrite your RPG program into pure Java and use the exact same API to provide the same capability to any other server on the network. This freedom and knowledge will also help you as a programmer to begin to integrate with other areas of technology in your company and will give you greater flexibility, not only in your programming options but as a valued member of the programming team.

And that's just the beginning! In addition to giving you the isolated capabilities of the service programs we'll discuss, I'll walk you through the process of identifying and implementing the classes and methods. So, once you get your RPG programs to start generating electronic documents and sending e-mails, you can further explore other options that are available and expand your service programs to implement more and more features. I hope this will be the beginning of a whole new level of programming using Java for you. Let's get started.

The Integrated Language Environment

The Integrated Language Environment differs from the Original Program Model in many ways. One of ILE's biggest differences is the benefit of being able to create modular code for maximum reusability. The modular capabilities of ILE go beyond those of subroutines, **COPY** files, and even subprograms. ILE actually lets you create multiple module objects and service programs that you can use as pieces of the program you're creating. You can also share those modules with other programs.

Another big ILE advantage, beyond the mechanical enhancements that benefit programmers, is a tangible improvement in performance. With ILE, instead of standalone programs, you create modules of code and then bind those modules to a main program. When you bind a module, you pay the overhead of initializing the shared module only on the first call to it. Subsequent references to the module will already have the module initialized.

Once you bind a module or service program to a program, the main program knows exactly where that program is and doesn't have to go looking for it. In contrast, when you call a subprogram from a main program, the main program calls the subprogram dynamically each time and must locate it each time.

Encapsulation is another great advantage in ILE. In OPM, your best attempt at modularizing code is to place reusable code into subroutines or subprograms. When you put code into subroutines, all the variables exist on a global scope. So, when you change a variable within a subroutine, the variable's value is also changed outside the subroutine. In ILE, you can create *procedures*, which have a local scope. In this environment, you can encapsulate your code within a procedure to create specialized functionality that you know will not impact the variable values in the rest of the program (unless you want it to, in which case you would deliberately create global variables that are accessible within the procedure). You can also create multiple, independent file references by taking advantage of separate activation groups.

ILE also provides better integration with other languages, additional opcodes and built-in functions (BIFs), fewer restrictions on the length of variable and field names, and many more features that I'll cover throughout the chapters.

Converting Existing OPM Source Code to ILE

The first step toward modernizing an RPG program is to convert the existing OPM source type of **RPG** to the ILE source type of **RPGLE**. I recommend keeping your original source code for a while during your transition to ILE and converting your code a member at a time.

ILE supports larger fields than OPM, so the source file into which you convert or create the source code must have a length of 112 characters: 100 characters for the source code itself and 12 characters for the source sequence numbers and the date. To set the record length, specify 112 for the **RCDLEN** parameter in the **CRTSRCPF** (Create Source Physical File) CL command.

To convert existing OPM RPG source code to ILE RPG source code, you can use the **CVTRPGSRC** (Convert RPG Source) command. This command converts the file layouts of the OPM source to the new ILE format. It also merges the I and E specifications into the new Definition (D) specification. It does not convert the code to free-format syntax. Be aware that once you convert your code to ILE, no command exists to convert it back to OPM.

One big thing you should keep in mind when converting code from OPM to ILE is your **COPY** files; before compiling these files, you'll need to convert them to ILE RPG. The **CVTRPGSRC** command's **EXPCPY(*YES)** option lets you include **COPY** file code in the converted RPG source; the **COPY** file is also converted to ILE. However, I don't recommend this option. Using **EXPCPY(*YES)** defeats the point of having a **COPY** file, which is to reuse the same code in multiple programs. If you specify this option, the code is copied into every program you convert, and you will have to maintain all that redundant code.

Unless you plan to convert all your programs to ILE at once, you may want to consider creating a new **COPY** source file member in ILE and retaining the OPM version as is. Doing so will let you convert one program at a time to ILE and then change the **COPY** references to point to the ILE version of the **COPY** file. This way, all your OPM programs will continue to work with the original OPM version.

Compiling ILE Source Code into a *PGM Object

Immediately after you have converted the code, you can compile it using the ILE compiler to have it behave exactly as it did before. You will no longer use the **CRTRPGPGM** (Create RPG Program) command to compile your source code. ILE provides some new ways to create an RPG ***PGM** object; we'll start with the simplest one, the **CRTBNDRPG** (Create Bound RPG Program) command.

If you were to compile the newly converted **RPGLE** source code, specifying only the source file and destination file parameters on the program call and taking the default on all the other parameters, you would create a program that would behave identically to the program that you created with the original OPM source code. With this point in mind, you could convert all your existing OPM code to

ILE and recompile it to behave as it originally did and then start taking advantage of all the new capabilities.

One of the big advantages of ILE is that you can create multiple modules and bind them together to form a final ***PGM** object. With **CRTBNDRPG**, you skip the step of manually creating a module, and the compiler creates the program object for you. During the compilation process, the compiler creates a temporary module and deletes it after the program object is created.

Here is the command you would use to create ILE source code that behaves like the original OPM program:

```
CRTBNDRPG PGM(AIRLIB/AIR01_01)   +
          SRCFILE(AIRSRC/AIRLIB) +
          DFTACTGRP(*YES)
```

I've specified the **DFTACTGRP** (Default activation group) parameter here even though ***YES** is its default value. I wanted to bring to your attention the fact that this parameter value is the key setting that indicates that the ILE source will behave like that of an OPM program — because OPM programs run in the default activation group.

Another way you could compile the program would be to manually create the module and then bind the module into a program object by using the **CRTRPGMOD** (Create RPG Module) and **CRTPGM** (Create Program) commands, respectively. When you compile the program using **CRTPGM**, you cannot put the program into the default activation group; this is not a valid option for the activation group parameter of the **CRTPGM** command. If you were to use the ***CALLER** activation group, you could call the ILE program from an OPM program, but this practice is not recommended.

We'll return to the topic of activation groups in more detail later in the chapter.

Modules

Modules, as I've indicated, are pieces of programs that you can put together to build a program. You cannot run a module directly; it must be a part of a program or service program for you to be able to access the logic of the module.

Within the module, you can have a main procedure, as well as subprocedures that you can make available for use with other modules or programs.

Procedures

When you use RPG subroutines, you stay within the same scope of the program in which each subroutine exists. This means that the variables you use are globally accessible to the entire program. If you change the value of a variable in a subroutine, the variable's value is also affected outside the subroutine. ILE procedures offer an improvement over subroutines by letting you encapsulate your subroutine logic so that the scope of the variables is relevant only to the segment of code within the procedure.

When you use subroutines, all the code must be contained within the RPG code of the calling program unless you use the **/COPY** statement, which still requires you to recompile all the programs using **/COPY** if you make any changes to the **COPY** file source code. If you were to manipulate the value of a variable within the subroutine, it could adversely affect programs that use that **COPY** file. All these features are undesirable in most situations and can be resolved using prototyping and procedures.

Prototyping

Every procedure that returns a value or accepts parameters must have a *prototype* defined in the main program. The prototype gives the compiler the call interface to the procedure. When you assign a prototype to a subprocedure, you specify the number of parameters, the types and sizes of the parameters, and the type and size of the returning value. This information enables parameter validation at compile time and provides a more programmer-friendly syntax in the code that calls the prototyped subprocedure.

Figure 2.1 shows the basic syntax for a prototype. The **PR** in the Definition Type entry (positions 24–25) on the first line of the prototype identifies this code as a prototype. You specify the return value on the **PR** definition line as well. Any parameters for the procedure are defined in the lines following the first line.

```
D <name>          PR     <return type>
D    <parms...>           <parm type> <parm keyword(s)>
```

Figure 2.1: Basic syntax for a prototype

Parameter Keywords

The following special keywords are available when you pass parameters:

- **const** — Specifies that the parameter cannot be changed within the proto-typed procedure. This option lets you send values into the parameter that do not match the type and size of the parameter that is defined. When you use the **const** keyword, the compiler makes a temporary copy of the variable being passed and converts it into the expected parameter type and size.

- **options(*NOPASS)** — Indicates that the parameter is optional. Once you specify a parameter as ***NOPASS**, any subsequent parameters must also be defined as ***NOPASS**. To identify the number of parameters actually passed, the subprocedure can use the **%parms** built-in function.

- **options(*OMIT)** — Used to indicate that a parameter is not required. This lets you specify the ***OMIT** keyword parameter when calling a procedure. The subprocedure can identify a parameter passed as ***OMIT** by using the **%addr** built-in function to check whether the parameter address is null.

- **options(*VARSIZE)** — Indicates that fewer characters than indicated may be passed. To identify the parameter's actual length, the subprocedure can use the **%len** built-in function.

- **options(*STRING)** — Automatically appends **x'00'** to the end of the bytes for use with Unix-type APIs.

- **options(*RIGHTADJ)** — Right adjusts the parameter.
- **value** — Indicates that the parameter is passed by value.

In addition to prototyping subprocedures, ILE lets you define prototypes for calls to external programs and procedures. Two optional keywords are used to prototype external calls:

- **extPgm** — Provides a call interface to an external program that is not bound to the main program. This type of call incurs the overhead time of dynamically finding the program. Within the main program, you use the name of the prototype to reference the external program.
- **extProc** — Provides a call interface to a bound procedure. Within the program, the name of the prototype references the external procedure.

If you specify neither **ExtPgm** nor **ExtProc**, the name of the prototype is the name of the procedure. In Chapter 3, we'll create a prototype to call the **QCMDEXC** (Execute Command) API as an external program.

Procedure Interface

As you've seen, the prototype provides the compiler with the call interface to the procedure. Within the procedure itself, the *procedure interface* duplicates the return value and parameters defined in the prototype but specifies **PI** in the Definition Type entry (positions 24–25) instead of the **PR** used on the prototype. Figure 2.2 shows the basic syntax for a procedure.

```
P <name>            B                      export (optional)
D <name>            PI       <return type>
D   <parms...>               <parm type> <parm keyword(s)>
D* Local variables
D <local var...>  S    <variable type>
C                       Code logic...
C                       Code logic...
C                       Code logic...
P <name>            E
```

Figure 2.2: Procedure syntax

The procedure code begins and ends with a P specification. You signal the beginning of the procedure with the letter B in position 24 of the P spec; the letter E in the same position of a concluding P spec marks the procedure's end. You indicate the name of the procedure at the beginning of the procedure code and may optionally also place the name on the ending line. If you want to make the procedure visible outside the program or service program that contains it, include the **EXPORT** keyword on the beginning line.

Activation Groups

Activation groups let you partition the resources, such as static storage and files, that your programs use. All programs, including both OPM and ILE programs, run within activation groups.

All OPM programs run in the default activation group. ILE programs can run in the default activation group, in the activation group of the calling program, in an activation group automatically named by the system, or in a named activation group. Activation groups are assigned to programs and service programs when they are compiled. You can decide which approach is best depending on the purpose of your application.

The Default Activation Group in OPM

Before ILE, there was no such thing as an activation group. The default activation group was born to provide backward compatibility with existing OPM programs. In OPM, when a program opens a file and applies overrides, the overrides continue to apply to any subsequently called programs because all programs are run in the default activation group.

However, if you call a program from the default activation group and the called program is in a different activation group, the file overrides do not apply. This behavior is something to consider as you begin to convert existing programs to ILE when those programs depend on overrides being established from the calling programs.

Activation Group Option *CALLER

In ILE, the ***CALLER** activation group option places the application into the activation group of the program that called it. In this case, file overrides from the calling program are carried over to the program in the ***CALLER** activation group and share the resources.

If an OPM program were to call an ILE program using the ***CALLER** activation group, the ILE program would run in the default activation group. Even though it is possible to run ILE programs this way, it is not recommended.

Activation Group Option *NEW

The ***NEW** activation group option creates a new activation group each time the application is called. This behavior ensures that you have a unique activation group for the job, which would provide you with file pointers that are independent of any calling programs.

The ***NEW** option is the most inefficient activation group method because it causes you to incur all the additional overhead of opening and closing the files. This consideration may not be an issue if you call a program only a few times, but if you call it repeatedly, you may notice the performance impact.

The system reclaims ***NEW** activation groups when the program using the activation group is returned to its original caller.

Named Activation Groups

Another activation group option is to specify the name of the activation group for the program. This option lets you keep the files open, and it reduces overhead when an application is called repeatedly. A named activation group remains active either until the activation group is reclaimed or until the job ends.

When I use this approach, I typically name the activation group after the program for which I'm using it. This practice helps if you're examining open files for the job to identify any file issues you may be debugging. When you perform a system request to display the open files, the activation group name also appears on the screen. If you see the same file open multiple times and in multiple activation groups, this naming convention will make it easy to identify which applications have the files open.

Use of Separate Activation Groups

Being accustomed to the OPM characteristics of the default activation group, you may not immediately understand why you would want separate activation groups, so let's look at a real-world example of why you might use them.

Suppose you've read a record from a file that contains a list of students and their associated grades. Now, you want to evaluate each student to determine his or her class rank and update the record with the rank value.

To perform this function in OPM, you would have to do the following:

1. Store the current values into variables.
2. Read through the entire file to gather the information from the file.
3. Store those result values into variables.
4. Reposition back to the original file record location.
5. Update the record.

In ILE, you can get the job done in two steps:

1. Call a procedure from a program in a different activation group.
2. Update the record.

Reclaiming Activation Groups

Activation groups are used exclusively for the job in which they are created. You cannot share an activation group across multiple jobs. To end an activation group, you execute the **RCLACTGRP** (Reclaim Activation Group) command.

This command closes any open files in the activation group and reclaims the static storage. You can think of **RCLACTGRP** as being somewhat like an ILE version of the **RCLRSC** (Reclaim Resources) command you use in OPM.

When a program crashes, the ***INLR** indicator may not get set on and the application may not close the files, so you could either sign off and back on again or call **RCLRSC**. But if the application were running in an activation group other than the default activation group, calling **RCLRSC** wouldn't close the files outside the default activation group; you would need to call the **RCLACTGRP** command.

You can designate which activation group to end by passing its name on the **RCLACTGRP** command, or you can specify ***ELIGIBLE** for the command's **ACTGRP** (Activation group) parameter to delete all activation groups that the job isn't using.

Using RCLACTGRP(*ELIGIBLE)

The **RCLACTGRP** command's ***ELIGIBLE** option deletes all activation groups that are not currently on the call stack. This option is useful when you're testing applications, and it can also provide a good cleanup utility when used at the initial point of entry into an ILE activation group from the default activation group.

Once you get beyond that point, you need to be aware of additional activation groups that you're using in both programs and service programs, and things begin to get more complicated when reclaiming the activation groups. You'll want to be more selective by specifying the activation group name when reclaiming activation groups. Otherwise, you could possibly reclaim activation groups that are active but not currently on the call stack. In this situation, an attempt to reuse an activation group that has been reclaimed could cause an error to occur.

Service Programs

One of the primary purposes of ILE is to enable programmers to create more modular applications to take advantage of program module reusability and increase performance. *Service programs* implement all these new features.

When you compile your RPG code as a service program instead of a program, you generate a ***SRVPGM** object instead of a ***PGM** object. You cannot call a service program directly; you must bind it to a program when you create it.

To create a service program, you create your modules and then use the **CRTSRVPGM** (Create Service Program) command to bind the modules together into a service program. When you create the service program, you can specify the modules you want to use and also bind another service program.

You will experience a dramatic performance improvement when you call a procedure from a service program versus calling a separate program. That's because when you call a separate program, the system has to determine where the program object is located and then initialize everything. When you call a service program, it is bound to the calling program, so the calling program knows exactly where the service program is — it doesn't have to go looking. And the service program has everything initialized only once, when it is first called. So, every subsequent call after the first already has all the resources ready.

In addition to the performance advantage, service programs promote code modularity for reusability and ease of understanding.

Exporting Procedures in a Service Program

When you put procedures into a service program, you'll obviously want to let other programs use them, but there may be some procedures that you want to keep private to the service program. Doing so provides reusability within the service program itself but prevents external programs from accessing those procedures.

In service programs, you must *export* procedures to provide access. You can control how you export the procedures in two different ways, and the choice is a matter of preference. You can specify the exports at compile time, or you can selectively specify the **EXPORT** keyword on the procedure and use the **EXPORT(*ALL)** option when you compile it.

Service programs can optionally contain a main procedure. If you do have a main procedure, that procedure is exported automatically.

Putting the Concepts to Work

Let's look at an example that uses procedures with prototypes, activation groups, and service programs. We'll use the simple case of a school that has a file called **STUDENTS** that contains basic information about each student, such as name, address, major, and a unique account number. A second file, **GRADES**, stores testing information and contains student grades that will be linked by account number. Figures 2.3 and 2.4 show the DDS for these two files.

```
A              R STFMT
A                STACCT        6S 0        COLHDG('ACCOUNT NUMBER')
A                STFNAM        32A         COLHDG('FIRST NAME')
A                STLNAM        32A         COLHDG('LAST NAME')
A                STADDR1       32A         COLHDG('ADDRESS LINE 1')
A                STADDR2       32A         COLHDG('ADDRESS LINE 2')
A                STCITY        32A         COLHDG('CITY')
A                STSTATE        2A         COLHDG('STATE')
A                STPOSTAL      12A         COLHDG('POSTAL')
A                STMAJOR       12A         COLHDG('MAJOR')
A              K STACCT
```

Figure 2.3: DDS source for AIRLIB/AIRSRC,STUDENTS file

```
A                                          UNIQUE
A              R SGFMT
A                SGACCT        6S 0        COLHDG('ACCOUNT NUMBER')
A                SGCLCODE      12A         COLHDG('CLASS CODE')
A                SGCLDESC      32A         COLHDG('CLASS DESCRIPTION')
A                SGCLTDTE       8S 0       COLHDG('TEST DATE')
A                SGCLGRADE      3S 0       COLHDG('TEST GRADE')
A              K SGACCT
A              K SGCLCODE
A              K SGCLTDTE
```

Figure 2.4: DDS source for AIRLIB/AIRSRC,GRADES file

To demonstrate the differences between OPM and ILE programming, we will build a simple program to apply the practical uses of ILE. We'll start with an OPM fixed-format application and evolve it through the remainder of the chapter to include the new features we've covered until we've implemented the functionality of the OPM program in an ILE program.

OPM Fixed-Format RPG Program

The overall purpose of the sample program is to display the rank of each student within his or her major. We'll accomplish this function by looping through the records in the **STUDENTS** file to obtain the rank and display it. Figure 2.5 shows the fixed-format OPM main program to retrieve and display student rankings.

```
FSTUDENTS   IF   E              K DISK
FGRADES     IF   E              K DISK
D*
DXSTUDENTS       E DS                    EXTNAME(STUDENTS)
DHSTUDENTS       E DS                    EXTNAME(STUDENTS)
D                                        PREFIX(H)
D displayBytes   S              52A
D rank           S              10I 0
D rankAlpha      S              10A
D currentTotal   S              10I 0
D currentCount   S              10I 0
D score          S               7S 4
D rankScore      S               7S 4
C       *START         SETLL    STUDENTS
C                      READ     STUDENTS                      69
C                      DOW      *IN69 = *OFF
C                      EVAL     HSTUDENTS = XSTUDENTS
C                      EXSR     GETRANK
C* Reposition STUDENTS file pointer
C       HSTACCT        CHAIN    STUDENTS                      69
C                      EXSR     DSPINFO
C                      READ     STUDENTS                      69
C                      ENDDO
C                      EVAL     *INLR = *ON
```

Figure 2.5: OPM fixed-format main program to get and display student rankings

When maintaining this program, you would need to know that the file pointer for the **STUDENTS** file is changed in the **GETRANK** subroutine, so you would have to store the initial values for the record of interest and then restore the values of both the record and the record position of the file being read after execution of the subroutine.

Subroutine **GETRANK** must determine each student's rank in relation to all the other students within that student's major. To achieve this, we'll have the student of interest go through the loop the first time to determine his or her test score and assume the highest rank of 1; then, we'll loop through the rest of the students to adjust the rank by pushing down anyone who has a higher score within the major. Figure 2.6 shows the OPM **GETRANK** subroutine.

```
C***************************************************************************
C* GETRANK: Retrieves the rank for students in the same major
C***************************************************************************
C       GETRANK       BEGSR
C                     EVAL      rank = 0
C* STACCT is initialized to the student of interest for first pass
C                     DOU       *IN67 = *ON
C                     EVAL      currentTotal = 0
C                     EVAL      currentCount = 0
C       STACCT        CHAIN     GRADES                              68
C                     DOW       *IN68 = *OFF
C                     EVAL      currentTotal = currentTotal + SGCLGRADE
C                     EVAL      currentCount = currentCount + 1
C       STACCT        READE     GRADES                              68
C                     ENDDO
C                     IF        currentCount = 0
C                     EVAL      score = 0
C                     ELSE
C                     EVAL      score = currentTotal / currentCount
C                     ENDIF
C* HSTACCT is set in the main program and is the student of interest
C                     IF        STACCT = HSTACCT
C                     EVAL      rank = 1
C                     EVAL      rankScore = score
C       *START        SETLL     STUDENTS
C                     ELSE
C                     IF        score > rankScore
C                     EVAL      rank = rank + 1
C                     ELSE
C                     ENDIF
C                     ENDIF
C                     DOU       (STACCT <> HSTACCT
C                               AND STMAJOR = HSTMAJOR)
C                               OR *IN67
C                     READ      STUDENTS                            67
C                     ENDDO
C                     ENDDO
C                     ENDSR
```

Figure 2.6: OPM subroutine GETRANK

The logic in this subroutine is fairly basic OPM logic that is intended to provide a practical example in a way that would require the use of the same file in the mainline program.

To complete the program, we'll use a second subroutine, **DSPINFO**, that displays the student's rank on the screen during execution (Figure 2.7).

```
C********************************************************************
C* DSPINFO: Displays the rank information
C********************************************************************
C        DSPINFO       BEGSR
C                      EVAL      displayBytes = '----------------'
C        displayBytes  DSPLY
C                      EVAL      displayBytes = 'First Name: '
C                                            + STFNAM
C        displayBytes  DSPLY
C                      EVAL      displayBytes = 'Last Name: '
C                                            + STLNAM
C        displayBytes  DSPLY
C                      EVAL      displayBytes = 'Major: '
C                                            + STMAJOR
C        displayBytes  DSPLY
C                      MOVE      rank          rankAlpha
C                      EVAL      displayBytes = 'Rank: '
C                                            + rankAlpha
C        displayBytes  DSPLY
C                      ENDSR
```

Figure 2.7: OPM subroutine DSPINFO

The sample program does separate the logic to make it reusable within the same program, but if you wanted to share this logic with another program, you would need to duplicate the code or put it into a **COPY** file, which would still require you to define all the files and variables.

ILE Fixed-Format RPG Program

Let's assume that the **GETRANK** subroutine has a general functionality that other programs can reuse, so we want to convert the subroutine into a procedure within a service program. Doing so will let us take advantage of the ability to easily bind the procedure to other programs, and it will let us use activation groups.

Figure 2.8 shows an ILE main program that uses a service program to provide the rank.

```
FSTUDENTS  IF   E         K DISK
D*
D/COPY AIRLIB/AIRSRC,SPAIRSAMP
D*
D displayBytes    S             52A
D rank            S             10I 0
D rankAlpha       S             10A
C*
C                     CALLP     Air_openFiles('MAINCAMPUS')
C        *START       SETLL     STUDENTS
C                     READ      STUDENTS                        69
C                     DOW       *IN69 = *OFF
C                     EVAL      rank = Air_getRank(STACCT)
C                     EXSR      DSPINFO
C                     READ      STUDENTS                        69
C                     ENDDO
C                     CALLP     Air_closeFiles()
C                     EVAL      *INLR = *ON
```

Figure 2.8: ILE fixed-format main program to get and display student rankings

You can see that the amount of code has been reduced by about a third. This program is a small one, but as you build more and more procedures into your service programs, you will notice the reduction in the code that uses the service programs. Less code is required because you don't have to redefine the files and variables that the procedure uses; you just need to define the prototype — something you can easily do by putting it into a **COPY** file.

You can also see that we don't have to reposition the file after using the **Air_getRank** procedure. That's because the service program will be in a different activation group, and the file pointer won't be affected in the mainline program.

I typically prefix the name of the prototype **COPY** file with **SP** and the service program with **SV**. This convention lets me easily identify the purpose of the code, and it groups objects together for easy searching when reviewing the available source code members. For this example, I've named the two source members **SPAIRSAMP** and **SVAIRSAMP**.

Another naming convention you'll see throughout this book is the prefix **Air_** added to procedure names to make it easy to identify procedures that are external to the main program and the service program that contains them.

Just because you have service programs doesn't mean you have to abandon subroutines. In this example, I left the **DSPINFO** subroutine alone. That's because **DSPINFO** is a special-purpose subroutine that will be used only with the program for which it was written. It is also being used on variables that are already defined in the mainline program. You could prototype this routine and redefine the variables, or just use a subroutine as usual.

Converting a Subroutine into a Procedure

When creating a procedure, you want to design it in a way that provides a "black box" interface to the functionality of the logic. In other words, you want to determine what final result you're looking for and what information is required to obtain it, with no other dependencies on the main program that uses the procedure (and no concern for how the procedure will affect the main program, for that matter).

In this case, we care only about the rank of a particular student within his or her major. We can determine the major from the account, so we simply need to pass in the student account number, and the rank will be represented by a number. How the rank is determined and what files are used should not be a concern for the programmer who reuses the procedure.

Now, we can create the prototype for the procedure. To do so, we specify the procedure name along with the **PR** notation and the return type on the first line of the prototype. Subsequent lines define the procedure's parameters — in this case, the account number. Figure 2.9 shows the prototype for the **Air_getRank** procedure.

```
D Air_getRank...
D                       PR              10I 0
D     argAccount                         6S 0 const
```

Figure 2.9: Prototype for procedure Air_getRank

This prototype uses the **const** keyword on the **argAccount** parameter definition to permit the main program to pass the value without the need for a predefined variable and also to support other data sizes. If you were to try to do this without specifying **const**, you would receive the compile error "Parameter 1 is not valid as a parameter passed by reference."

We can use **const** in this case because we know that we won't be changing the **argAccount** value within the procedure. The use of **const** also will let other programmers know that the value being passed in will not be changed.

For this example, the prototype is put into a separate source code member called **SPAIRSAMP**. Following the previously discussed naming conventions, the **SP** prefix is used to easily identify a **COPY** file for service program prototypes. The remaining portions of the service program source name and the prototype name are duplicated to associate the two files with each other. This naming style is not required, but it helps identify the purpose of the files.

The Procedure

Figure 2.10 shows the **GETRANK** subroutine after it has been converted into the **Air_getRank** procedure within a service program. This part of the code will be created in a source file member separate from the main source code. The type of the source member will still be **RPGLE**. This source file member may contain multiple procedures that will be made accessible from the service program.

```
 *-----------------------------------------------------------------
 * Air_getRank: Retrieves the rank for students in the same major
 *-----------------------------------------------------------------
P Air_getRank...
P                     B                    export
D Air_getRank...
D                     PI          10I 0
D    argAccount                    6S 0 const
D* Local Variables
D currentTotal        S           10I 0
D currentCount        S           10I 0
D score               S            7S 4
D rankScore           S            7S 4
D rank                S           10I 0
```

```
C                       EVAL      rank = 0
C          argAccount   CHAIN     STUDENTS                                    69
C                       EVAL      HSTUDENTS = XSTUDENTS
C                       DOU       *IN69 = *ON
C                       EVAL      currentTotal = 0
C                       EVAL      currentCount = 0
C          STACCT       CHAIN     GRADES                                      68
C                       DOW       *IN68 = *OFF
C                       EVAL      currentTotal = currentTotal + SGCLGRADE
C                       EVAL      currentCount = currentCount + 1
C          STACCT       READE     GRADES                                      68
C                       ENDDO
C                       IF        currentCount = 0
C                       EVAL      score = 0
C                       ELSE
C                       EVAL      score = currentTotal / currentCount
C                       ENDIF
C                       IF        STACCT = HSTACCT
C                       EVAL      rank = 1
C                       EVAL      rankScore = score
C          *START       SETLL     STUDENTS
C                       ELSE
C                       IF        score > rankScore
C                       EVAL      rank = rank + 1
C                       ELSE
C                       ENDIF
C                       ENDIF
C                       DOU       (STACCT <> HSTACCT
C                                 AND STMAJOR = HSTMAJOR)
C                                 OR *IN69
C                       READ      STUDENTS                                    69
C                       ENDDO
C                       ENDDO
C                       RETURN    rank
P              E
```

Figure 2.10: ILE fixed-format procedure Air_getRank

If you were to chop off the top and bottom of this procedure, you would see that, with the exception of the variable names, the logic is exactly the same as the subroutine.

This procedure did not need to go into a service program. We could have placed it right into the same source member as the main program. But putting it into a service program makes it easily reusable by other programs.

It is possible to share a procedure with other programs from within a main program by putting the procedure in the source code member of the main program and exporting it, but doing so would impose the dependencies of other programs onto this one, and it would force the procedure to be contained within the same activation group as the main program.

It could be cumbersome if you have one programmer who changes a procedure that is being used by another program while another programmer is changing the main program. In such cases, you may need to coordinate your release efforts. If you put your reusable procedures into service programs, any programmer who uses one of those procedures can modify the programs that use the procedure without prohibiting or waiting for your changes to be made and released.

Cohesion

Procedures are normally placed into service programs when they have a well-focused purpose and are general enough to be used by multiple programs. In object-oriented design terminology, this state is referred to as *cohesion*. The more focused a procedure is, the higher the cohesion it has. High cohesion is a goal to shoot for when designing procedures in service programs.

High cohesion not only promotes reusability but also takes advantage of providing solid code. This is because you'll be reusing code that already has been demonstrated to work somewhere else, and you won't have to go through the design and testing process from scratch. At the beginning of the next project, you'll be starting with some proven code.

Identifying the Activation Groups on Open Files

If we display the open files for the job (Figure 2.11), you can see that the **STUDENTS** file is opened twice. You can also see that the file instances are identified as being in different activation groups. Not only does this approach enable independent file pointers, but it also lets you open and close a file within the service program and change member overrides without affecting the file in the mainline program.

```
Job . . :     MCPRESS21Z     User . . :   SNYDERTOM        Number . .
Number of open data paths . . . . . . . . . . :      6


                            Member/
File          Library       Device        Scope        Activation Group
QDSPMNU       QSYS          MCPRESS21Z     *ACTGRPDFN   0000000002  *DFTACTGRP
QDUODSPF      QPDA          MCPRESS21Z     *ACTGRPDFN   0000000002  *DFTACTGRP
QDUT80        QSYS          MCPRESS21Z     *ACTGRPDFN   0000000002  *DFTACTGRP
STUDENTS      AIRLIB        MAINCAMPUS     *ACTGRPDFN   0000000030  AIR02_02
STUDENTS      AIRLIB        MAINCAMPUS     *ACTGRPDFN   0000000031  SVAIRSAMP
GRADES        AIRLIB        MAINCAMPUS     *ACTGRPDFN   0000000031  SVAIRSAMP
```

Figure 2.11: Open file activation groups

For this example, I specified the name of the activation group for the main program as **AIR02_02** at compile time. That's why you see the **STUDENTS** file opened once in the **AIR02_02** activation group and once in the **SVAIRSAMP** activation group of the service program. If I had compiled either the program or the service program using *NEW for the activation group, the activation group would have had a randomly generated name.

If we were to compile both the service program and the main program into the same activation group, we would have the same issues as the original program that did not use activation groups. The file pointer would be set to the end of the file after the first call to the **Air_getRank** procedure, and the program would terminate after processing the first student.

We could force the behavior of having both the main program and the service program in the same activation group by specifying the *CALLER activation group on the service program. With this setting, the service program would use the same activation group as any program that uses it.

I don't advise using *CALLER on programs that are called by OPM programs. Although your program would be compiled and run, you could receive unpredictable results because you would be trying to run an ILE program in the default activation group, which is intended for OPM programs.

Using Files in a Service Program

Because we are using files in the service program, I have also created procedures to open and close the files. This was done so that we could override the files to a specified member; it also gives us control over the opening and closing of the files so that we can change the overrides during program execution.

Figure 2.12 shows the prototypes for the procedures in service program **SVAIRSAMP** to open and close the files.

```
D Air_openFiles...
D                          PR              1N
D  argMember                              10A
D Air_closeFiles...
D                          PR              1N
```

Figure 2.12: Prototypes to open and close the service program files

Figure 2.13 shows the procedure to open the files.

```
    *---------------------------------------------------------------
    * Air_openFiles: Opens the files for the specified member
    *---------------------------------------------------------------
P Air_openFiles...
P                    B                       export
D Air_openFiles...
D                    PI              1N
D  argMember                        10A
D* Local Variables
D  string           S              1000A
C*
C                    EVAL        STRING = 'OVRDBF FILE(STUDENTS)'
C                                + ' MBR(' + %trim(argMember)
C                                + ')'
C                    Z-ADD       1000            STRLEN
C                    CALL        'QCMDEXC'
C                    PARM                        STRING
C                    PARM                        STRLEN          15 5
C*
C                    EVAL        STRING = 'OVRDBF FILE(GRADES)'
C                                + ' MBR(' + %trim(argMember)
C                                + ')'
C                    Z-ADD       1000            STRLEN
C                    CALL        'QCMDEXC'
```

```
C                     PARM                     STRING
C                     PARM                     STRLEN         15 5
C*
C                     OPEN      STUDENTS                           59
C    N59              OPEN      GRADES                             59
C                     RETURN    *IN59
P              E
```

Figure 2.13: Procedure to open the service program files

I know what you may be thinking. We're working with procedures, activation groups, and we're still using **CALL QCMDEXC** in fixed-format RPG. Where is the free-format stuff? We're getting there. Activation groups are a radically new concept, and I don't want to overcomplicate the objective by introducing too many things at once. Don't worry; before you know it, we'll have this common API wrapped up and tucked into a service program for easy reuse.

Figure 2.14 shows the nice, simple procedure to close the files.

```
    *----------------------------------------------------------------
    * Air_closeFiles: Closes the files
    *----------------------------------------------------------------
P Air_closeFiles...
P                     B                        export
D Air_closeFiles...
D                     PI              1N
C                     CLOSE     STUDENTS                           59
C    N59              CLOSE     GRADES                             59
C                     RETURN    *IN59
P              E
```

Figure 2.14: Procedure to close the service program files

Providing simple procedures to open and close the files in the service program helps you to take full advantage of the separate activation groups because you can search through multiple physical file members in the service program's activation group without affecting the files in the calling program.

Compiler Directives

Compiler directives are handy when you begin using prototypes, procedures, and constants in your RPG code. Using these directives, you can include code into modules that can be reused by different modules that may be used together without conflicts.

/COPY and /INCLUDE

The **/COPY** and **/INCLUDE** compiler directives both provide the same capabilities, except that the Structured Query Language (SQL) precompiler does not process **INCLUDE** files. These directives let you create a segment of code that you can save outside the mainline program code and include into the source code at compile time. The code to be copied can be either a source member or a file in the integrated file system (IFS). You can make the inclusion of the code conditional by using the **/DEFINE** directive with the conditional **/IF** and **/ELSE** directives.

/DEFINE and /UNDEFINE

You use the **/DEFINE** and **/UNDEFINE** directives to indicate whether a condition name is added to the list of defined conditions used by the compiler. The condition names you use need not be declared before use.

/IF, /ELSE, /ELSEIF, /ENDIF

The **/IF**, **/ELSE**, **/ELSEIF**, and **/ENDIF** directives let you identify segments of code that should be included or excluded during compile time based on the condition name or keyword being evaluated. You can use these directives to check whether a specified condition has been either **DEFINED** or **NOT DEFINED**. The result of the check can be used as a conditional Boolean value to determine the compiler's behavior.

In addition to evaluating condition names, you can use **/IF**, **/ELSE**, and **/ELSEIF** to evaluate special predefined conditions. Table 2.1 provides a list of the keywords used to test for these conditions.

Table 2.1: Special conditions for the /IF, /ELSE, and /ELSEIF compiler directives	
/IF, /ELSE, /ELSIF keyword	Purpose
*ILERPG	Identifies the use of an ILE RPG IV compiler
*VxRxMx	Determines whether the operating system is greater than or equal to VxRxMx
*CRTBNDRPG	Identifies the use of the CRTBNDRPG compile command
*CRTRPGMOD	Identifies the use of the CRTRPGMOD compile command

/EXEC SQL and /END-EXEC

/EXEC SQL and **/END-EXEC** are compiler directives used with the **CRTSQLRPGI** (Create SQL ILE RPG Object) compiler to mark the beginning and end of segments of code that use SQL.

/FREE and /END-FREE

The **/FREE** and **/END-FREE** compiler directives mark the beginning and end of segments of free-format RPG code. We'll discuss free-format RPG in detail in Chapter 3.

Compiler Directives Example

Figure 2.15 shows some RPG code that implements most of the preceding compiler directives.

```
D/define ALPHA_MODE
D/if defined(ALPHA_MODE)
D a               S              5A    inz('Hello')
D b               S              5A    inz(' RPG')
D c               S             10A
D/else
D a               S             10I 0 inz(1)
```

```
D b               S              10I 0 inz(2)
D c               S              10I 0
D/endif
D d               S              10A
D*
D displayBytes    S              52A
C*
C                 EVAL       c = a + b
C                 MOVE       c                    d
 /free
                  displayBytes = 'Results: ' + %trim(d);
                  DSPLY      displayBytes;
 /end-free
 /if defined(*ILERPG)
C      'RPG ILE'  DSPLY
 /else
 /endif
C/if defined(*CRTBNDRPG)
C      'CRTBNDRPG' DSPLY
C/else
C/endif
C/if defined(*CRTRPGMOD)
C      'CRTRPGMOD' DSPLY
C/else
C/endif
C/if defined(*V5R1M0)
C      '>= V5R1M0' DSPLY
C/else
C/endif
C                 EVAL       *INLR = *ON
```

Figure 2.15: Mixed-format compiler directives program

To view the results of the **DSPLY** strings, display the job log. Figure 2.16 shows the results for the sample program.

```
> CALL AIR02_01
   DSPLY   Results: Hello RPG
   DSPLY   RPG ILE
   DSPLY   CRTBNDRPG
   DSPLY   >= V5R1M0
```

Figure 2.16: DSPLY output from compiler directives program

If you were to comment out the first line of the program, which defines the **ALPHA_MODE** condition name, the "Results: Hello RPG" line in the output would change to "Results: 0000000003".

You may notice a few things about this sample program, especially if you are unfamiliar with the compiler directives. First, the **a**, **b**, and **c** variables are coded twice. You would think that the compiler would complain about these variables being declared already, but it won't. And what about the **EVAL** statement that adds **a** and **b** together? How does the compiler know whether you are concatenating bytes or performing an arithmetic operation on numbers? These typical compiler errors will not occur because the compiler won't even see the second declaration. It will see only the declarations contained in the conditional branch that is determined by the condition name.

The **/IF**, **/ELSE**, and **/ENDIF** directives don't care whether they are on a C spec or a D spec. In fact, you don't even need to indicate a spec at all. You can see these directives used with both C and D specs in the example.

The **/FREE** and **/END-FREE** directives are a different story; you *cannot* use a spec letter with these, or the compiler will complain about it. The **/FREE** and **/END-FREE** directives must be the first and last lines, respectively, for any segments of code that use the free-format RPG syntax. When you use free-format syntax, you must end each line with a semicolon (;).

You'll see a lot more of the free-format syntax in the next chapter, where we get into the details of coding free-format RPG.

3

Advanced ILE RPG

Free-formatted RPG lets you code your RPG in a more readable style, using indentation, blank lines, and free-form expressions to make it easier to see what the code is doing. You may already consider fixed-format RPG to be easily readable, but once you start working with procedures, you'll see that you would be making quite a few redundant **CALLP**s if you couldn't use the free-format syntax.

As you start to evolve your code, you will begin to appreciate the readability of the free format. Table 3.1 lists some of the operation codes available in free-format RPG. The list grows with each new release.

Table 3.1: Free-format RPG operation codes					
ACQ	DOW	EVAL	ITER	READ	SETGT
BEGSR	DSPLY	EVALR	LEAVE	READC	SETLL
CALLP	DUMP	EXCEPT	LEAVESR	READE	SORTA
CHAIN	ELSE	EXFMT	MONITOR	READP	TEST
CLEAR	ENDDO	EXSR	NEXT	READPE	UNLOCK
CLOSE	ENDFOR	FEOD	ON-ERROR	REL	UPDATE
COMMIT	ENDIF	FOR	OPEN	RESET	WHEN
DEALLOC	ENDMON	FORCE	OTHER	RETURN	WRITE
DELETE	ENDSL	IF	OUT	ROLBK	
DOU	ENDSR	IN	POST	SELECT	

When you code free-format RPG, you must indicate where the free-format code begins and ends by specifying the **/FREE** and **/END-FREE** compiler directives, respectively, beginning in position 7. The compiler defaults to fixed-format RPG, and you can mix fixed- and free-format RPG code. When using free-format RPG, you cannot use the H, F, D, I, C, or O specification statements; this rule also applies to the beginning and ending **/FREE** and **/END-FREE** lines.

Free-Format RPG

Let's take the example we covered in Chapter 2 and convert it to free format so you can see a working example of free-format code. We will create a program called **AIR03_01** that will contain the main program and the **DSPINFO** subroutine to display the results. We'll place the **Air_getRank** procedure into a service program called **SVAIRSAMP**, which will contain two additional procedures to open and close the files with a file override.

Figure 3.1 shows the free-format RPG main program, **AIR03_01**.

```
FSTUDENTS   IF    E          K DISK
D*
D/COPY AIRLIB/AIRSRC,SPAIRSAMP
D*
D displayBytes    S              52A
D rank            S              10I 0
D rankAlpha       S              10A
C*
 /free
  Air_openFiles('MAINCAMPUS');
  setll *START STUDENTS;
  read STUDENTS;
  dow not %eof(STUDENTS);
    rank = Air_getRank(STACCT);
    exsr DSPINFO;
    read STUDENTS;
  enddo;
  Air_closeFiles();
  *inlr = *ON;
```

Figure 3.1: Free-format main program AIR03_01 to get and display student rankings

Reviewing this free-format code, you can note some differences from the fixed-format version:

- The free-format code begins with the **/FREE** directive.
- Each free-format line ends with a semicolon (;).
- In the free-format code, position is no longer used to determine syntax, so you can indent the source code for readability.
- You can call procedures without using the **CALLP** operation, as seen here with the calls to procedures **Air_openFiles** and **Air_closeFiles**.
- File I/O operations do not use indicators.
- The **%eof** built-in function determines when the end of file is encountered.
- Factor 1 fields are coded after the operation code, not before it.

Free-Format CALLP

The **CALLP** operation is not required in the free-format main program when calling **Air_openFiles** and **Air_closeFiles**, which override the applicable files used in the service program to the **MAINCAMPUS** physical file member. Because we aren't using the return values from these procedures, we can just reference the procedures in the program to be executed.

Determining the Status of Free-Format File Operations

For the **SETLL** operation, the ***START** value that is normally positioned before the operation code in fixed formatting as Factor 1 now follows **SETLL**. This is usually where you'll place Factor 1 when using the free-format syntax.

On the **READ** command, we no longer need to use the end-of-file indicator. Instead, the free-format program looks for the end of the file using the **%eof** built-in function. If the end of file is found, **%eof** returns ***ON**; otherwise, it returns ***OFF**. When you use **%eof**, the file name is optional; if you specify no file name, the function returns the **%eof** value for the most recent file I/O operation.

The **%eof** BIF not only returns the value for the last **READ**; it also is updated for **CHAIN**, **OPEN**, **READC**, **READE**, **READP**, **READPE**, **SETGT**, **SETLL**, and **WRITE** operations. So, if you were reading from one file and writing to another file within the same loop, the **%eof** value could change on the write unless you specify the file name on the **%eof** for the status that controls the loop.

The **%eof** function is the primary BIF we'll use throughout the book to determine file I/O status, but it is not the only BIF you can use. For example, the **%equal**, **%error**, and **%found** functions are also available. I'll introduce some of my other favorite BIFs later in the chapter.

Free-Format EVAL

You no longer need to explicitly code the **EVAL** operation code when using a procedure to return a value. Instead, you can simply use the equal sign (=), which returns the value to the left side of the expression from the procedure, equation, or operation on the right side of the expression.

Free-Format Subroutines

You can code subroutines right into the free-format code, delineating them with the **BEGSR** and **ENDSR** free-format operation codes. Such a code segment is a continuation of the main program, so the **/FREE** statement continues to apply. Figure 3.2 shows the code for the free-format **DSPINFO** subroutine.

```
//-----------------------------------------------------------
// DSPINFO: Displays the rank information
//-----------------------------------------------------------
begsr DSPINFO;
  displayBytes = '----------------';
  DSPLY displayBytes;
  displayBytes = 'First Name: ' + STFNAM;
  DSPLY displayBytes;
  displayBytes = 'Last Name: ' + STLNAM;
  DSPLY displayBytes;
  displayBytes = 'Major: ' + STMAJOR;
  DSPLY displayBytes;
/end-free
```

```
C* OPCODE 'MOVE' IS NOT AVAILABLE IN FREE-FORMAT
C                    MOVE      rank           rankAlpha
  /free
     displayBytes = 'Rank: ' + rankAlpha;
     DSPLY displayBytes;
   endsr;
  /end-free
```

Figure 3.2: AIR03_01 free-format subroutine DSPINFO

The subroutine begins and ends within free-format RPG using the **BEGSR** and **ENDSR** free-format RPG operation codes (although it does switch back to a single fixed-format RPG statement to execute the **MOVE** operation code, which is not available in free-format RPG). We could have implemented this functionality differently, but I wanted to illustrate the capability of switching between formats as well as to note that **MOVE** is not a valid free-format operation code.

I like to provide comments at the beginning of my procedures to give some notes about the purpose of each subroutine. In fixed-format RPG, you can use an asterisk (*) with the specification you're working with to indicate a comment. In free-format RPG, you simply code two forward slashes (//).

Java Note

Providing comments at the beginning of a subroutine or procedure comes with some additional capabilities in Java. A tool called Java-Doc lets you retrieve comments that are coded in a specific format to provide automated documentation in HTML format that describes the available classes and methods. We'll discuss JavaDoc further in the next chapter.

Using F and D Specs in a Service Program

Figure 3.3 shows the File Description and Definition specifications for service program **SVAIRSAMP**. In this program, we want independent file descriptors, so we'll define them in the service program and use a named activation group. The **SPAIRSAMP** source code will contain all the prototypes for the service program, so you could copy those prototypes into the service program and also reuse them in other programs that use the service program.

```
FSTUDENTS   IF   E              K DISK      usropn
FGRADES     IF   E              K DISK      usropn
D*
DXSTUDENTS        E DS                      EXTNAME(STUDENTS)
DHSTUDENTS        E DS                      EXTNAME(STUDENTS)
D                                           PREFIX(H)
D*
D/COPY AIRLIB/AIRSRC,SPAIRSAMP
```

Figure 3.3: SVAIRSAMP File Description and Definition specifications

Figure 3.4 shows the free-format **Air_getRank** procedure, which you can compare with its fixed-format counterpart in Chapter 2 to see how the two formats differ.

```
     *-------------------------------------------------------------------
     * Air_getRank: Retrieves the rank for students in the same major
     *-------------------------------------------------------------------
     P Air_getRank...
     P                   B                        export
     D Air_getRank...
     D                   PI          10I 0
     D   argAccount                   6S 0 const
     D* Local Variables
     D currentTotal     S           10I 0
     D currentCount     S           10I 0
     D score            S            7S 4
     D rankScore        S            7S 4
     D rank             S           10I 0
      /free
        rank = 0;
        chain argAccount STUDENTS;
        HSTUDENTS = XSTUDENTS;
        dou %eof(STUDENTS);
          currentTotal = 0;
          currentCount = 0;
          chain STACCT GRADES;
          dow not %eof(GRADES);
            currentTotal = currentTotal + SGCLGRADE;
            currentCount = currentCount + 1;
            reade STACCT GRADES;
          enddo;
          if currentCount = 0;
            score = 0;
          else;
            score = currentTotal / currentCount;
          endif;
```

```
      if STACCT = HSTACCT;
        rank = 1;
        rankScore = score;
        setll *START STUDENTS;
      else;
        if score > rankScore;
          rank = rank + 1;
        else;
        endif;
      endif;
      dou (STACCT <> HSTACCT AND STMAJOR = HSTMAJOR)
        or %eof(STUDENTS);
        read STUDENTS;
      enddo;
    enddo;
    return rank;
  /end-free
P                       E
```

Figure 3.4: SVAIRSAMP free-format procedure Air_getRank

One of the newly introduced concepts in procedure **Air_getRank** is the use of the **CHAIN** operation code, which is formatted similarly to the free-format **SETLL** operation code used in the main program, with Factor 1 following the **CHAIN** operation code.

You can also see the assignment of the data structures. The operation **HSTUDENTS = XSTUDENTS** copies the contents of the **XSTUDENTS** data structure into the **HSTUDENTS** data structure.

Procedure **Air_getRank** also contains nested loops that are controlled by the reading of different files. The logic flow in this procedure does not require us to specify the file names on the **%eof** BIFs, but doing so helps to ensure proper execution for any future enhancements that may change the flow of the program logic.

Using a Prototype with the QCMDEXC API

We covered the functionality of the **Air_openFiles** and **Air_closeFiles** procedures in Chapter 2. Now, let's introduce a new concept by creating a prototype for the commonly used **QCMDEXC** API and dropping it into the generic **SPAIRFUNC** service program prototype source file. Figure 3.5 shows the prototype for **QCMDEXC**.

```
D ExecuteCommand...
D                      PR                    extPgm('QCMDEXC')
D  argInCommand                 65535A      const options(*varsize)
D  argInLength                  15P 5 const
```

Figure 3.5: Prototype for QCMDEXC API

The arguments should be starting to look familiar to you, but notice the use of **extPgm** in the keyword field of the prototype. This keyword tells the compiler that you will be accessing an external program with this prototype, and the arguments will match the specified parameters on the API. (For **QCMDEXC**, you could also specify the optional **IGC** process control parameter.) When you use **extPgm**, all the parameters must be passed by reference.

Now that we've prototyped the **QCMDEXC** API, we can use this new prototype when applying the file overrides in our free-format **Air_openFiles** procedure (Figure 3.6).

```
 *------------------------------------------------------------------
 * Air_openFiles: Opens the files for the specified member
 *------------------------------------------------------------------
P Air_openFiles...
P                      B                    export
D Air_openFiles...
D                      PI             1N
D  argMember                 10A      const
D* Local Variables
D  retVal        S              1N
D  svString      S           1000A    varying
 /free
  retVal = *OFF;
  svString = 'OVRDBF FILE(STUDENTS) '
          + 'MBR(' + %trim(argMember) + ')';
  ExecuteCommand(svString: %len(svString));
  svString = 'OVRDBF FILE(GRADES) '
          + 'MBR(' + %trim(argMember) + ')';
  ExecuteCommand(svString: %len(svString));
  monitor;
    open STUDENTS;
    open GRADES;
```

```
   on-error;
     eval retVal = *ON;
   endmon;
   return retVal;
  /end-free
 P                        E
```

Figure 3.6: SVAIRSAMP free-format procedure Air_openFiles with QCMDEXC

Monitoring for Exceptions

Procedure **Air_openFiles** performs some basic exception handling using the **MONITOR** operation (which is also available in fixed-format coding). As you start to become familiar with Java, you will see similar capabilities achieved with a combination of Java's **try** and **catch**.

RPG's **MONITOR** operation code is similar to Java's **try** keyword. If an exception occurs within a monitored section of code, the program flow jumps to the exception-handling section of code contained in the **ON-ERROR** code segment, which is similar to **catch** in Java. You can also have multiple **ON-ERROR** exception handlers that evaluate the status code to determine which exception-handling code will be executed. You use the **MONITOR** operation to start the monitor group and use the **ENDMON** operation to end it.

For the **Air_openFiles** example, we could have used different techniques to perform exception handling when opening a file. For example, we could have coded the **(e)** operation extender on the **OPEN** operation to handle exceptions. Before execution of the command, special BIF values would be set to zero (**0**); you could then check for specific exceptions, such as **%ERROR**, **%STATUS**, and **%OPEN**, after the command was executed.

And that's not all! You can take even more control over your exception handing by creating user-written condition handlers using APIs **CEEHDLR** (Register a User-Written Condition Handler) and **CEEHDLU** (Unregister a User-Written Condition Handler). With these APIs, you can specify a procedure to be executed when an exception occurs and define the next system action to take: **RESUME**, **PERCOLATE**, or **PROMOTE**.

You can also use the *PSSR subroutine to handle program errors and use the INFSR subroutine for file errors. If you don't specify any exception handling, the default RPG error handler takes over.

Built-in Functions

Some built-in functions furnish additional functionality beyond the existing operation codes, and others provide a new format for existing operation codes. As you've no doubt noticed, built-in functions always start with the percent sign (%).

This section introduces the BIFs I most frequently use. This is not a complete list of the available built-in functions, but it should cover most of the ones we'll use in this book.

String Manipulation

I was once asked what my favorite BIF was, and I immediately said %trim. When I initially started out integrating RPG with Java, I would go through all my code repeatedly when experiencing problems, and the issue always seemed to come down to the strings I was using with Java, because the spaces were being used and they were not being trimmed. Today, I can't say that I don't still have those issues, but now one of the first things I look for is a missing %trim.

The %trim function is just one of several useful string-related BIFs:

%TRIM(string)
The %trim function returns the string that results from removing the leading and trailing blanks from a string passed in as the parameter.

%TRIML(string)
The %trimL function returns a string that is the result of removing only the leading blanks from the string passed in as the parameter.

%TRIMR(string)
The %trimR function returns a string that is the result of removing only the trailing blanks from the string passed in as the parameter.

%SUBST(string:start{:length})

The **%subst** function returns the portion of the string that is passed in as the first parameter beginning at the position indicated in the second parameter. If you do not specify the third parameter (a length), **%subst** returns the portion of the string from the starting position to the end of the string. If you specify the third parameter, the function returns the part of the string beginning at the starting position through the number of characters specified in the third parameter. The first character position of the string parameter has a starting index value of 1.

You can also use the **%subst** function on the left side of an **EVAL** statement to set a specific set of bytes within a character string.

%XLATE(from-characters: to-characters: string{: start position})

The **%xlate** function translates all instances of the "from" characters specified in the first parameter into the "to" characters specified in the second parameter. The returned value will have the character translations performed on the string that is passed in the third parameter. You can optionally specify the starting position of the translations.

%CHECK(comparator: base {:start})

The **%check** function checks the characters of the base string to make sure all the comparator characters are contained within the base. If all the characters in the base are found within the comparator, the result is zero. If a character is found in the base that is not contained in the comparator, the function returns the position of the first character in the base that is not contained in the comparator.

%CHECKR(comparator: base {:start})

The **%checkR** function is exactly the same as **%check** except it proceeds from right to left instead of left to right, as **%check** does. **%checkR** is useful for finding unspecified characters from the back of a string.

Using String-Manipulation BIFs to Preprocess External Files

Dealing with interface files from external systems is a good real-world example of the usefulness of some string-manipulation BIFs.

Suppose a file provided by an external system is not available in XML format, so you must process an ASCII text file. I've dealt with lots of systems that provided this type of information in many possible permutations. If it's possible to do it, you are sure to see it someday in such a file. You have to be able to handle the file and process it, especially if it contains data that generates revenue; you don't want to reject or misinterpret a single record. So, you'll want to preprocess the data and convert it into a usable format.

Figure 3.7 shows a simple program that emulates a worst-case file record, read without the file input/output complexities to distract from the main objective of string manipulation. The program accomplishes this by creating a simple string to represent a read operation that acts as a single line of data from an external file.

```
D inputBytes       S              42A
D subBytes         S              10A
D numberBytes      S              10A
D junkInBytes      S              10A
D junkOutBytes     S              10A
D displayBytes     S              52A
D posi             S              10I 0
D* XLATE STRUCTURE FOR LOWER- TO UPPER-CASE CONVERSION + X'3A' FOR E'*
D lc               S              27A
D uc               S              27A
C*
 /free
   // Lower-case and upper-case characters
   lc = 'abcdefghijklmnopqrstuvwxyz';
   uc = 'ABCDEFGHIJKLMNOPQRSTUVWXYZ';
   // ALSO include conversion of acute accent "E'" to "E" in Cafe' ***
   lc = %TRIM(LC) + X'3A';
   uc = %TRIM(UC) + 'E';
   junkInBytes = ':"''-,';
   junkOutBytes = '      ';
   numberBytes = '1234567890';
   inputBytes = '    621 '
              + 'Caf' + X'3A'
              + ', "Air" ''Book'':'
              + ' 1114-0812     ';
   displayBytes = '[' + inputBytes + ']';
   DSPLY displayBytes;
   // trim
```

```
displayBytes = '%trim['
                    + %trim(inputBytes)
                    + ']';
DSPLY displayBytes;
// trimR
displayBytes = '%trimR['
                    + %trimR(inputBytes)
                    + ']';
DSPLY displayBytes;
// trimL
displayBytes = '%trimL['
                    + %trimL(inputBytes)
                    + ']';
DSPLY displayBytes;
// Using %Check to Get the Front Number
posi = %check(numberBytes:%trimL(inputBytes));
subBytes = %subst(%trimL(inputBytes):1:posi);
displayBytes = 'Front # ['
                    + %trim(subBytes)
                    + ']';
DSPLY displayBytes;
// Using %checkR to Get the Back Number
posi = %checkR(numberBytes:%trimR(inputBytes));
subBytes = %subst(%trimR(inputBytes):posi+1);
displayBytes = 'Back # ['
                    + %trim(subBytes)
                    + ']';
DSPLY displayBytes;
// XLATE to UPPER Case
displayBytes = 'lc->UC['
                    + %xlate(lc:uc:inputBytes)
                    + ']';
DSPLY displayBytes;
// Strip the Junk
displayBytes = 'junk['
                    + %xlate(junkInBytes:junkOutBytes:inputBytes)
                    + ']';
DSPLY displayBytes;
// All Cleaned Up
displayBytes = 'clean['
                    + %trim(%xlate(lc:uc:
                      %xlate(junkInBytes:junkOutBytes:inputBytes)))
                    + ']';
DSPLY displayBytes;
*inlr = *ON;
/end-free
```

Figure 3.7: String-manipulation BIF program

Figure 3.8 shows the output you should expect to see after running the program.

```
> CALL AIR03_07
    DSPLY  [    621 Caf , "Air" 'Book': 1114-0812        ]
    DSPLY  %trim[621 Caf , "Air" 'Book': 1114-0812]
    DSPLY  %trimR[    621 Caf , "Air" 'Book': 1114-0812]
    DSPLY  %trimL[621 Caf , "Air" 'Book': 1114-0812        ]
    DSPLY  Front # [621]
    DSPLY  Back # [0812]
    DSPLY  lc->UC[    621 CAFE, "AIR" 'BOOK': 1114-0812        ]
    DSPLY  junk[    621 Caf    Air    Book    1114 0812        ]
    DSPLY  clean[621 CAFE    AIR    BOOK    1114 0812]
```

Figure 3.8: String-manipulation BIF program output

Let's review the code. The string (**inputBytes**) includes spaces at the beginning and end of the string, an acute accent e (**é**), double and single quotation marks (**"** and **'**), a colon (:), and a hyphen (-) between the last two numbers, just for good measure. In the output, brackets surround the resulting strings to identify any leading and trailing blanks.

- After the **%trim** function is executed, both the leading and trailing blanks are removed.

- After **%trimR** is executed, only the trailing blanks are removed.

- After **%trimL** is executed, only the leading blanks are removed.

- Using a combination of **%check** and **%trimL**, the sample program retrieves the first numeric value, which could have been passed as a number in a right-justified field.

- Using a combination of **%checkR** and **%trimR**, the program retrieves the last numeric value, which could have been passed as a number in a left-justified field.

- To retrieve the numbers at both the front and back of the string, the program uses the **%subst** BIF to pull the specified characters from the main string.

- In the output, the **lc->UC** line demonstrates how the **%xlate** BIF provides one way to convert all the lowercase letters to upper case, with an additional conversion for the acute accent e.

- The **junk** line shows the **%xlate** BIF in action again, removing any characters that you may find undesirable in your database when bringing in the information.
- Last, the **clean** line has the kitchen sink thrown at it, applying all the modifications to the data to provide the intended clean results.

You may laugh, but I've actually had files that contained every one of these instances in a single file. No lie!

Now, back to the BIFs. Let's see what else we can do with some new ones.

Bit Operations

Bit operations are useful when you're working with Unix-type APIs, and some Java classes also use bits. These operations are handy as well for code sets that can be reduced by logically ORing constants together to reduce the number of defined constants — a technique you'll see used later in the book for wrapping text around images in iText.

Most of the BIFs discussed in this book are available as of V5R1, but the bitwise logical BIFs became available in V5R2:

%BITAND(expression: expression {:expression...})
The **%bitAND** function evaluates as *ON when all the bits are set on; otherwise, the result is *OFF.

%BITOR(expression: expression {:expression...})
The **%bitOR** function evaluates as *ON when any bits are set on; otherwise, the result is *OFF.

%BITNOT(expression)
The **%bitNOT** function evaluates as *ON when any bit is set off; otherwise, the result is *OFF.

%BITXOR(expression: expression)
The **%bitXOR** function evaluates as *ON when only one bit is set on and the rest are set off; otherwise, the result is *OFF.

When it comes to bit operations, you can use different data types for your operations; all that matters is how many bytes the data type uses. The functions all behave the same when manipulating the bits. Bits are bits, but when you use variables with the bit operators, all the variables involved must be of the same type.

Characters use one byte of space for each character. Integers have four allowable sizes: 3, 5, 10, and 20. Table 3.2 summarizes the bytes and ranges for signed integers.

Table 3.2: Integer bytes and ranges		
Integer	Number of bytes	Range
3I 0	1	−128 to 127
5I 0	2	−32768 to 32767
10I 0	4	−2147483648 to 2147483647
20I 0	8	−9223372036854775808 to 9223372036854775807

Unsigned integers also have four allowable sizes: 3, 5, 10, and 20. Unsigned does not support negative numbers, so the bit used for the sign in integers is available for the number in unsigned numbers. Table 3.3 summarizes the bytes and ranges for unsigned integers.

Table 3.3: Unsigned integer bytes and ranges		
Unsigned integer	Number of bytes	Range
3U 0	1	0 to 255
5U 0	2	0 to 65535
10U 0	4	0 to 4294967295
20U 0	8	0 to 18446744073709551615

Figure 3.9 shows a sample free-format program that uses the bit operation BIFs.

```
D airChar          S               2A
D airInt           S               5I 0
D airUnsigned1     S               5U 0
D airUnsigned2     S               5U 0
D airResult        S               5U 0
D airResultBig     S              10U 0
D displayBytes     S              52A
C*
```

```
/free
  // All of these variables take two bytes of space.
  airChar = x'FFFF';
  airInt = x'2222';

  // airUnsigned1 and 2 have alternating bits assigned.
  // airUnsigned1 = x'5555' = binary'0101 0101 0101 0101'
  // airUnsigned2 = x'AAAA' = binary'1010 1010 1010 1010'
  airUnsigned1 = x'5555';
  airUnsigned2 = x'AAAA';

  airResult = %bitAND(airUnsigned1: airUnsigned2);
  // airResult = x'0000' = binary'0000 0000 0000 0000'

  airResult = %bitOR(airUnsigned1: airUnsigned2);
  // airResult = x'FFFF' = binary'1111 1111 1111 1111'

  airResultBig = %bitXOR(airUnsigned1: airUnsigned2);
  // airResultBig
  //    = x'0000FFFF'
  //    = binary'0000 0000 0000 0000 1111 1111 1111 1111'

  airResult = %bitNOT(airUnsigned1);
  // airResult = x'AAAA' = binary'1010 1010 1010 1010'
  *inlr = *ON;
/end-free
```

Figure 3.9: Bit operation BIF program

The **airChar** and **airInt** variables accept the hexadecimal values into the two bytes of available space, but you cannot use these values with the bit operators unless both the expressions and the result are also of the same type.

Variable **airResult** is of type unsigned integer, so the expressions must also be of type unsigned integer. Although they must be the same type, they need not be the same size, as illustrated with the use of **airResultBig**, which has a size of **10U 0**.

Quantification BIFs

A few other built-in functions will prove themselves useful in your free-format RPG programs and over the course of this book:

%PARMS

The **%parms** function returns the number of parameters that were passed in to a procedure. If the number of parameters cannot be determined, the value – 1 is returned. You use **%parms** when you have a procedure that specifies the **options(*NOPASS)** keyword on the variable declaration of the list of input parameters to indicate that a parameter is optional.

%ELEM

The **%elem** function returns the number of elements in a multiple-element variable of an array or a multiple-occurrence data structure. This BIF doesn't tell you the number of populated elements; it tells you the total number of elements that are declared for the variable.

%SIZE(variable{:*ALL})

The **%size** function returns the size of the specified variable. If you pass in the name of a multiple-element variable, such as an array, the BIF returns the variable size of a single element. If you pass in the optional second parameter *ALL, the function returns the size of all the elements, so you would receive the same results as **%SIZE(array) * %ELEM(array)**.

%LEN(expression)

You use the **%len** function to get or set the length of a variable. If the variable is a varying-length variable, the function retrieves the value stored in the first two bytes, which indicate the number of bytes in the variable that represent the data. If the variable is neither varying nor numeric, the return value is the same as the **%size** of the variable, which is the size allocated to the variable when it was declared. If the variable is numeric, the return value identifies the precision of the number.

You can also use **%len** to set the length of the variable on the left side of an **EVAL** statement, but only for varying variables.

The sample program in Figure 3.10 defines the results of the quantification BIFs and throws in a little bit of variable scoping along the way.

```
D/COPY AIRLIB/AIRSRC,SPAIRFUNC
D Air_quantify      PR              10I 0
D   arg1                            10A    const varying options(*varsize)
D   arg2                            10A    const varying options(*varsize)
```

```
D   argEOL                          10A    const varying
D                                          options(*nopass: *omit: *varsize)
D   argBold                         1N     options(*nopass: *omit)
D*
D airResult        S               10I 0
D airBold          S                1N
D displayBytes     S               52A
C*
 /free
   // All of these variables take two bytes of space.
   airBold = *ON;
   dis    playBytes = 'Result Size:';
   airResult = Air_quantify('Bold ': 'Line':*OMIT: airBold);
   displayBytes = %trim(displayBytes) + ' '
                     + %trim(%editc(airResult:'Z'));
   DSPLY displayBytes;
   *inlr = *ON;
 /end-free
```

Figure 3.10: Quantification main program with prototype for Air_quantify

The mainline program looks easy enough, but why is the **displayBytes** variable initialized in a different location when we could just assign it with the results? I did this deliberately to provide an example of variable scoping. When you look at the quantification procedure (Figure 3.11), you can see that **displayBytes** is declared again and the value is changed within the procedure, but the value will not be changed in the main program.

```
P Air_quantify      B                      EXPORT
*
D Air_quantify      PI              10I 0
D   arg1                            10A    const varying options(*varsize)
D   arg2                            10A    const varying options(*varsize)
D   argEOL                          10A    const varying
D                                          options(*nopass: *OMIT: *varsize)
D   argBold                          1N    options(*nopass: *OMIT)
 * LOCAL VARIABLES *
D displayBytes     S               52A
D svReturn         S               10I 0
D svBold           S                1N
D svEOL            S               10A
D svArray          S               10A    DIM(20)
D svOccur          S               25A    DIM(35)
 /free
   svReturn = *ZEROS;
   displayBytes = 'array [size] '
                     + %trim(%editc(%size(svArray):'Z'))
```

```
                        + ' [elem] '
                        + %trim(%editc(%elem(svArray):'Z'));
      DSPLY displayBytes;
      displayBytes = 'occur [size] '
                        + %trim(%editc(%size(svOccur):'Z'))
                        + ' [elem] '
                        + %trim(%editc(%elem(svOccur):'Z'));
      DSPLY displayBytes;
      displayBytes = 'len[1] ' + %trim(%editc(%len(arg1):'Z'))
                        + ' len[2] ' + %trim(%editc(%len(arg2):'Z'));
      DSPLY displayBytes;
      displayBytes = 'size[1] ' + %trim(%editc(%size(arg1):'Z'))
                        + ' size[2] ' + %trim(%editc(%size(arg2):'Z'));
      DSPLY displayBytes;
      svEOL = EBCDIC_CR + EBCDIC_LF;
      if %parms > 2;
        if %addr(argEOL) <> *NULL;
          eval svEOL = argEOL;
        else;
        endif;
      else;
      endif;
      displayBytes = 'argEol size: ' + %trim(%editc(%size(svEOL):'Z'))
                    + ' length: ' + %trim(%editc(%len(svEOL):'Z'));
      DSPLY displayBytes;
      displayBytes = 'Required: '
                    + arg1 + arg2
                    + svEOL;
      DSPLY displayBytes;
      svBold = *OFF;
      if %parms > 3;
        if %addr(argBold) <> *NULL;
          svBold = argBold;
        else;
        endif;
      else;
      endif;
      if svBold;
        eval displayBytes = '<b>'
                        + %trim(displayBytes)
                        + '</b>';
      else;
      endif;
      DSPLY displayBytes;
      svReturn = %len(%trim(displayBytes));
      return svReturn;
     /end-free
    C*
    P                         E
```

Figure 3.11: Quantification procedure illustrating use of quantification BIFs

Figure 3.12 shows the results of running the program.

```
> call AIRO3_10
   DSPLY   array [size] 10 [elem] 20
   DSPLY   occur [size] 25 [elem] 35
   DSPLY   len[1] 5 len[2] 4
   DSPLY   size[1] 12 size[2] 12
   DSPLY   argEol size: 10 length: 10
   DSPLY   Required: Bold Line█
   DSPLY   <b>Required: Bold Line█</b>
   DSPLY   Result Size: 28
```

Figure 3.12: Quantification program output

The size of the **10A** varying fields is 12 because the first two bytes are used to store the length value of the data in the **10A** character fields.

The length of **argEOL** is the same as the size. This is because **argEOL** is not a varying field, so the length of the variable includes every character in the variable.

To Learn More

There are plenty more BIFs out there to explore. The functions covered here have been selectively included to provide details about their functionality for use in future chapters. For more information about these and all the other BIFs available to you, see IBM's *ILE RPG Reference*. Another great source of information about BIFs and free-format RPG is the book *Free-Format RPG IV* by Jim Martin (MC Press, 2005), which presents useful combinations of various methods to provide easily reusable procedures.

APIs

Application programming interfaces represent the next step beyond built-in functions and operation codes. APIs fully satisfy the goal of procedures discussed in Chapter 3, which is to provide functionality with no dependencies on the main program that calls it. All you need to know is the functionality of the API and which parameters to use with it.

APIs provide lower-level access to the system than built-in functions and operation codes do. BIFs and operation codes actually use APIs, but they give RPG and CL a high-level language means of accessing the APIs' functionality, preventing you from worrying about the details.

There are many APIs to choose from, and IBM provides a useful API finder that you can use to search for APIs by name or by category. The API finder is available at the IBM i Information Center (*http://publib.boulder.ibm.com/iseries*) under **Programming|Application programming interfaces**.

We will use three APIs extensively when working with Java. In this final part of the chapter, we'll discuss these APIs and create some RPG-friendly procedures for reuse in future chapters.

Converting Between EBCDIC and ASCII

The **iconv()** (Code Conversion) API converts from one Coded Character Set Identifier (CCSID) to another. There is an extensive set of CCSIDs from which to choose, but we will be interested primarily in the EBCDIC code set and the ASCII code set; you can use the **iconv()** API to convert between these two character sets. This API requires the use of a conversion descriptor, which needs to be opened and closed.

Using **iconv()** is a three-step process:

1. Open the conversion descriptor.
2. Convert a buffer of characters using the conversion descriptor.
3. Close the conversion descriptor.

The ability to convert between EBCDIC and ASCII is useful when RPG and Java communicate with each other using the Java Native Interface (JNI), which we'll begin discussing in Chapter 5. You can also use the **iconv()** API to convert character sets for international applications.

Table 3.4 lists some commonly used CCSIDs. A complete list of CCSIDs is available at *http://www.ibm.com/servers/eserver/iseries/software/globalization/ccsid.html*.

Table 3.4: Commonly used coded character set identifiers	
Encoding	**CCSID**
EBCDIC	37
ASCII	367
ISO-8859-1	819
UTF-8	1208

ISO-8859 is an extension of the ASCII code set that leaves the first 128 characters intact. You could use ISO-8859 encoding instead of ASCII to implement a more extensive set of characters.

UTF-8 extends the ASCII code set even further by extending the ISO-8859 character set and keeping the first 256 characters intact. UTF-16 and UTF-32 also support ASCII and ISO-8859, but the number of bits per character increases from 8 to 16 and 32, respectively, so they are not exactly the same.

An Alternative: The QDCXLATE API

The **QDCXLATE** (Convert Data) API is an alternative to using the **iconv()** API. **QDCXLATE** uses tables to convert from one character set to the other. The most recent tables used to support EBCDIC and ASCII are **QTCPEBC** and **QTCPASC**, respectively. This option may be sufficient for simple cases, and you can also create custom tables for use with the **QDCXLATE** API. The **iconv()** API may be more complicated than **QDCXLATE**, but it is also more flexible and current.

Opening the Conversion Descriptor

The **QtqIconvOpen()** (Code Conversion Allocation) API returns a conversion descriptor that performs the conversions specified in the **tocode** and **fromcode** CCSID values passed to the API. We will be converting between the EBCDIC and ASCII CCSIDs. The EBCDIC value can be set to the zero value to indicate the default system CCSID.

Figure 3.13 shows the RPG prototype for the **QtqIconvOpen()** API.

```
D* Open the conversion descriptor

D QtqIconvOpen     PR                    extProc('QtqIconvOpen')
D                                        like(iconv_t)
D   argToCCSID                           like(QtqCode_t) const
D   argFromCCSID                         like(QtqCode_t) const
```

Figure 3.13: Prototype for QtqIconvOpen() API

The API takes two parameters:

- **argToCCSID** — A pointer to a **QtqCode** data structure that contains the CCSID to convert *to*.

- **argFromCCSID** — A pointer to a **QtqCode** data structure that contains the CCSID to convert *from*.

Figure 3.14 shows the **QtqCode_t** data structure, which is defined in the **QSYSINC/QRPGLESRC,QTQICONV** source file.

```
DQtqCode_t          DS
D QTQCCSID                  1      4B 0
D QTQCA                     5      8B 0
D QTQSA                     9     12B 0
D QTQSA00                  13     16B 0
D QTQLO                    17     20B 0
D QTQMEO                   21     24B 0
D QTQERVED02               25     32
```

Figure 3.14: QtqCode_t data structure from QSYSINC/QRPGLESRC,QTQICONV

API **QtqIconvOpen()** returns the conversion descriptor in an **iconv_t** data structure. This data structure (Figure 3.15) is defined in the **QSYSINC/ QRPGLESRC,ICONV** source file.

```
D*definition of iconv_t type
Diconv_t             DS
D ICORV                     1      4B 0
D ICOC                      5     52B 0 DIM(00012)
```

Figure 3.15: iconv_t data structure from QSYSINC/QRPGLESRC,ICONV

An alternative API called **iconv_open()** (Code Conversion Allocation) provides the same functionality as **QtqIconvOpen()**. The only difference is in the interface, which uses characters instead of the **QtqCode_t** data structure.

Converting the CCSID Using the Conversion Descriptor

The **iconv()** API performs the actual CCSID conversion using the conversion descriptor returned from the **QtqIconvOpen()** API. You can use **iconv()** repeatedly with the same conversion descriptor without having to open and close the descriptor for each use. Figure 3.16 shows the RPG prototype for the **iconv()** API.

```
D* Convert CCSID from input buffer to output buffer
D Iconv           PR              ExtProc('iconv')
D  argConvDesc                    like(iconv_t) value
D  argInBuffer                *
D  argInBytes                10I 0
D  argOutBuffer               *
D  argOutBytes               10I 0
```

Figure 3.16: Prototype for iconv() API

The original characters to be converted are placed into the input buffer, and the results are returned in the output buffer.

Closing the Conversion Descriptor

A third API, **iconv_close()** (Code Conversion Deallocation), closes the conversion descriptor. You will want to call this API when you're finished using the conversion descriptor (Figure 3.17).

```
D* Close the conversion descriptor

D iconv_close     PR         10I 0 ExtProc('iconv_close')
D  argConvDesc                    like(iconv_t) value
```

Figure 3.17: Prototype for iconv_close() API

Creating the Custom Procedures

You can use the three **iconv()** APIs just as they are, or you can create custom procedures to simplify the APIs and make them more RPG-friendly.

Procedure **Air_openConverter** (Figure 3.18) simplifies the use of the **QtqIconvOpen()** API by requiring only the two numbers that represent the CCSIDs with which you want to work. All the other details of initializing the data structures are handled within the custom procedure.

```
     *------------------------------------------------------------------
     * Air_openConverter: Opens the conversion descriptor for iconv()
     *------------------------------------------------------------------
P Air_openConverter...
P                         B                    export
D Air_openConverter...
D                         PI                   likeDs(iconv_t)
D    argToCCSID                    10I 0
D    argFromCCSID                  10I 0 options(*nopass)
D* Local Variables
D from              DS                   likeDs(QtqCode_t)
D to                DS                   likeDs(QtqCode_t)
D cd                DS                   likeDs(iconv_t)
D*****************************************************************************
 /free
   // Set the target CCSID
   to = *ALLx'00';
   to.QTQCCSID = argToCCSID;
   to.QTQSA00 = 1;
   // If Specified, Set the From CCSID
   from = *ALLx'00';
   if %PARMS < 2;
     from.QTQCCSID = 0;
   else;
     from.QTQCCSID = argFromCCSID;
   endif;
   from.QTQSA00 = 1;
   // If Specified, Set the From CCSID
   cd = QtqIconvOpen(to: from);
   if (cd.ICORV < *zeros);
     // FAILURE
   else;
     // SUCCESS
```

```
       endif;
       return cd;
      /end-free
     P                    E
```

Figure 3.18: Procedure Air_openConverter

The final result we are looking for with the use of these APIs is to convert between EBCDIC and ASCII. So, let's eliminate the details of pointers, buffers, and APIs and create a simple procedure that we can use to pass in the string we want to convert and the conversion descriptor that is returned for **Air_openConverter** (Figure 3.19).

```
     *----------------------------------------------------------------
     * Air_convert: Converts the CCSIDs of conversion descriptor
     *----------------------------------------------------------------
     P Air_convert...
     P                     B                  EXPORT
     D Air_convert...
     D                     PI       65535A    varying
     D   argCd                                likeDs(iconv_t)
     D   argInString                65535A    const varying
     D****************************************************************
     D inBuf          S       65535A
     D inBufPtr       S            *
     D inBufBytes     S          10I 0
     D outBuf         S       65535A
     D outBufPtr      S            *
     D outBufBytes    S          10I 0
     D bytesIn        S          10I 0
     D bytesOut       S          10I 0
     D outReturn      S       65535A    varying
     D****************************************************************
      /free
        inBuf = argInString;
        inBufPtr = %addr(inBuf);
        // Set to hex zeros or will initialize to EBCDIC spaces
        outBuf = *ALLx'00';
        outBufPtr = %addr(outBuf);
        // Do not trimR, use Varying and %len()
        inBufBytes = %len(argInString);
        outBufBytes = %size(outBuf);
        bytesIn = outBufBytes;
        iconv(argCd: inBufPtr: inBufBytes:
                     outBufPtr: outBufBytes);
        bytesOut = bytesIn - outBufBytes;
```

```
  outReturn = %subst(outBuf:1:bytesOut);
  return outReturn;
 /end-free
P                       E
```

Figure 3.19: Procedure Air_convert

Procedure **Air_closeConverter** (Figure 3.20) does nothing additional to support the **iconv_close()** API, but I created a custom procedure to keep the three associated APIs standardized. This step will also make it easier to understand the code and prepare for any future enhancements or exception handling.

```
  *----------------------------------------------------------------
  * Air_closeConverter: Closes the conversion descriptor
  *----------------------------------------------------------------
P Air_closeConverter...
P                B                    EXPORT
D Air_closeConverter...
D                PI
D   argCd                             likeDs(iconv_t)
D***************************************************************************
 /free
  iconv_close(argCd);
 /end-free
P                E
```

Figure 3.20: Procedure Air_closeConverter

Now that we have three simple and clean procedures to take advantage of the capabilities the APIs provide, let's put together a program that uses all these procedures in a worst-case scenario. Figure 3.21 shows the sample RPG program.

```
D***************************************************************************
D*    SAMPLE USE OF CCSID CONVERSIONS
D***************************************************************************
D to                DS               likeDs(QtqCode_t)
D from              DS               likeDs(QtqCode_t)
D cd                DS               likeDs(iconv_t)
D ebcdicString      S        10A     varying
D asciiString       S        10A     varying
D toCCSID           S        10I 0
D***************************************************************************
```

```
/free
 toCCSID = 1208;
 ebcdicString = '@AS/400@';
 cd = Air_openConverter(toCCSID);
 asciiString = Air_convert(cd: ebcdicString);
 Air_closeConverter(cd);
 *inLr = *ON;
/end-free
```

Figure 3.21: Main program demonstrating use of custom CCSID procedures

If you were to debug this program and place a breakpoint immediately after the execution of the **Air_convert** procedure and display the variable values, you would see the results shown in Figure 3.22.

```
eval ebcdicString = '@AS/400@       '
eval ebcdicString:x = 0008B5C1 E261F4F0 F0B50000 ....

eval asciiString = '    ë□□□□'
eval asciiString:x = 00084041 532F3430 30400000 ....
```

Figure 3.22: CCSID conversion program output

You can verify that the conversion was successful by manually checking each character in the EBCDIC and ASCII translation table provided in Appendix A.

As you can see here, there is minimal complexity. We were able to remove the need for pointers and complex data structures, with the exception of the conversion descriptor implementation of the **iconv_t** data structure. I contemplated putting a global structure in the service program, but I decided not to because I wanted to support multiple construction descriptors in the application.

You could simplify your conversions by creating a single procedure to convert between different CCSIDs that would open the conversion descriptor, perform the conversion, and then close the conversion descriptor. But then you would be putting additional overhead into programs that might use this functionality repeatedly in an application. So, I chose to separate the three steps to permit the reuse of the conversion descriptor without the need to repeatedly open and close it. You always face a tradeoff between simplicity and speed, and you may choose to take a different approach, but this code seems simple enough.

Note: When using the **iconv()** API to convert between CCSIDs, do not use a variable with the **varying** keyword because **iconv()** will convert the first two bytes of the value, which contain the length of the data. A variable with the **varying** attribute will not display the characters represented in the first two bytes unless you view the variable's hexadecimal value.

4

Introduction to Java

Although this book is not intended to teach you Java, successfully integrating RPG with Java will require you to understand some basic Java concepts. For this reason, we'll discuss Java from a very high-level view. The Java topics you'll learn about in this chapter will help you to understand how the RPG wrappers are written to access the Java class files. A familiarity with these concepts will also be useful should you decide to expand your RPG wrapper library to contain new or custom Java applications.

Java Classes

In Java, a *class* is a template for the behavior of each Java object that is created. A class also provides the capability to define generic behaviors for all the objects that you create as instances of the class.

Every piece of Java code is written within a class. The name of the file that contains the source code for the class ends with the file extension **.java**. When you compile this code, a file with the **.class** extension is created.

Java Methods

A Java *method* is similar to an RPG procedure. Both Java methods and RPG procedures use a specified parameter list that is validated during compile time. Methods are contained within classes and usually implement get or set operations to retrieve values for the particular instance of the class upon which a method is being used.

All classes have at least one method, which exists whether you code it or not. This method is the *constructor method*, and it is used to create a new instance of the class. If you do not include a constructor method in your class, a default constructor is assigned to the class automatically.

Java Objects

When a Java object is initialized, memory is allocated for the object that is being created. You create an object by specifying the **new** keyword on the constructor method of the class. The **new** operator allocates the memory for the object and returns a variable, called a *reference variable*, that refers to the memory location used to store the object.

The object will also have a *state*. The object's state is like a snapshot of all the values of the variables contained within the object.

RPG Note

You can think of a class in Java as being comparable to an RPG program object. The source code contains the logic of the program and is compiled into an executable program. This comparison is not 100 percent accurate, however, because Java classes are actually compiled into byte-code for execution by the Java Virtual Machine (JVM).

RPG Note

When you call an RPG program, the program allocates memory for itself and all its variables and places itself on the call stack. When you run the program, the variables are changed within the program, reflecting the program's state. If the program crashes and you select D (from the familiar C, D, I, and R options) to dump the program, the dump will list all the values that the variables had when the program crashed. You can think of that RPG call stack dump of values as the state of the RPG object instance at the time the program crashed.

Let's get started with our first piece of Java code. For an example, we'll create a generic class to be used to represent a person. We'll name this class **AirPerson**. Figure 4.1 shows the Java code for the class.

```
/**********************************************************
 * The <B>AirPerson</B> class is a generic class
 * intended to be extended to exploit inheritance.
 * @author Tom Snyder
 **********************************************************/
public class AirPerson
 {
 /**
  *  Default Constructor is optional
  */
 public AirPerson()
   {
   }
 }
```

Figure 4.1: AirPerson class with constructor method

Because the class name is **AirPerson**, the source code must be contained in a Java source file named **AirPerson.java**. The constructor method, **AirPerson()**, has the exact same name as the class and is case-sensitive. This particular class has no code between the curly braces that follow the **AirPerson()** constructor method, so the constructor will behave exactly like the default constructor.

Another acceptable name for this class could have been simply **Person**. However, because the name **Person** is so generic, there might very well be another class named **Person** in use elsewhere in the application. Giving a unique name to the class helps avoid any ambiguity. An alternative is to fully qualify the class name, a method you'll learn about in the next section. The choice is a matter of preference, and either technique is acceptable.

Java Packages

Java programmers typically organize classes into *packages*. A package groups code for easy distribution and provides a way to reference the classes contained in the package using unique naming conventions that include the package name. Sun's naming convention suggests using your company's Internet domain name as the starting point for package names, specifying the domain in reverse order to ensure uniqueness. For example, a package created by a programmer at a company whose domain name is **twowolvesout.com** would begin with **com.twowolvesout**.

When importing a package into a program, you can specify an asterisk (*) after the package name — **com.twowolvesout.*** — to make all the classes of the package accessible from the program. To include only a single class from the package, you use the fully qualified class reference in your import statement — **com. twowolvesout.AirClass**, for example.

When I'm using multiple classes from a package, I typically name the classes in a way that will ensure uniqueness most of the time, and then I include the package in the import statement. If I'm using only one class from the package, I specify the fully qualified class name on the import statement.

The package reference actually represents the physical location of the class files in the directory structure of your storage device. So, **com.twowolvesout.AirClass** represents the file **com/twowolvesout/AirClass.class** in the directory structure, with the root directory of the package being relative to the class path.

Java Subpackages

Packages can be contained within packages to provide better organization of code. Such *subpackages* represent the same directory structure as a package by creating subdirectories within the main directory of the package. Using the asterisk in an import statement to include a package within the code specifies all the contents of the specified package, but it does not include any subpackages.

RPG Note

Java programmers use packages to group classes into a unique reference location. The idea is similar to what you do when you install third-party RPG programs on your IBM i system and put them into their own library. By specifying the library name with the program name, you can ensure the use of the third-party programs.

Similarly, if you had a generic program that was named the same as another program higher in your library list, you could access the generic program by including the library name to access it. This practice is comparable to using the fully qualified package name with the class in Java.

For example, if you created a subpackage named **air** within the **com.twowolvesout** package and you wanted to specify the packages using import statements, you would have to import both the **com.twowolvesout.*** package and the **com.twowolvesout. air.*** package to include the main package's classes as well as the classes contained within the **air** subpackage. If the **air** subpackage contained a class named **AirSub-Class**, you would refer to this class using the full name of **com.twowolvesout.air. AirSubClass** within your code.

Jar Files

Java Archive (Jar) files are commonly used to distribute Java packages, and you can place these files into your class path for access from your applications. We'll use this technique for the open-source projects we'll work with in later chapters.

Jar files are similar to the commonly used Zip format and contain an optional manifest file that indicates the main class to be used as the entry point of execution. This information lets the Jar file be executed as an application.

Jar files can contain multiple files, and they are organized in a directory structure that can be accessed from the class path in which they are placed.

Import

When you write Java code, you most likely will use classes from outside the package in which you are working. To do this, you must *import* the classes to provide access to your new program or class. To identify classes from other packages to use within your program, you use the **import** keyword. You specify any import statements immediately after the optional package name, which you would place on the first line.

As I noted previously, you can specify a wild card to include all the classes for a particular package or subpackage, or you can specify a single class to import. The ability to import methods depends on the access that is specified for the methods; we'll discuss this topic soon, when we get into public and private access control.

Class Path

The *class path* is like your library list in RPG. It tells the Java runtime environment where to find all the classes that are being used by your program/class when it is compiled. If you specify a package to import in your Java code and the package is not found in your class path, the Java compiler will throw an error.

When you use a class in your Java code, you can simply specify the class name without the full package name; in this case, the class either must be included in one of the packages defined in the import statements or must be contained within the same package. The compiler will search your class path and use the first class it finds in the first package in the class path. This behavior is similar to searching the library list when referencing a program or file.

If you instead specify the fully qualified class name to include the package name, the program will use the class from the specified package for ambiguously named classes.

Static Methods

You can assign the **static** attribute to a method of a class to identify the method as unique to the class and not specific to an instance of the class.

RPG Note

If an RPG program refers to a Java class that is not found in the class path, the RPG program will compile with no trouble. You'll discover the problem when the RPG program tries to use the class.

RPG Note

A physical file has a *file definition* to describe the fields that make up the data. When you populate the file with data, you create *records* within that file. You could think of each one of these records as an *instance* of the file definition. When you look at the records within the physical file, each record is in the same format that matches the file definition.

Because the file definition does not depend on which record you're looking at, you could say that the file definition is a static attribute of the file. If you were interested in a specific field of data within a record, this would depend on the record because each record is non-static and could contain a different value.

Main Method

The **main** method is the entry point for a Java application. The JVM looks for a method named **main** to use as the starting point of execution. Therefore, you must always have at least one class that has a **main** method to begin execution. After that, you can reference all the other classes from the class that contains the main entry point.

Naming Conventions

It is a Java naming standard to begin variable names and methods with a lowercase letter and to begin class references with an uppercase letter. So, **AccountNumber** indicates a class, and **accountNumber** implies a variable name. This naming style is not a requirement for the compiler, but its use is strongly encouraged.

Camel case is an additional Java naming convention used for standardization as well as compliance with the JavaBeans specifications. When a variable name contains more than one "word," the camel case style uses lowercase letters for most of the name, switching to upper case to identify the beginning of subsequent words. For example, a variable representing an account number would be **accountNumber** in camel case.

Public and Private Access Control

The **public** Java attribute specifies that a class, method, or variable is visible to other classes for use, regardless of the package to which the class, method, or variable belongs. As long as a class imports the package of the public class, method, or variable (or is part of the same package), the class will be able to access it.

The **private** attribute indicates that the method or variable is visible only to the class within which it is defined. Java programmers usually make variables private to force access to variables through methods instead of via direct manipulation. The **private** attribute aids modular coding and helps ensure consistent behavior.

Two less commonly used access modifiers, **protected** and **default**, provide access control within a package of classes. If you specify no access control keyword, the default access control is assigned.

Encapsulation and the JavaBeans Naming Standards

In RPG, you may have variables that are defined in the D specifications and used globally throughout the entire program and shared within subroutines. When you review the source code of an RPG program, you

> **RPG Note**
>
> When we discussed service programs in Chapter 3, we talked about exporting procedures to make them visible to the programs that use them. This practice is equivalent to using public and private access modifiers. A procedure that is exported in a service program is equivalent to a public method in Java.

may have subroutines that seem to serve a clear purpose. However, unanticipated changes to the values of variables within a subroutine may alter the expected results of the subsequent code. Or, another programmer might make changes to the subroutine that modify the variable in the subroutine and break the code.

To help with this problem, an RPG procedure can use global variables defined in the D specifications or use variables that are declared within the procedure with a scope of usage that is limited to the procedure (as we discussed in Chapter 2). In Java, you are strongly encouraged to *encapsulate* the variables you define within a class by making the variables private and providing access to them only through publicly accessible methods so that no one can modify the variable values directly.

When you force access to variables through methods, public access to the variables is not available, and other programmers can't write code that directly accesses the variables. You thus gain greater control over your code and help ensure stable results in future releases of the code, without the threat of breaking the code of another program that uses your classes. There are always exceptions to the rule, but following the JavaBeans specifications for variable access is usually best.

One example of an exception to the rule of always making your mutable (changeable) variables private is providing a publicly accessible variable that lets a program cancel execution of a method by changing the variable to exit the method as soon as possible. This is a good feature when you have multiple threads and want one thread to be able to tell another to stop as soon as possible in a controlled manner. You can do this by providing a publicly accessible **boolean** variable that the program checks during each iteration of a loop to see whether it should exit.

Another typical exception to the making-all-variables-private rule is when you want to define constants that are associated with a class; in this case, you can provide publicly accessible variables without the need for get and set methods because you would never be changing the values of the constants.

In most cases, you will want to restrict access to variables through methods on the first version of your program; then, you won't have to worry about changing the access in future versions. Even if you have no customized exception handling at the time of release, you should still make the variable private and provide the procedure for future implementation of additional logic.

Let's add some basic variables to our **AirPerson** class to allow the first and last name to be assigned to the object. We'll declare the variables as private and force access through some methods (Figure 4.2).

```java
package com.twowolvesout.air;
/**********************************************************
 * The <B>AirPerson</B> class is a generic class
 * intended to be extended to exploit inheritance.
 * @author Tom Snyder
 **********************************************************/
public class AirPerson
  {
  /**
   *  Default Constructor is optional
   */
  public AirPerson()
    {
    }
  /**
   * Returns the first name of the person
   * @return firstName The String value of the first name
   */
```

```java
public String getFirstName()
  {
  return firstName;
  }
/**
 * Sets the first name of the person
 * @param inString The first name of the person
 */
public void setFirstName(String inString)
  {
  firstName = inString;
  }
/**
 * Returns the last name of the person
 * @return lastName The String value of the last name
 */
public String getLastName()
  {
  return lastName;
  }
/**
 * Sets the last name of the person
 * @param inString The last name of the person
 */
public void setLastName(String inString)
  {
  lastName = inString;
  }
private String firstName;
private String lastName;
}
```

Figure 4.2: AirPerson class using access methods to promote encapsulation

Notice the comments included in this Java code. These notations are written in a specific format to enable the JavaDoc automated documentation tool to produce HTML documentation describing the class and its methods. We'll discuss JavaDocs in greater detail later in the chapter.

The JavaBeans naming standards specify the way publicly accessible methods are named. According to these standards, if you are going to change the value of a variable, the method name will start with **set**. If you are retrieving the value of a variable, you will use the **get** prefix on the method name. The rest of the method name should match the variable name that is being referenced, using the camel case naming convention. The methods defined in the preceding figure — **getFirstName**, **setFirstName**, **getLastName**, and **setLastName** — follow this naming style.

We could define other methods to perform additional formatting on the results of the data we are retrieving. Figure 4.3 shows a new method, **getReportName**, that provides added functionality to format the names when they are used on reports.

```java
/**
 * Returns the name of the person to be used on reports
 * @return reportName
 */
public String getReportName()
   {
   String reportName = null;
   reportName = this.getLastName().trim() + ", "
             + this.getFirstName().trim();
   return reportName;
   }
```

Figure 4.3: AirPerson class getReportName method

The **getReportName** method is a simple method that could be expanded to do additional verification (e.g., to check whether either of the values is null) and perform some more extensive logic. But for this discussion, we'll keep the logic at a minimum for conceptual purposes.

The use of the keyword **this** in this method is optional. It serves to clarify the code by indicating that the method is being called on the current instance. You could remove **this** from the code and it would execute exactly the same way.

This may seem like a lot of unnecessary code to write now, but this way of coding in Java has many practical purposes, and I strongly recommend that you initiate your Java programming in this manner. One particular reason is to ensure proper synchronization when you're dealing with multiple threads. I don't want to wander too far down the road of complexity with Java development for this book, but I do want to emphasize the importance of the naming standards that have been established to get you off to a good start.

Inheritance and Polymorphism

Two more important concepts, inheritance and polymorphism, are fundamental to a basic understanding of Java. I couldn't really come up with any comparisons to these topics in RPG, so I'll just cover these concepts in a way that is relevant to their implementation in future chapters.

Inheritance

Inheritance is a powerful feature of Java that lets you build a class to be an extension of an existing class. In doing so, you automatically provide your new class with the methods and constructor of the class you are extending.

Almost every Java application uses inheritance because every new class that is created extends, at the very least, the **Object** class. Therefore, every class you build has access to the methods in the **Object** class. If you create a new class that does not specify which class to extend, the **Object** class is understood.

The **Object** class is the most basic class to extend. You could create a new class, which would already be a subclass of the **Object** class, that could happen to be multiple levels of inheritance beyond the **Object** class.

To indicate which class you are extending, you use the Java keyword **extends**. You can extend only a single class; you cannot extend multiple classes.

Let's create a new class that inherits from (i.e., extends) our **AirPerson** class and has the characteristics of any other person, along with a few extras. We'll name the class **AirEmployee**, and we'll add a new characteristic, **rank**. Figure 4.4 shows the Java code for the new class.

```
package com.twowolvesout.air;
/************************************************************
 * The <B>AirEmployee</B> class is a subclass of AirPerson
 * @author Tom Snyder
 ************************************************************/
public class AirEmployee extends AirPerson
   {
```

```
/**
 *  Default Constructor is optional
 */
public AirEmployee()
  {
  }
/**
 * Returns the rank of the employee
 * @return rank The String value of the rank
 */
public String getRank()
  {
  return rank;
  }
/**
 * Sets the rank of the employee
 * @param inString The String value to set as the rank
 *                  of the employee
 */
public void setRank(String inString)
  {
  rank = inString;
  }
public static void main(String[] args)
  {
  AirEmployee test = new AirEmployee();
  test.setFirstName("Cynthia");
  test.setRank("Captain");
  System.out.println("First Name - " + test.getFirstName());
  }
private String rank;
}
```

Figure 4.4: AirEmployee class extending AirPerson class

When we use the JVM to execute this class, the **main** method is executed, and the output shown in Figure 4.5 is generated:

```
First Name - Cynthia
```

Figure 4.5: AirEmployee main procedure output

Although we did not code the **setFirstName** and **getFirstName** methods in this class, we are still able to use them in the **main** method. That's because the **AirEmployee** class inherits these methods from the parent class, due to the use of the **extends** keyword to indicate that the new class is a subclass of **AirPerson**.

Polymorphism

Another important feature of Java, *polymorphism*, exploits the characteristics of inheritance to give flexibility to your programs. When you have a subclass that extends a parent class, you know that both classes must support the methods of the parent class. So, you could use the parent class as the "least common denominator" to determine the methods that are guaranteed to be in both classes and then use that rule to your advantage.

In the examples so far, we have created two classes: **AirPerson** and **AirEmployee**. Let's modify the previous **main** method using these two classes to demonstrate the characteristics of polymorphism. Figure 4.6 shows the modified **AirEmployee** main method.

```
public static void main(String[] args)
  {
  //   Create New Objects
  AirPerson person = new AirPerson();
  AirPerson personEmployee = new AirEmployee();
  AirEmployee employee = new AirEmployee();

  //   Set the name values
  person.setFirstName("Mia");
  person.setLastName("Snyder");
  personEmployee.setFirstName("Raven");
  personEmployee.setLastName("Snyder");
  employee.setFirstName("Jade");
  employee.setLastName("Snyder");
  employee.setRank("Admiral");

  // Display the results
  System.out.println("Person Name - "
                     + person.getReportName());
  System.out.println("Object toString - "
                     + person.toString());
  System.out.println("PersonEmployee Name - "
                     + personEmployee.getReportName());
  System.out.println("Object toString - "
                     + personEmployee.toString());
```

```
System.out.println("Employee Name - "
                    + employee.getReportName());
System.out.println("Object toString - "
                    + employee.toString());
}
```

Figure 4.6: AirEmployee main method demonstrating polymorphism

Running the **main** method of this Java class generates output similar to that shown in Figure 4.7.

```
Person Name - Snyder, Mia
Object toString - com.twowolvesout.air.AirPerson@1b5430
PersonEmployee Name - Snyder, Raven
Object toString - com.twowolvesout.air.AirEmployee@1b5420
Employee Name - Snyder, Jade
Object toString - com.twowolvesout.air.AirEmployee@1b5410
```

Figure 4.7: AirEmployee polymorphic main method output

Notice that even though the **personEmployee** reference variable is of type **AirPerson**, it is being assigned to an object of type **AirEmployee**; this is polymorphism. We can do this because the **AirPerson** type is only required to have all the available methods of its type. Because **AirEmployee** extends **AirPerson**, we know that we will have all the required attributes and possibly more.

When printing the person's and employee's report name, each class will look for the defined method within the class to which the reference variable is pointing. If the method is not defined within the current class, the compiler will work upward through the inheritance chain to find and execute the first class that contains a method that matches the parameter list. In this case, both the person and the employee will use the **AirPerson getReportName** method to retrieve the name.

I mentioned earlier that all objects are subclasses of the **Object** class. The **Object** class is where the **toString** method is contained, so both the person and the employee will use the **toString** method from that class. The **toString** method returns the class name followed by the at symbol (@) and some memory address information. (Your memory addresses will likely differ from those shown in the figure.)

Overriding

Java programmers use a technique called *overriding* with inheritance when the subclass being built contains a method with the same name and parameters as the parent class. Instead of reusing the method that was created in the parent class, this technique overrides the parent's method in favor of the new method that is defined for the subclass.

For an example, let us override the **toString** method in the **AirPerson** class to provide more programmer-friendly information (Figure 4.8). Java programmers commonly use this technique to assist in debugging applications.

```java
/**
 * Returns the first and last name
 * @return first and last name
 */
public String toString()
   {
   return "First: " + getFirstName() + ", "
          + "Last: " + getLastName();
   }
```

Figure 4.8: AirPerson toString method overriding Object method

In addition, to take advantage of the added information in the **AirEmployee** class, let's override the **getReportName** method to use the employee's rank in the output (Figure 4.9).

```java
/**
 * Returns the name of the employee to be used on reports
 * @return reportName
 */
public String getReportName()
   {
   String reportName = null;
   if (rank == null)
      {
      reportName = "???: ";
      }
   else
      {
      reportName = rank.trim() + ": ";
      }
```

```
reportName = reportName
            + this.getLastName().trim()
            + ", " + this.getFirstName().trim();
return reportName;
}
```

Figure 4.9: AirEmployee getReportName overriding AirPerson method

Now, running the **main** method in **AirEmployee** with the **toString** method over-ridden in **AirPerson** and the **getReportName** method overridden in **AirEmployee** produces the results shown in Figure 4.10.

```
Person Name - Snyder, Mia
Object toString - First: Mia, Last: Snyder
PersonEmployee Name - ???: Snyder, Raven
Object toString - First: Raven, Last: Snyder
Employee Name - Admiral: Snyder, Jade
Object toString - First: Jade, Last: Snyder
```

Figure 4.10: Results of main method in Figure 4.6 with methods overridden

The **toString** method in **AirPerson** overrides the **toString** method of the **Object** class and will be used for all the objects created in this example.

Which **getReportName** method is used will be determined by the object that is being referenced, regardless of the type of the reference variable:

- The **getReportName** method will use the **AirPerson** method only for the **person** reference variable, because this variable points to an **AirPerson** object.

- The **personEmployee** is interesting because it uses a reference variable type of **AirPerson** but points to an **AirEmployee** object. So, it will use the **AirEmployee getReportName** method.

- The employee will use the **AirEmployee getReportName** method because it is an **AirEmployee**.

Even though the **personEmployee** points to an **AirEmployee** and will use the **getReportName** method from the **AirEmployee** class, there is no way to set the rank. This is because the reference variable is of type **AirPerson**, which does not have a **setRank** method available to use.

This is a pretty involved example of overriding in Java, so don't worry if you don't fully comprehend every detail. If you understand the **toString** overrides of the **Object** class and how they work, that should be good enough for you to grasp the concepts in future chapters.

Overloading

Overloading occurs when two methods have the same name but different parameter lists and possibly different return types. The compiler determines which method to use according to the parameters that are sent.

For the **AirEmployee** class, let's create another **getReportName** method that has the same method name but a different parameter list (Figure 4.11).

```
/**
 * Returns the name of the employee to be used on reports
 * @param isPersonFormat
 * @return reportName
 */
public String getReportName(boolean isPersonFormat)
  {
  String reportName = null;
  if (isPersonFormat)
    {
    reportName = super.getReportName();
    }
  else
    {
    reportName = this.getReportName();
    }
  return reportName;
  }
```

Figure 4.11: AirEmployee getReportName method overloading with different parameters

For this new **getReportName** method, we have indicated a single parameter of a type **boolean** that will determine whether the **getReportName** method will be used by the **AirEmployee** class or whether the **getReportName** method of the parent class should be used.

We can modify the main procedure to implement the new overloaded method as shown in Figure 4.12.

```java
public static void main(String[] args)
   {
   //  Create New Objects
   AirEmployee employee = new AirEmployee();

   //  Set the name values
   employee.setFirstName("Jade");
   employee.setLastName("Snyder");
   employee.setRank("Admiral");

   //  Display the results
   System.out.println("Employee Name (Person Format) - "
                       + employee.getReportName(true));
   System.out.println("Employee Name (Employee Format) - "
                       + employee.getReportName(false));
   System.out.println("Employee Name (No Parameters) - "
                       + employee.getReportName());
   System.out.println("Object toString - "
                       + employee.toString());
   }
```

Figure 4.12: AirEmployee main method demonstrating overloading

This would generate the results shown in Figure 4.13.

```
Employee Name (Person Format) - Snyder, Jade
Employee Name (Employee Format) - Admiral: Snyder, Jade
Employee Name (No Parameters) - Admiral: Snyder, Jade
Object toString - First: Jade, Last: Snyder
```

Figure 4.13: AirEmployee main method output using overloading

In the overloaded **getReportName** method, the Java keyword **super** indicates that we are referring to the parent class using inheritance. The **this** keyword indicates that we are referring to the current class instance.

When we use the **getReportName** method within the overloaded method, you can see that there are no parameters, so the compiler uses the other method to determine the results. This example demonstrates a good way to reuse code and gain flexibility by providing an alternative feature to your class with minimal coding.

Interface

A Java *interface* defines the methods that must be supported within a class, without providing any of the logic that will be used to support them. So, when you define an interface and you implement it on a class, the class must have the methods defined with the specified parameters in the interface.

Suppose you had a report that you wanted to write that included both employees and customers. The employees would inherit the **getReportName** method from the **AirPerson** class and also override it in **AirEmployee**, but **AirCustomer** might not be a subclass of **AirPerson**. So, you cannot define a polymorphic reference to the object to obtain the report name using inheritance. However, you can support this functionality by creating an interface that requires all the classes that use it to provide a **getReportName** method. Figure 4.14 shows this interface, called **AirReportable**.

```
package com.twowolvesout.air;
public interface AirReportable
    {
    public String getReportName();
    }
```

Figure 4.14: AirReportable interface

When declaring an interface, you use the **interface** keyword. Then, any methods being used by the interface contain the method name and parameters. There is no logic, and no curly braces; you simply place a semicolon after the opening and closing parentheses of the parameter list, forcing the classes that implement the interface to support these methods.

To indicate the use of the interface on a class, you use the **implements** keyword (Figure 4.15).

```
public class AirPerson implements AirReportable
```

Figure 4.15: AirPerson class implementing AirReportable interface

If we implement this interface on the **AirPerson** class, it will also be supported on every subclass of **AirPerson**. This makes sense because the subclasses are automatically provided with the methods of the class from which they inherit.

Now, we can create the **AirCustomer** class to implement the **AirReportable** interface that will contain different information in the **getReportName** results.

The **AirCustomer** class will have a **businessName** and an **accountType** with respective get and set methods. Because the **AirCustomer** class implements the **AirReportable** interface, it must include the **getReportName** method or it will not compile. Figure 4.16 shows the **AirCustomer** class code.

```java
package com.twowolvesout.air;
/***********************************************************
 * The <B>AirCustomer</B> class is a generic class
 * intended to implement the AirReportable Interface
 * @author Tom Snyder
 ***********************************************************/
public class AirCustomer implements AirReportable
  {
  /**
   *  Default Constructor is optional
   */
  public AirCustomer()
    {
    }
  /**
   * Returns the first name of the person
   * @return firstName The String value of the first name
   */
  public String getBusinessName()
    {
    return businessName;
    }
  /**
   * Sets the first name of the person
   * @param inString The String value to set as the first name
   *                  of the person
   */
  public void setBusinessName(String inString)
    {
    businessName = inString;
    }
  /**
```

```
 * Returns the last name of the person
 * @return lastName The String value of the last name
 */
public String getAccountType()
  {
  return accountType;
  }
/**
 * Sets the last name of the person
 * @param inString The String value to set as the last name
 *                   of the person
 */
public void setAccountType(String inString)
  {
  accountType = inString;
  }
/**
 * Returns the name of the person to be used on reports
 * @return reportName
 */
public String getReportName()
  {
  String reportName = null;
  reportName = this.getBusinessName().trim() + ", "
               + this.getAccountType().trim();
  return reportName;
  }
private String businessName;
private String accountType;
}
```

Figure 4.16: AirCustomer class implementing AirReportable interface

Next, we can create a method in the **AirCustomer** class that accepts an **AirReportable** parameter that doesn't care what class is being sent in as long as it has a **getReportName** method, which is a requirement for the **AirReportable** interface (Figure 4.17).

```
public static void print(AirReportable inReportable)
  {
  System.out.println("Reportable Name: "
                      + inReportable.getReportName());
  }
```

Figure 4.17: Static print method using an interface for a parameter

Because the **print** method accepts an object as a parameter and does not depend on the instance that contains it, we can make it a static method. This method could be in any of the classes we've created so far, or it could be in a different class altogether. For this example, we can arbitrarily place it into the **AirCustomer** class.

Now, let's create a **main** method that puts it all together (Figure 4.18).

```
public static void main(String[] args)
    {
    AirCustomer customer = new AirCustomer();
    customer.setBusinessName("MC Press");
    customer.setAccountType("National");

    AirEmployee employee = new AirEmployee();
    employee.setRank("President");
    employee.setFirstName("Merrikay");
    employee.setLastName("Lee");

    AirEmployee employeeExec = new AirEmployee();
    employeeExec.setRank("Executive Editor");
    employeeExec.setFirstName("Victoria");
    employeeExec.setLastName("Mack");

    AirPerson person = new AirPerson();
    person.setFirstName("Tom");
    person.setLastName("Snyder");

    AirCustomer.print(customer);
    AirCustomer.print(employee);
    AirCustomer.print(employeeExec);
    AirCustomer.print(person);
    }
```

Figure 4.18: Main method using an interface for a parameter

When you run this **main** method, you will see that the **print** method uses the **getReportName** method of each associated class. Because **print** is a static method — that is, associated with the class instead of a particular instance — we can use the class name to reference the method: **AirCustomer.print(. . .)**. If the **main** method were contained in the **AirCustomer** class, we could simply reference the **print** method without the class in front of it.

Figure 4.19 shows the output produced by the **main** method in the preceding figure.

```
Reportable Name: MC Press, National
Reportable Name: President: Lee, Merrikay
Reportable Name: Executive Editor: Mack, Victoria
Reportable Name: Snyder, Tom
```

Figure 4.19: Output for main method in Figure 4.18

We now have a **print** method that will take anything with a **getReportName** method that you can throw at it, from completely different inheritance chains and in completely different formats, depending on the information provided.

An interface is the solution when you want a subclass to have the same attributes as multiple parent classes. You can extend only one class, but you can implement multiple interfaces. So, this solution lets your class be polymorphic with all the parent classes and also with any other classes that implement the interfaces that are supported by your class.

Integrated Development Environment

An integrated development environment (IDE) is a useful development tool for programmers. As an RPG programmer, you are probably familiar with Programming Development Manager (PDM) and may use it as your primary development tool. IDEs provide a common development environment for programmers of all different languages, including Java. They commonly feature syntax checking, compilers, and debuggers all within one application that may support multiple languages.

Eclipse is an open-source IDE for Java development. You can download and install Eclipse for free, and it is available for multiple operating systems. IBM WebSphere Development Studio client (WDSC), which is built on the open-source Eclipse IDE, is a useful tool for RPG and Java hybrid developers. Although WDSC is about to be discontinued, it is being replaced with Rational Developer for System i (RDi).

JavaDoc

JavaDoc is a useful documentation tool provided with the Java Development Kit. When writing Java code, the programmer can include comments that will be made accessible by the JavaDoc application to create standardized HTML pages that describe the behavior of classes. These JavaDocs are very useful when developing code that is intended to be built and distributed for other programmers to use. Some IDEs display the JavaDoc information when listing available methods and variables.

You write JavaDocs in your Java code immediately before a class, method, or field. The JavaDoc comments are written in HTML or standard text, starting with /** and ending with */. There are also special inline tags that start with the @ symbol to provide common information, such as parameters and return values.

As we have been developing the examples in this chapter, we have been creating JavaDoc comments within the classes. Let's look at the fruits of our labor by generating the JavaDocs for the **AirEmployee** class and analyzing the results. Figure 4.20 shows the JavaDoc segment that contains the **AirEmployee** class information.

com.twowolvesout.air
Class AirEmployee

```
java.lang.Object
  └ com.twowolvesout.air.AirPerson
      └ com.twowolvesout.air.AirEmployee
```

All Implemented Interfaces:
   com.twowolvesout.air.AirReportable

```
public class AirEmployee
extends com.twowolvesout.air.AirPerson
```

The **AirEmployee** class is a subclass of AirPerson

Author:
   Tom Snyder

Constructor Summary

```
AirEmployee()
```
       Default Constructor is optional

Figure 4.20: JavaDoc segment illustrating AirEmployee class information

Starting at the top of this segment of the **AirEmployee** JavaDoc, you can determine that the **AirEmployee** class is contained in the **com.twowolvesout.air** package and that it extends the **AirPerson** class. You can also see that it implements the **AirReportable** interface.

The keyword **@author** is specially formatted to display the author information from the comments in the code. The constructor is given a special section to let you know how you can create instances of the class.

Figure 4.21 shows the JavaDocs method information for the **AirEmployee** class.

Method Summary	
java.lang.String	**getRank**() Returns the rank of the employee
java.lang.String	**getReportName**() Returns the name of the employee to be used on
java.lang.String	**getReportName**(boolean isPersonFormat) Returns the name of the employee to be used on
static void	**main**(java.lang.String[] args)
void	**setRank**(java.lang.String inString) Sets the rank of the employee

Methods inherited from class com.twowolvesout.air.AirPerson
getFirstName, getLastName, setFirstName, setLastName, toString

Methods inherited from class java.lang.Object
equals, getClass, hashCode, notify, notifyAll, wait, wait, wait

Figure 4.21: JavaDoc segment illustrating AirEmployee method information

You can see all the methods that are available directly from the class, and you also get a list of all the methods that are available from the classes from which **AirEmployee** inherits. The method summary documents the return types and parameters that are used with the methods. Next to the methods, you can see some of the comments that we put into the special JavaDoc comments of the code.

Below the tables in the JavaDocs, you will see more detail about each of the methods available from the class. In Figure 4.22, you can see from the JavaDocs that the **getReportName** method overrides the method in **AirPerson**.

---

getReportName

`public java.lang.String` **`getReportName`**`()`

Returns the name of the employee to be used on reports

Specified by:
`getReportName` in interface `com.twowolvesout.air.AirReportable`
Overrides:
`getReportName` in class `com.twowolvesout.air.AirPerson`
Returns:
reportName

---

getReportName

`public java.lang.String` **`getReportName`**`(boolean isPersonFormat)`

Returns the name of the employee to be used on reports.

Parameters:
`isPersonFormat` - determines the format of the output.
Returns:
reportName

Figure 4.22: JavaDoc segment illustrating AirEmployee detailed method information

Java 1.4.2 JavaDocs

For this book, all references will be to Version 1.4.2 of Java, so you'll find the relevant JavaDocs at *http://java.sun.com/j2se/1.4.2/docs/api*. If you're using a different version of Java, replace the "1.4.2" in this URL with your version number.

Now you know how to read a JavaDoc for a Java class and understand what most of the nomenclature means. This knowledge will enable you to determine the functionality and implementation of the classes without the need to know how the logic works. Using the information provided in this chapter, you can explore the online JavaDocs for the open-source projects in this book (Table 4.1) and expand the capabilities and implement new ones as new versions of the packages become available.

Table 4.1: Online JavaDocs for open-source projects used in this book	
Open source project	Online JavaDocs
iText for PDF files	http://www.1t3xt.info/api
POI for Excel files	http://poi.apache.org/apidocs
JavaMail for e-mail	http://java.sun.com/products/javamail/javadocs

A Good Foundation

This chapter is merely the tip of the iceberg when it comes to all the capabilities and complexities of Java programming. It is intended only to provide you with some conceptual examples of how Java works. Yes, you saw some coding examples, but these are intended to convey the concepts more than the syntax. To me, a sample of code is worth a thousand words. I like to have concrete examples that I can wrap my brain around.

When it is all said and done, for the objective that we are trying to achieve of integrating Java with RPG, you'll find the JavaDocs discussion to be the most useful information — the culmination of all the conceptual information provided in the preceding topics. If you can decipher the JavaDocs and understand the nomenclature being used on the classes, you will be able to evaluate the examples used in this book and delve deeper into the additional capabilities that are available to evolve the service programs to provide more capabilities to your programs.

Sure, you could start with the code provided in this book, but I'm certain that once you master the use of the procedures, you'll want to start getting into other features that go beyond what is provided here. Who knows, you may even want to download a completely different open-source project and build service programs for that to use. With the information in this book, you should be able to successfully do just that!

5

Java and RPG

This chapter is crucial for all the chapters to come. In it, you'll expand your programming capabilities beyond what RPG alone has to offer by learning how to access Java from RPG. We'll wrap RPG code around some Java classes and methods to be placed into service programs. These wrappers will let you create service programs to handle most of the Java interaction, and you'll be able to use the Java classes from within RPG with minimal impact on your RPG code.

The techniques discussed in this chapter promote all the encouraged programming practices of code modularity. But one of the biggest benefits I've found is that you can give these new capabilities to your fellow RPG programmers to use, coding in nothing more than RPG. You can thus take advantage of current skill sets as you gradually enhance existing applications by adding incremental enhancements to your current software.

Determining the Current Version of Java

Before beginning to use Java on your IBM i system, you should determine the current version of Java that is installed. To do so:

1. Start the Qshell command environment by entering **STRQSH** at the command line.

2. In Qshell, enter **java -version**.

If you have Qshell and a Java Virtual Machine installed on your system, you should see a display similar to the one shown in Figure 5.1 (your system may report a different version). For this book, I recommend using Version 1.4.2 or later to ensure you can support the code examples.

```
                          QSH Command Entry
   $
 > java -version
   java version "1.4.2"
   Java(TM) 2 Runtime Environment, Standard Edition (build 1.4.2_16-b05)
   Classic VM (build 1.4, build JDK-1.4, native threads, jitc_de)
```

Figure 5.1: Determining the current Java version using Qshell

Java is diligent at providing backward compatibility, but it is not forward-compatible, so you need to pay attention to your current Java version. In other words, if you have Java 1.4.2 on your system, you can run Java classes all the way back to Version 1.0, but you *cannot* use anything that was compiled using a newer version of Java than 1.4.2. For example, if you were to compile a program using the Java 1.6 compiler while using Version 1.4.2 as your runtime environment, the classes would not run.

Java Invocation API

Java's Invocation API, which you'll see in action later, lets you create a JVM within an RPG program and gives you access to all the functionality Java has to offer. The API is part of the Java Native Interface (JNI), which is included in the Java development kit and provides the capability to embed the JVM into native applications.

The **QJVAJNI** or **QJVAJNI64** service program provides the JNI Invocation API functionality. These service programs are included in the system binding directory, so you don't need to specify them when creating your RPG program.

Accessing Java Objects from Within RPG

To create reference variables within RPG for Java objects, you specify the variable as type **O** (Object) in column 40 of the D specification. Then, use the **CLASS** keyword to indicate the Java object being referred, entering ***JAVA** as the first parameter and specifying the Java class as a character string for the second parameter. This character string must fully qualify the object and the Java package that contains it.

Let's begin by creating a reference to a Java **String** object. The **String** object is a common object included in the JDK. It is contained in the **java.lang** package, so the character string to identify the class must be in the Java format of **'java.lang. String'**. It's important to note that the reference to the class is case-sensitive.

Figure 5.2 shows the code to declare an RPG variable that refers to a Java **String** object.

```
D string          S              O   CLASS(*JAVA:'java.lang.String')
```

Figure 5.2: RPG object variable for reference to Java String object

The Java **String** class is an important class that enables communications from RPG to Java because RPG stores strings in an array of bytes, while Java typically uses its **String** object to pass text as parameters to objects and methods.

At this point, we have declared an RPG variable that refers to a Java **String** object, but we don't have a **String** object yet. We have only a reference to a **String** object that is not yet initialized, so it is pointing to nowhere. It's like a zoned variable that was not initialized before an attempt to display it in a DDS menu; it will blow up because it doesn't have a value.

Note that you cannot define fields of type **O** as subfields of data structures, but it is possible to have arrays of type **O** fields. I found this fact to be of significance when I was creating procedures and wanted to return more than one object.

Accessing Java Methods from Within RPG

As you know from the preceding chapter, Java classes have methods, which are similar to procedures in RPG. To access a Java method from RPG, you can prototype the method. The prototype specifies the Java method that is assigned to the prototype and lets the compiler check syntax within the RPG program, although it does not give the compiler the ability to check the prototype against the actual Java class. The compiler assumes you set up the prototype correctly.

The **extProc** extended keyword tells the RPG compiler that you are defining an external procedure. If you do not use **extProc**, the compiler assumes you're defining a procedure with the same name as the external method. You can define external procedures for C, CL, Cobol, Java, and RPG. To define Java methods, you use the special keyword *__JAVA__ as the first parameter of **extProc**. The second parameter identifies the fully qualified class, and the third parameter is the method name.

When sending information from Java to RPG, you need to convert the Java **String** back to the array of bytes used in RPG. The Java **String** class includes the **getBytes** method to provide this capability. Figure 5.3 shows how you would write the prototype to access the **getBytes** method.

```
D String_getBytes...
D                     PR        65535A    varying
D                                         extproc(*JAVA:
D                                         'java.lang.String':
D                                         'getBytes')
```

Figure 5.3: RPG prototype for getBytes method of String class

This example uses 65,535 as the field length because that is the maximum field length supported by RPG. In practice, you could use any value less than or equal to 65,535 that you find adequate.

To provide a comprehensive naming strategy when using Java from within RPG, we could establish the standard naming convention illustrated in the figure for Java methods, which specifies the class name followed by the method name, separated by an underscore to represent the period in Java.

Java Object Constructors

Let's put some of the Java information from Chapter 4 to use now by giving RPG the ability to create a new object. We do this using the constructor method of the class. When the object is constructed, the reference variable will identify the location of the memory allocated to the object.

We call the constructor method of the class by specifying the special keyword ***CONSTRUCTOR** as the method name in **extProc**. In the Java language, you construct objects by using the **new** keyword, so we'll name the procedure **new_String**, using an underscore to represent the separation of the keyword **new** from the class name that you would code in Java.

Figure 5.4 shows the prototype for the constructor method of the **String** class.

```
D new_String      PR                      like(jstring)
D                                         extproc(*JAVA:
D                                         'java.lang.String':
D                                         *CONSTRUCTOR)
D argBytes                    65535A      varying const
```

Figure 5.4: RPG prototype for constructor method of String class

> **Java Note**
>
> In some languages, variables that contain references to memory locations are called *pointers*. In the Java world, such a variable is called a *reference variable*. Quite a few Java advocates out there would scoff at you for calling it a pointer instead of a reference variable, so try to refer to it as a reference variable.
>
> This outspoken demand for the term "reference variable" ties back to memory management in languages such as C. In Java, the memory management is handled automatically within the JVM, eliminating all the administrative coding needed to manage memory and preventing programs from experiencing memory leaks. (Unfortunately, when using JNI, as we'll be doing from RPG, you must perform all garbage collection manually.)
>
> When you use a constructor to create a Java object, the memory is allocated on something called a *heap*. The reference variables that refer to the newly created object reside on the stack and determine the location of the object on the heap.

The QSYSINC/QRPGLESRC,JNI File

Included with the System Openness Includes library provided by IBM is the **QSYSINC/QRPGLESRC,JNI** file. If you don't have this file, you can install licensed program 5722SS1, option 13, to obtain it.

The JNI file provides field definitions for the Java data types (e.g., **jint**, **jfloat**, **jlong**) and creates RPG variables with these names and their comparable attributes in RPG. The file also contains prototypes for the most commonly used Java objects and methods. As you begin developing custom RPG wrappers for Java functions, you will find that you'll be creating more prototypes for Java objects and methods that you'll want to put into a common service program, which is the primary objective of this chapter.

The JNI file uses several different compiler directives to include or exclude certain segments of code during compile time. We'll use the conditional names **OS400_JVM_12** and **JNI_COPY_ALL** throughout our code to indicate additional code to be used in the JNI file. If you were to look into the **QSYSINC/QRPGLESRC,JNI** file on your system, you would see the impact that the **JNI_COPY_ALL** and **OS400_JVM_12** variables have on the amount of code that is included.

Java Primitive Types

Not every Java variable is an **Object**. There are some variables, called *primitives*, for which memory is allocated when the variables are declared. Table 5.1 lists the Java primitive types and their RPG equivalents.

Table 5.1: Java primitive types and RPG equivalents			
Java type	Native type	Storage	RPG variable
boolean	jboolean	Unsigned 8 bits	1 U
byte	jbyte	Signed 8 bits	1 I
char	jchar	Unsigned 16 bits	2 C
short	jshort	Signed 16 bits	2I 0
int	jint	Signed 32 bits	4I 0
long	jlong	Signed 64 bits	8I 0

Table 5.1: Java primitive types and RPG equivalents (Continued)			
float	jfloat	32 bits	4F
double	jdouble	64 bits	8F
void	void	N/A	N/A

The primitive types are defined, with their RPG equivalents, in the **QSYSINC/QRPGLESRC,JNI** file. The variable definitions in **QSYSINC/QRPGLESRC,JNI** are extremely useful, as you'll see when we start coding, because you can refer to the Java data type reference in the JNI file instead of having to remember the actual size of the variable in RPG, as the code in Figure 5.5 demonstrates.

```
 *-----------------------------------------------------------------
 * Java data types
 *-----------------------------------------------------------------
 * The jlongJNI type should be used for parameters passed by value
 * or return values for JNI functions.
 *-----------------------------------------------------------------
D                   DS                        BASED(JNItypes_P)
D  argInLength                      15P 5 const
D  jbyte                      1      1I 0
D  jshort                     1      2I 0
D  jint                       1      4I 0
D  jlong                      1      8I 0
D     jlongJNI                      8A    OVERLAY(jlong)
D  jboolean                   1      1U 0
D  jchar                      1      2C
D  jfloat                     1      4F
D  jdouble                    1      8F
D  jsize                      1      4I 0
D*-----------------------------------------------------------------
```

Figure 5.5: Java data types in QSYSINC/QRPGLESRC,JNI

Referring to External Jar Files

IBM i systems use **/QIBM/UserData/Java400/ext** as the default location for optional packages, which used to be called standard extensions. If you place your Java Jar files into this directory in the integrated file system, no further action is required to make the files visible to your application.

The problem with putting your Java files in the default directory is that you'll need to keep track of which Jar files are yours and which are provided by IBM whenever you migrate, upgrade, or restore from backup. You'll also need to make sure you don't overwrite the IBM-provided files, and your files may start to get out of control. I've learned that it is not good to manually update files that are provided with the operating system, and that even though you know what the files should be and you have the knowledge to do it, you should order the PTF that provides the upgrade for you.

Some "real-world" background will help bring this point home. When I was trying to automate iSeries Access updates for our clients, I looked into the automated updates feature in the iSeries Access client and found that the location being used was **/QIBM/ProdData/Access**. I compared the contents against the files contained on the installation CD and found that they were exactly the same, which makes sense — it was just doing an installation across the network using the IFS.

Being impatient, I decided to manually replace the files in **/QIBM/ProdData/Access** with the latest iSeries Access installation files. Everything worked great — until it came time to update OS/400. The last thing you want to encounter on your crucial server during an operating system upgrade is an error. Well, when OS/400 is being upgraded, it validates the existence of files from the previous version and generates errors during the upgrade if the files are not what is expected. Then the boss is standing there, stressing the importance of getting the system back online and finding you to be the cause of the problem.

After that incident, I realized that I was being overeager with the automation and that the frequency of the client updates with the server operating system were more than adequate. For more immediate updates, PTFs were the way to go. I also found the option to specify the location of the updates on the client, but this required additional configuration during the initial install, and I decided to go with the automated updates in the **/QIBM/ProdData/Access** location. But now I'm getting way off topic.

The point of this story is that I do *not* recommend using the default **/QIBM/User-Data/Java400/ext** location for your additional Java packages. Even though doing so is easier and works just fine, I don't believe it's worth the risk of inadvertently overwriting IBM-provided files and cluttering up the directory with files that you may lose track of.

The SVAIRJAVA Service Program

During the rest of this chapter, we'll walk through the creation of the **AIRLIB/ AIRSRC,SVAIRJAVA** service program. Service program **SVAIRJAVA** is intended to give you a starting point from which to extend the JNI file capabilities. This service program is provided for you to modify and enhance to suit your needs.

You can include the service program in all your RPG programs that will use Java. **SVAIRJAVA** takes all the lower-level Java operations that you won't want to have to deal with every time you want to use Java from within RPG, and it puts them into an easy-to-use service program that you can install and share with other RPG programmers at your shop.

Because **SVAIRJAVA** is the most generic service program that deals directly with the JVM, it is primarily a compilation of IBM and Sun Microsystems code, with additional enhancements to handle the nuances of dealing with Java from RPG. This service program provides all the things I believe should be included in the **QSYSINC/QRPGLESRC,JNI** file.

The JNI and **SVAIRJAVA** resources are building blocks to use with other Java resources to extend beyond the current capabilities of RPG alone. Using such fundamental components of Java for their own sake alone would be inefficient in RPG and would gain you no additional capabilities. But when we get to the following chapters, you'll begin to use Java resources with the capabilities of Excel, PDFs, and e-mail that require access to these fundamental features.

Installing External Jar Files on the IFS

Organization and standardization are key components to expediting your code development and managing your resources. Throughout this book, I want not only to show you the syntax of the code but also to share the best practice methods I have formulated during my evolution into the Java world.

I will assume that you'll want to install your external Jar files in a custom location on your IFS to keep the files organized and isolated from the IBM folders. For the examples provided here, we'll use the custom folder location of **/Public/Java** off the root directory of the IFS. You can create any folder you like on your system or go with the default optional package location of the JVM and not use a custom location at all, but you'll have to change the references in the service program to make it work if you do so. I've put comments in the code so you can easily change this setting.

To let the RPG program know where the external files are located, you execute the **ADDENVVAR** (Add Environment Variable) command. This step is similar to modifying a library list to make a program or file visible to the job.

For the **SVAIRJAVA** service program, we'll create a main procedure that we'll use to set the environment variables to point to the external Jars we'll be using in future chapters. This procedure would also be helpful if you decided to declare some global variables and wanted to initialize them at the beginning. Another possibility would be to apply any initial file overrides and open the files. For this service program, we'll simply set the environment variables.

Figure 5.6 shows the RPG main procedure for the **SVAIRJAVA** service program.

```
D/DEFINE OS400_JVM_12
D/DEFINE JNI_COPY_ALL
D/COPY QSYSINC/QRPGLESRC,JNI
D/COPY AIRLIB/AIRSRC,SPAIRFUNC
D/COPY AIRLIB/AIRSRC,SPAIRJAVA
D fd0              S             10I 0
D fd1              S             10I 0
D fd2              S             10I 0
D i                S             10I 0
D displayBytes     S             52A
D localPath        S           2048A   varying
D commandString    S           2048A   varying
C****************************************************************************
C* Add the environment variable to let the application know where
C* the Jar files are.
C****************************************************************************
```

```
/free
 //----------------------------------
 //---       POI for Excel        ---
 //----------------------------------
 localPath = %trim(localPath)
           + ':/Public/Java/Excel_POI'
           + '/poi-3.0.2-FINAL-20080204.jar';
 //----------------------------------
 //---       iText for PDF        ---
 //----------------------------------
 localPath = %TRIM(localPath)
           + ':/Public/Java'
           + '/PDF_iText/iText-2.1.2u.jar';
 //--------------------------------------
 // JAF - JavaBeans Activation Framework
 // JAF and JavaMail for Email
 //--------------------------------------
 localPath = %TRIM(localPath)
           + ':/Public/Java'
           + '/JavaMail/activation.jar';
 localPath = %trim(localPath)
           + ':/Public/Java'
           + '/JavaMail/mail.jar';
 //------------------------------------------------------
 // Put the entire class path together and implement.
 //------------------------------------------------------
 commandString = 'ADDENVVAR ENVVAR(CLASSPATH) '
               + 'VALUE('''.:'
               + %TRIM(localPath)
               + ''') REPLACE(*YES)';
 monitor;
   ExecuteCommand(%trim(commandString):%len(%trim(commandString)));
 on-error;
   displayBytes = 'ERROR occurred on Class Path!';
   DSPLY displayBytes;
 endmon;
 // Call getJNIEnv() to:
 // - Ensure first three file descriptors are open
 // - Start JVM, if not started
 // - Attach to JVM, if already started
 getJNIEnv();
 return;
/end-free
```

Figure 5.6: SVAIRJAVA service program main procedure

An important point to make about **ADDENVVAR** when using Jar files is that you need to point the command directly to the file with the **.jar** extension. If the files are not contained in a Jar file, you can reference the directory that contains the files.

You can have only one JVM per job, and you cannot change the class path of the JVM once it is started, so make sure you include all the required Jar references needed for the entire job once you start the JVM. Once you end the JVM for the job, you cannot restart it.

At the end of the main procedure, a call is made to the **getJNIEnv** procedure. The call to **getJNIEnv** starts the JVM or attaches to the existing JVM if one is already started. The **getJNIEnv** procedure also ensures that the first three file descriptors — which we'll be discussing next — are open.

Standard JVM Streams: STDIN, STDOUT, and STDERR

Java offers a lot of flexibility and many capabilities, and I could brag it up all day, but unless I address the following topic, you'll experience strange behaviors when executing the code. These concepts may seem to take the fun out of the programming, and the following discussion may strike you as somewhat in-depth, but don't be discouraged. I'm just trying to get you on to solid ground before playing with the code.

Using the JVM in Batch from RPG

Java has three standard streams that are assumed to be open when the JVM is started:

- **STDIN**
- **STDOUT**
- **STDERR**

STDIN (which is file descriptor, or fd, 0) is used for standard input, **STDOUT** (fd 1) is used for standard output, and **STDERR** (fd 2) is used for dumping errors. Being an RPG programmer, the standard JVM stream files were not the first thing I was interested in learning about in Java. But I quickly became acquainted with them when my programs worked interactively but crashed when I submitted them to batch.

When you run programs interactively on an IBM i system, the input, output, and error streams are initialized automatically. However, when you run the programs in batch, the standard JVM streams are not automatically opened.

To avoid any problem, you just need to ensure that at least three file descriptors open when you start the JVM. The standard stream files that are expected to exist for the JVM will be assigned to the first three file descriptors: 0, 1, and 2. This is one of the little nuances you have to deal with when using the IBM i version of Java, which was initially designed for Unix.

To open the file descriptors, we'll use the **open** API to open the files. This API opens a file or directory and returns the file descriptor.

Several other APIs are available for use with the IFS. For the purposes of service program **SVAIRJAVA**, we'll use only **open**. That's because we won't be doing anything with the file once we have it open; we just need to make sure that the first three file descriptors are in use to satisfy the JVM.

Figure 5.7 shows the RPG prototype for the **open** API.

```
D IFSOpen         PR              10I 0 extproc('open')
D  argPath                         *     value options(*STRING)
D  argFlag                        10I 0 value
D  argMode                        10U 0 value options(*NOPASS)
D  argToConv                      10U 0 value options(*NOPASS)
D  argFromConv                    10U 0 value options(*NOPASS)
```

Figure 5.7: RPG prototype for open API

The first parameter is a pointer to a null-terminated path name. The **options(*STRING)** keyword specified on this parameter will ensure that the null-terminator is appended to the string you are using.

The second parameter specifies the file status flags and file access modes of the file to be opened. Table 5.2 lists the three valid modes you can specify in this field; the **QSYSINC/H,FCNTL** file defines these values.

Table 5.2: Values for flag parameter of open API		
File access mode	Description	Value
O_RDONLY	Read only	1
O_WRONLY	Write only	2
O_RDWR	Read/write	4

If the open is successful, the **open** API returns a number representing the file descriptor. If the open fails, the API returns a value of −1.

We'll put the **IFSOpen** prototype for the **open** API into our **SPAIRFUNC** prototype file, along with our previously prototyped APIs for general reuse. Service program **SVAIRJAVA** will use this prototype file to ensure that the first three file descriptors are opened.

As you become more familiar with Java, you may find a need to use **STDIN**, **STDOUT**, and **STDERR**, but for the intentions of this book we will satisfy the minimum requirements by ensuring that the first three file descriptors are open when the JVM starts by using a common Unix practice of pointing the files to **/dev/null**. This is an actual file on the system, so you need to either make sure this file exists in the IFS or point to another file that you know exists.

Starting and Destroying the JVM

When a JVM is created, it will run either until it is destroyed or until the job is ended. You can manually start and destroy the JVM. Only one JVM can run for each job, so once you destroy a job, you cannot restore it. The class path is established during startup, when the JVM is initialized. Once the JVM is started, you cannot change the class path.

Having only one JVM per job works out pretty well because you pay all the overhead time of having the JVM start up the first time, and then it is reused for each subsequent call to the JVM throughout the duration of the job. So, just make sure you specify the entire class path during the initial call to the JVM. (Another option is to submit each use of the JVM to batch, a technique that would create a separate JVM for each batch job.)

Starting the JVM

Before using any Java code, you need to get the JNI environment pointer. Procedure **getJNIEnv** (Figure 5.8), which is called by our main procedure, looks for an existing JVM to attach to. If no JVM already exists, the procedure creates one for the job.

```
P*****************************************************************
P*  getJNIEnv
P*****************************************************************
P getJNIEnv...
P                 B                   EXPORT
D getJNIEnv...
D                 PI                *
D rc              s                   LIKE(jint)
D jvm             s                 * DIM(1)
D env             s                 *
D bufLen          s                   LIKE(jsize) INZ(%elem(jvm))
D nVMs            s                   LIKE(jsize)
D initArgs        DS                  LIKEDS(JDK1_1InitArgs)
D attachArgs      DS                  LIKEDS(JDK1_1AttachArgs)
D fd              s         10I 0
 /free
   // First, ensure STDIN, STDOUT, and STDERR are open
   fd = IFSopen('/dev/null': O_RDWR);
   if (fd = -1);
     // '/dev/null' does not exist in your IFS
     // You can create it or use another known good file.
   else;
     dow ( fd < 2 );
       fd = IFSopen('/dev/null': O_RDWR);
     enddo;
   endif;
   // Second, attach to existing JVM
   //      OR create new JVM if not already running
   rc = JNI_GetCreatedJavaVMs(jvm:bufLen:nVMs);
   if (rc = 0 and nVMs > 0);
     attachArgs = *ALLX'00';
     JavaVM_P = jvm(1);
     rc = AttachCurrentThread(jvm(1):env:%addr(attachArgs));
   else;
```

```
  initArgs = *ALLX'00';
  rc = JNI_GetDefaultJavaVMInitArgs(%addr(attachArgs));
  if (rc = 0);
    rc = JNI_CreateJavaVM(jvm(1):env:%addr(initArgs));
  else;
  endif;
 endif;
 if (rc = 0);
   return env;
 else;
   return *NULL;
 endif;
 /end-free
P                    E
```

Figure 5.8: Getting a pointer to the JNI environment

You could let the JVM start automatically, but I have found that doing so sometimes causes problems when I'm running more than one Java program in a job. So, I always make sure to manually do this first to provide reliable and consistent results.

The procedure also makes sure that the first three file descriptors are open to ensure proper execution when the RPG program is run in batch.

Destroying the JVM

The JVM clean ups automatically when the job that invoked it ends. This cleanup activity includes reclaiming the resources and ending the JVM. You can destroy the JVM manually if you prefer. Figure 5.9 shows procedure **destroyJVM**, which destroys the JNI environment.

```
P****************************************************************
P* destroyJVM
P****************************************************************
P destroyJVM      B                   export
D destroyJVM      PI             N
D jvm             S                   like(JavaVM_p) dim(1)
D bufLen          S                   like(jsize) INZ(%elem(jvm))
D nVMs            S                   like(jSize)
D rc              S             10I 0
/free
```

```
      rc = JNI_GetCreatedJavaVMs (jvm : bufLen : nVMs);
      if (rc = 0 AND nVMs > 0);
        JavaVM_P = jvm(1);
        rc = DestroyJavaVM(jvm(1));
        if (rc = 0);
          return *ON;
        else;
        endif;
      else;
      endif;
      return *OFF;
   /end-free
   P                       E
```

Figure 5.9: Destroying the JNI environment

JNI Service Program QJVAJNI

You may be wondering to yourself, "Where do all these JNI procedures come from, and how do I 'auto-magically' have access to them?" Well, when you compile your RPG program, the binding directory **QUSAPIBD** is included automatically. This directory includes a service program names **QJVAJNI**, which gives you access to the JNI functionality from RPG.

Thread-Safe RPG with THREAD(*SERIALIZE)

RPG supports multithreading as of V4R4. RPG cannot initialize multiple threads in versions earlier than V6R1, but you can use it in a multithreaded environment. Because RPG uses global variables that are applicable to a job and you could have multiple Java threads running in the same job, you need to make sure the RPG module is *serialized* so that the global variables aren't being manipulated by two different Java threads at the same time. To do so, you use the **THREAD(*SERIALIZE)** keyword in the H specification. This setting indicates that only one thread can run within the module at a time.

I don't want to go too in-depth into multiple threading, but I do want to provide a high-level view so that you can understand why it's necessary to serialize the RPG module. Let's look at a simple RPG program segment and the impact of multiple threads.

Suppose we have a section of code (Figure 5.10) that opens a file, reads the first record, and then closes the file. Let's consider the bad things that could happen without serialization.

```
C                 OPEN      FILE
C                 READ      FILE
C                 CLOSE     FILE
```

Figure 5.10: Simple multithread RPG code

Let's assume that two Java threads in the same job are executing the RPG code shown in the figure. The first thread executes the **OPEN FILE** statement. Then the second thread tries to run the **OPEN FILE** statement and fails because it's trying to **OPEN** an already opened file. Let's assume you've handled the error and it wasn't a showstopper. The second thread keeps on running and successfully executes the **READ FILE** statement followed by the **CLOSE FILE** statement. Now, the first thread comes back, and what do you think happens? That's right. The first thread tries to **READ FILE** after the second thread has already closed the file, and now you have a program crash.

If you specify **THREAD(*SERIALIZE)** in the H specification for the module, the second thread will be prevented from accessing the module until the first thread is done. So, in the preceding scenario, the first thread executes the first statement, and the second thread comes in. But, because you specified **THREAD(*SERIALIZE)**, the second thread is prevented from entering the module and must wait until the first thread has exited the module. In this case, both threads will open, read, and close the file without any issues.

The **THREAD(*SERIALIZE)** option takes care of most multithreaded situations, but it does not address all of them. There are still shared data cases that you need to address, such as modules that use **EXPORT/IMPORT** keywords on the D specifications, files that are shared across modules, or pointers that are shared between programs.

Java Note

In Java, this behavior is called *synchronization*. Every object in Java has a built-in lock that is implemented when you use the **synchronized** keyword on the method. Serialization does exist in Java, but it has a totally different meaning.

When you start using **THREAD(*SERIALIZE)** in your programs, there is one new condition you'll have to deal with, and that is that you cannot use external indicators (***INU1**–***INU8**) in your programs.

I recommend including the following three lines of code in every RPG program you use with Java:

- **THREAD(*SERIALIZE)** in the H specification
- **/DEFINE OS400_JVM_12**
- **/COPY QSYSINC/QRPGLESRC,JNI**

Garbage Collection

RPG uses JNI to load the JVM in the native application of RPG. When you program in Java, the JVM normally recognizes when an object is no longer being used and frees the resources that are no longer referenced by the program. But, because RPG uses JNI to run the JVM, only the RPG program knows when a resource is finished being used, so you will want to manually free resources to avoid excessive allocation of unused memory.

The JNI file provides the **DeleteLocalRef** function, which you can use directly from an RPG program to remove local object references, but the **freeLocalRef** wrapper procedure shown in Figure 5.11 retrieves the JNI interface pointer for use with **DeleteLocalRef**.

```
p*****************************************************************
P*   freeLocalRef(Ref)
p*****************************************************************
P freeLocalRef...
P                     B                   EXPORT
D freeLocalRef...
D                     PI
D  inRefObject                            like(jobject)
D  env                S                 * static inz(*null)
/free
  if (env = *NULL);
    env = getJNIEnv();
  else;
  endif;
```

```
  JNIENV_p = env;
  DeleteLocalRef(env: inRefObject);
/end-free
P                          E
```

Figure 5.11: Making a local reference eligible for deletion in the JVM

You can also free references in bulk by using the JNI function **pushLocalFrame** at the beginning of a section of RPG code. Then, you could call the **popLocalFrame** function to release all the objects.

The **beginObjectGroup** procedure (Figure 5.12) uses the **PushLocalFrame** RPG procedure to create a local reference frame for a specified number of object references. If insufficient memory exists, you'll receive an error.

```
P*********************************************************************
P* beginObjectGroup creates a new group of object references
P*     on the stack that can be released all at once
P*********************************************************************
P beginObjectGroup...
P                         B                     EXPORT
D beginObjectGroup...
D                        PI             10I 0
D inCapacity                            10I 0 value options(*nopass)
D*
D env            S                        *
D rc             S              10I 0
D capacity       S              10I 0 inz(100)
/free
  if (%parms >= 1);
    capacity = inCapacity;
  else;
  endif;
  env = getJNIEnv();
  if (env = *NULL);
    return JNI_ERR;
  else;
  endif;
  JNIENV_p = env;
  rc = PushLocalFrame(JNIENV_p : capacity);
  if  (rc <> 0);
    return JNI_ERR;
  else;
  endif;
```

```
      return JNI_OK;
   /end-free
   P                 E
```

Figure 5.12: Procedure to push a local frame

When you are finished with the objects, you can call the **endObjectGroup**
procedure (Figure 5.13) to pop the frame to free all the local references that were
created since the last **PushLocalFrame** procedure was called.

```
P******************************************************************
P* endObjectGroup releases a group of object references
P******************************************************************
P endObjectGroup...
P                 B                   EXPORT
D endObjectGroup...
D                 PI          10I 0
D  inRefObject                        like(jObject) const
D                                     options(*nopass)
D  outNewObject                       like(jObject)
D                                     options(*nopass)
D refObject       S                   like(jObject) inz(*NULL)
D newObject       S                   like(jObject)
/free
 JNIENV_p = getJNIEnv();
  if (JNIENV_p = *NULL);
  return JNI_ERR;
  endif;
  if %parms >= 1;
    refObject = inRefObject;
  else;
  endif;
  newObject = PopLocalFrame (JNIENV_p: refObject);
  if %parms >= 2;
    outNewObject = newObject;
  else;
  endif;
  return JNI_OK;
/end-free
P                 E
```

Figure 5.13: Procedure to pop a local frame

You can find pure Java versions of these procedures on the Sun Microsystems
Web site. The RPG code, with some minor modifications, can be found in the *ILE
RPG Programmer's Guide*.

Hello World

We now have all of our foundation procedures established. Let's build a Hello World program that creates a Java **String** object, sets the value to **'Hello World'**, and retrieves the bytes back into RPG for display (Figure 5.14).

```
 H THREAD(*SERIALIZE)
 D********************************************************************
 D*   How to Compile:
 D*
 D*    (1. CREATE THE MODULE)
 D*    CRTRPGMOD MODULE(AIRLIB/AIR05_01) SRCFILE(AIRLIB/AIRSRC) +
 D*              DBGVIEW(*ALL) INDENT('.')
 D*
 D*    (2. CREATE THE PROGRAM)
 D*    CRTPGM PGM(AIRLIB/AIR05_01)
 D*    MODULE(AIRLIB/AIR05_01)
 D*    BNDSRVPGM(AIRLIB/SVAIRFUNC AIRLIB/SVAIRJAVA)
 D*              ACTGRP(AIR05_01)
 D********************************************************************
 D*** PROTOTYPES ***
 D/COPY QSYSINC/QRPGLESRC,JNI
 D/COPY AIRLIB/AIRSRC,SPAIRJAVA
 D airString       S                      like(jString)
 D displayBytes    S              52A
  /free
    JNIEnv_p = getJNIEnv();
    airString = new_String('Hello World');
    displayBytes = String_getBytes(airString);
    DSPLY displayBytes;
    freeLocalRef(airString);
    *inlr = *ON;
  /end-free
```

Figure 5.14: RPG–Java Hello World program

If you were to run this program, you would see the expected "Hello World" output displayed on your screen. The figure shows the small amount of code that is required to implement most of the capabilities discussed in this chapter:

- The **/COPY QSYSINC/QRPGLESRC,JNI** statement includes all the prototypes and data types that are provided by IBM.

- The **/COPY AIRLIB/AIRSRC,SPAIRJAVA** statement provides access to the Java **String** methods and basic Java procedures.

- The **like(jString)** usage on the **airString** variable provides a reference variable for the Java **String** object.

- The **getJNIEnv** procedure ensures that the **STDIN**, **STDOUT**, and **STDERR** streams are open.

- The **getJNIEnv** procedure looks for an existing JVM and attaches to it, if one exists. If a JVM does not already exist, the procedure creates a new one.

- The **new_String** procedure calls the constructor method of the **String** class to create a new object and return the reference variable to the **String** object.

- The **String_getBytes** procedure converts the **String** content back into EBCDIC bytes to be used within RPG.

- The **freeLocalRef** procedure manually releases the memory allocated to the object that is referred to by the **airString** reference variable.

Now you can see the notable capabilities that we have provided by taking the front-end time to create these highly useful RPG procedures to handle all the complexities of using Java from RPG.

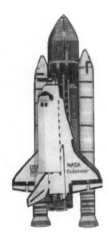

6

Java Native Interface

In this chapter, we delve into some advanced topics related to the Java Native Interface. This material is the final step in your preparation for the open-source projects that make up the rest of this book. If you feel as if you're in a bit over your head already, don't worry — it's all smooth sailing after this chapter.

Advanced JNI

RPG gives you access only to Java methods; it does *not* provide access to fields within a class. For the reasons I touched on in discussing encapsulation in Chapter 4, it's normally not a good idea to allow access to fields within a class. Instead, the recommendation is to accomplish all variable access using publicly accessible setter and getter methods. At times, however, there could be a good reason to break this rule, and you may need to handle those situations. This section shows you how to do that.

It's funny because when I needed to access a field from a class, I thought it would be the simplest thing. Then, I discovered that you can't access variables directly using RPG. The only way to do it involves an advanced topic: calling JNI functions directly to gain access to publicly accessible variables.

So far, we've talked about accessing Java through special keywords and letting RPG do most of the grunt work to handle the details involved in working with JNI. Now, you get to see more of the details from behind the scenes.

The first thing to note when accessing JNI functions from RPG is that you don't use the ***JAVA** parameter on the **extProc** keyword; otherwise, we wouldn't need to go down to the JNI level. Another thing to consider is that RPG uses EBCDIC characters, whereas Java uses Unicode characters. For the two environments to communicate, we need to use the common ASCII character set. RPG normally performs the EBCDIC-to-ASCII conversions automatically, but when you deal directly with JNI, you must perform the conversions manually.

The Java Virtual Machine (JVM) uses the Unicode character set internally, but when it communicates outside itself, it uses the character set specified by the **file.encoding** property, a system property of the JVM. If necessary, you can override the **file.encoding** property when the JVM is started up.

The default encoding is typically the ISO-8859 character set. ISO-8859 is an extension of the ASCII character set, and you may be using a different international encoding. You can find more international encodings on the Sun Microsystems Web site at *http://java.sun.com/j2se/1.4.2/docs/guide/intl/ encoding.doc.html*. For references throughout this book, I'll refer to the character set used to communicate between RPG and Java simply as "ASCII."

Fortunately for us, we've already created some convenient procedures (in Chapter 3) to perform EBCDIC-to-ASCII conversions: **Air_openConverter**, **Air_convert**, and **Air_closeConverter**. If you choose not to use these procedures, you can employ the **QDCXLATE** (Convert Data) API, or you can perform the conversions manually and hard code them into the application by entering the hexadecimal code values.

Finding the Class

The JNI function **FindClass** searches for a fully qualified class name within the **CLASSPATH** of the specified JNI environment. The class name must be in ASCII format and must have each period (.) replaced with a forward slash (/) to indicate the directory structure of the class.

Figure 6.1 shows the RPG prototype for the **FindClass** function. You'll find this prototype (and the others we'll discuss here) in the IBM-provided **QSYSINC/ QRPGLESRC,JNI** file.

```
D*------------------------------------------------------------------
D*    jclass (*FindClass)
D*       (JNIEnv *env, const char *name);
D*------------------------------------------------------------------
D FindClass       PR                    LIKE(jclass)
D                                       EXTPROC(*CWIDEN
D                                       : JNINativeInterface.
D                                         FindClass_P)
D env                                   LIKE(JNIEnv_P) VALUE
D name                        *         OPTIONS(*STRING) VALUE
```

Figure 6.1: JNI FindClass function prototype in QSYSINC/QRPGLESRC,JNI

The **FindClass** function accepts two parameters:

- **JNIEnv *env** — The JNI interface pointer
- **const char *name** — The class name

Identifying Fields of a Class

The **GetFieldID** JNI function identifies the field of the specified class. Figure 6.2 shows the prototype for the function.

```
D*------------------------------------------------------------------
D*    jfieldID (*GetFieldID)
D*       (JNIEnv *env, jclass clazz, const char *name, const char *sig);
D*------------------------------------------------------------------
D GetFieldID      PR                    LIKE(jfieldID)
D                                       EXTPROC(*CWIDEN
D                                       : JNINativeInterface.
D                                         GetFieldID_P)
```

```
D argEnv                        LIKE(JNIEnv_P) VALUE
D argClass                      LIKE(jclass) VALUE
D argName              *        OPTIONS(*STRING) VALUE
D argSignature         *        OPTIONS(*STRING) VALUE
```

Figure 6.2: JNI GetFieldID function prototype in QSYSINC/QRPGLESRC,JNI

The procedure expects four parameters and returns the field ID of the instance variable of the specified class:

- **JNIEnv *env** — The JNI interface pointer
- **jclass clazz** — A Java class object
- **const char *name** — The field name
- **const char *sig** — The JNI type signature of the field of interest (more about type signatures later)

Identifying Methods of a Class

In addition to retrieving an identifier to a field within a class, you can obtain an identifier to a method by using the **GetMethodID** or **GetStaticMethodID** JNI function. **GetMethodID** is available to work with instance (non-static) methods of classes. **GetStaticMethodID** identifies static methods of a class.

Figure 6.3 shows the prototype for the **GetStaticMethodID** function.

```
D*------------------------------------------------------------------
D*      jmethodID (*GetStaticMethodID)
D*        (JNIEnv *env, jclass clazz, const char *name, const char *sig);
D*------------------------------------------------------------------
D GetStaticMethodID...
D                 PR                    LIKE(jmethodID)
D                                       EXTPROC(*CWIDEN
D                                       : JNINativeInterface.
D                                         GetStaticMethodID_P)
D env                                   LIKE(JNIEnv_P) VALUE
D clazz                                 LIKE(jclass) VALUE
D name                         *        OPTIONS(*STRING) VALUE
D sig                          *        OPTIONS(*STRING) VALUE
```

Figure 6.3: JNI GetStaticMethodID prototype in QSYSINC/QRPGLESRC,JNI

The function expects four parameters and returns the method ID of the static method of the specified class:

- **JNIEnv *env** — The JNI interface pointer
- **jclass clazz** — A Java class object
- **const char *name** — The method name
- **const char *sig** — The JNI type signature of the method of interest

In this chapter, our focus is on JNI field access. You'll see a working example of JNI method access in Chapter 13.

JNI Type Signatures

The JNI *type signature* provides the unique identifier of methods, including methods that use overloaded methods that have different parameters and return types. Table 6.1 lists the available type signatures.

Table 6.1: Java type signatures used with JNI

Java type	Type signature
boolean	Z
byte	B
char	C
short	S
int	I
long	J
float	F
double	D
void	V
fully-qualified-class	L fully-qualified-class
method type	(arg-types) ret-type
array	[

Get<type>Field and Set<type>Field Routines

JNI functions provide access to the instance variables of a class using the field ID obtained from the **GetFieldID** function:

> **Get<type>Field (JNIEnv *env, jobject obj, jfieldID fieldID)**
> The **Get<type>Field** routines retrieve the *value* of the instance variable of the specified class using the field ID. The routines accept three parameters:

- **JNIEnv *env** — The JNI interface pointer
- **jobject obj** — A Java object (must not be null)
- **fieldID** — The field ID retrieved using **GetFieldID**

> **Set<type>Field (JNIEnv *env, jobject obj, jfieldID fieldID, <type> variable)**
> The **Set<type>Field** routines set the *value* of the instance variable of the specified class using the **fieldID**. The parameters are the same as for **Get<type>Field**, plus an additional field that matches the type of the set procedure.

Table 6.2 lists the JNI **get<type>Field** and **set<type>Field** functions whose prototypes are defined in the **QSYSINC/QRPGLESRC,JNI** file.

Table 6.2: Get<type>Field and Set<type>Field JNI functions

Native type	Get<type>Field	Set<type>Field
jobject	GetObjectField	SetObjectField
jboolean	GetBooleanField	SetBooleanField
jbyte	GetByteField	SetByteField
jchar	GetCharField	SetCharField
jshort	GetShortField	SetShortField
jint	GetIntField	SetIntField
jlong	GetLongField	SetLongField
jfloat	GetFloatField	SetFloatField
jdouble	GetDoubleField	SetDoubleField

RPG Example of JNI Concepts

The JNI functions are a bit too general to easily explain in words, so let me attempt to provide a conceptual example of these functions using an RPG program.

Suppose we have some raw data that contains several fields' worth of information, but the positions of the fields are not identified. We'll represent the raw data using a data structure named **DimensionRaw** that contains a single field, and we'll represent the several fields' worth of data in that one field.

Once we know the layout of the data, we can create another data structure that contains field sizes and overlays to structure the data in a usable manner. In this example, we'll call this second data structure **Dimension** in preparation for the next example.

Figure 6.4 shows the sample RPG program, and Figure 6.5 shows the program's output. This may strike you as a senseless program, but if we focus on the concepts being presented, it will help to represent the JNI functionality of the **FindClass**, **GetFieldID**, and **Get<type>Field** functions.

```
D Dimension        DS                      qualified
D  field1                   1    3A
D  field2                   4    6A
D  field3                   7    9A
D  field4                  10   12A
D  width_I                       3S 0 overlay(field2)
D  width_B                       3A   overlay(field2)
D  height_I                      3S 0 overlay(field4)
D  height_B                      3A   overlay(field4)
D*
D DimensionRaw     DS
D  dimRaw                   1   12A
D*
D  displayBytes     S            52A
C*
 /free
   dimRaw = 'xxx001xxx002';
   displayBytes = 'Raw: ' + %trim(dimRaw);
   dsply displayBytes;
   // Push Raw Dimension into Structured Dimension
   Dimension = DimensionRaw;
```

```
displayBytes = 'fieldId(width_I) '
             + %trim(%editc(Dimension.width_I:'Z'));
dsply displayBytes;
displayBytes = 'fieldId(width_B) '
             + %trim(Dimension.width_B);
dsply displayBytes;
displayBytes = 'fieldId(height_I) '
             + %trim(%editc(Dimension.height_I:'Z'));
dsply displayBytes;
displayBytes = 'fieldId(height_B) '
             + %trim(Dimension.height_B);
dsply displayBytes;
*inlr = *ON;
/end-free
```

Figure 6.4: RPG program illustrating JNI concepts

```
DSPLY    Raw: xxx001xxx002
DSPLY    fieldId(width_I) 1
DSPLY    fieldId(width_B) 001
DSPLY    fieldId(height_I) 2
DSPLY    fieldId(height_B) 002
```

Figure 6.5: Program output illustrating JNI concepts

First, the program creates the raw data. This is valid data, and we could work with it if we knew all the positions of the data, but it would be inflexible to work with and the program would break if any small change occurred to the data layout. So, we push the data into the **Dimension** data structure to make working with it easier.

You can think of the **FindClass** procedure as being kind of like the qualified **Dimension** data structure. **Dimension** is the name of a data structure that has fields contained within it. Similarly, **FindClass** retrieves a reference to a class that is located within your class path.

The field names that are specified after the qualified data structure name provide a parallel to the **GetFieldID** procedure. If we were interested in the **width_I** field of the **Dimension** data structure, we would refer to that location as **Dimension.**

width_I. The **width_I** field is dependent on the data structure that contains it, just as **GetFieldID** depends on the results of the **FindClass** procedure.

This example provides multiple ways to access the same data, with the use of **Dimension.width_I**, which is a zoned variable, and **Dimension.width_B**, which is a variable made up of character bytes. This is similar to the **Get<type>Field** procedures. Once you have the field name, you will determine the expected results according to the type specified.

RPG Code Sample to Access Java Instance Variables

Now that we've defined the required JNI functions, let's walk through a simple code example to access Java instance variables using Java.

The **Dimension** class lets you store both the height and the width values in a single object. This class, which is included with the JDK, is commonly used as a parameter for other classes.

Our primary objective in using **Dimension** is to exploit the publicly accessible fields **height** and **width**. The width and height values are simple integers, which is a good starting point for understanding the JNI functions. A look at the Java-Docs for the **Dimension** class (Figure 6.6) shows that the height and width are publicly accessible.

Field Summary	
int	height The height dimension; negative values can be used.
int	width The width dimension; negative values can be used.

Figure 6.6: JavaDoc for java.awt.Dimension of publicly accessible variables

Figure 6.7 shows the three constructors available for the **Dimension** class. We'll use the default constructor (**Dimension()**) and then access the public variables directly to set them to the desired values.

Constructor Summary
`Dimension`() Creates an instance of `Dimension` with a width of zero and a height of zero.
`Dimension`(`Dimension` d) Creates an instance of `Dimension` whose width and height are the same as for the specified dimension.
`Dimension`(int width, int height) Constructs a `Dimension` and initializes it to the specified width and specified height.

Figure 6.7: JavaDoc for java.awt.Dimension constructor methods

The JavaDoc method summary (Figure 6.8) shows the getter and setter methods that are available for the **Dimension** class. We won't be using any of these methods for this example.

Method Summary	
double	`getHeight`() Returns the height of this dimension in double precision.
double	`getWidth`() Returns the width of this dimension in double precision.
void	`setSize`(int width, int height) Sets the size of this `Dimension` object to the specified width and height.

Figure 6.8: JavaDoc for java.awt.Dimension public accessor methods

Figure 6.9 provides the Java code to create an instance of the **Dimension** class and then set the width and height by directly accessing the public variables.

```
package com.airbook.util;
import java.awt.*;
/**********************************************************
 * Accessing publicly accessible variables to demonstrate
 * the use of JNI in RPG.
 **********************************************************/
public class AirDimensionJni
```

```
    {
  public AirDimensionJni()
     {
     Dimension dim = new Dimension();
     // Retrieve the publicly accessible field values
     // of the Dimension instance on Initialization
     widthBefore = dim.width;
     heightBefore = dim.height;
     dim.width = 1;
     dim.height = 2;
     widthAfter = dim.width;
     heightAfter = dim.height;
     }
  public void print()
     {
     System.out.println("Before");
     System.out.println("Width: " + widthBefore
                    + " Height: " + heightBefore);
     System.out.println("After");
     System.out.println("Width: " + widthAfter
                + " Height: " + heightAfter);
     }
  public static void main(String[] args) throws Exception
     {
     AirDimensionJni test = new AirDimensionJni();
     test.print();
     System.exit(0);
     }
  private int widthBefore;
  private int heightBefore;
  private int widthAfter;
  private int heightAfter;
  }
```

Figure 6.9: Java class directly accessing variables of java.awt.Dimension

After running the **main** method of the **AirDimensionJni** class, you'll see the output depicted in Figure 6.10.

```
Before
Width: 0 Height: 0
After
Width: 1 Height: 2
```

Figure 6.10: Output of Java class directly accessing variables of java.awt.Dimension

Accessing the public variables in Java seems easy enough. It looks just like accessing qualified data structures in RPG. We won't be creating much Java code, but we'll use it here to assist with the transition into RPG code using Java. This way, you can look at some Java code segments that might illustrate a desired capability and make them accessible through RPG.

Figure 6.11 shows the first part of an RPG program to accomplish the same goal as the preceding Java code. The first step is to use the CCSID conversion procedures to convert the EBCDIC characters to ASCII for communications with JNI.

```
H THREAD(*SERIALIZE)
D new_Dimension...
D                       PR              O   EXTPROC(*JAVA
D                                           :'java.awt.Dimension'
D                                           :*CONSTRUCTOR)
D*
D dim              S                   O   CLASS(*JAVA
D                                           :'java.awt.Dimension')
D dimClass         S                       Like(jclass)
D displayString    S              52A
D cd               DS                      likeDs(iconv_t)
D ebcdicString     S            1024A
D asciiDimension   S            1024A
D asciiWidth       S            1024A
D asciiHeight      S            1024A
D asciiSignature   S            1024A
D toCCSID          S             10I 0
D widthBefore      S             10I 0
D heightBefore     S             10I 0
D widthAfter       S             10I 0
D heightAfter      S             10I 0
D widthId          S                      Like(jfieldID)
D heightId         S                      Like(jfieldID)
D**************************************************************************
D/DEFINE OS400_JVM_12
D/DEFINE JNI_COPY_FIELD_FUNCTIONS
D/COPY QSYSINC/QRPGLESRC,JNI
D/COPY AIRLIB/AIRSRC,SPAIRFUNC
D/COPY AIRLIB/AIRSRC,SPAIRJAVA
C/EJECT
 /free
   // Create/Attach to JVM
   CallP JavaServiceProgram();
   JNIEnv_P = getJNIEnv();
```

```
// Create conversion descriptor for CCSID conversions
toCCSID = 1208;
cd = Air_openConverter(toCCSID);
// Java classes are typically identified with period separators
// But, when using JNI you must change the '.' to '/'
// ASCII java.awt.Dimension
ebcdicString = 'java/awt/Dimension';
asciiDimension = Air_convert(cd: %trim(ebcdicString));
// The JNI type signature for int = 'I'
ebcdicString = 'I';
asciiSignature = Air_convert(cd: %trim(ebcdicString));
// ASCII width
ebcdicString = 'width';
asciiWidth = Air_convert(cd: %trim(ebcdicString));
// ASCII height
ebcdicString = 'height';
asciiHeight = Air_convert(cd: %trim(ebcdicString));
```

Figure 6.11: RPG program directly accessing java.awt.Dimension variables (part 1 of 4)

After execution of this code, we will have all the characters converted from EBCDIC to ASCII for use with the JNI procedures. Note that the program changes the periods to slashes for use with JNI.

Next, we create an instance of the **Dimension** class to get and set the values (Figure 6.12). For this example, we use RPG to call the constructor method of the **Dimension** class using **extProc** with the ***JAVA** and ***CONSTRUCTOR** parameters, but you could keep going in JNI if you wanted to using the **NewObject** JNI function.

```
// Get an instance of the Dimension class
dim = new_Dimension();
// Get the Class reference using JNI
dimClass = FindClass(JNIEnv_P:%trim(asciiDimension));
if (dimClass = *null);
  displayString = 'Dimension FindClass Error';
  dsply displayString;
else;
endif;
```

Figure 6.12: RPG program directly accessing java.awt.Dimension variables (part 2 of 4)

The **dim** variable now contains the reference to the constructed **Dimension** object. This step is similar to the **dimRaw** variable receiving the raw data in

Figure 6.4. We have the valid data, the memory has been allocated, and the fields have been initialized, but we don't know all the positions of the data.

The **FindClass** procedure defines the class and returns the results to the **dimClass** variable, which is similar to the qualified **Dimension** data structure defined in our RPG concept program in Figure 6.4.

In Figure 6.13, the program uses the **GetFieldID** procedure to determine the field information to retrieve from the class referred to in the **dimClass** variable, just as the variable name used in Figure 6.4 used a combination of the qualified data structure and the field name.

```
// Get the Field references within the Class
widthId = GetFieldID(JNIEnv_P:dimClass:
                     %trim(asciiWidth):
                     %trim(asciiSignature));
heightId = GetFieldID(JNIEnv_P:dimClass:
                     %trim(asciiHeight):
                     %trim(asciiSignature));
// Retrieve the publicly accessible field values
// of the Dimension instance on initialization
widthBefore = getIntField(JNIEnv_P:dim:widthId);
heightBefore = getIntField(JNIEnv_P:dim:heightId);
```

Figure 6.13: RPG program directly accessing java.awt.Dimension variables (part 3 of 4)

Java provides the ability to override the methods, so you usually have to specify the signature of what you're referencing when you use JNI. The width is an integer variable, so the signature in this case will be the ASCII "I" value, according to the information given in Table 6.1.

The preceding segment of code also retrieves the values for the width and height using the **getIntField** procedure. This procedure returns the field data from the instance of the **dim** object. **getIntField** is one of the **Get<type>Field** procedures mentioned earlier and is one of the options listed in Table 6.2.

Because we are communicating between RPG and Java using JNI, we must convert any string references between EBCDIC and ASCII before they can be properly implemented in the JNI procedures. Pay close attention to the case of the letters, and remember to replace the periods with slashes.

Now that you know how to "get" the values, let's look at how to "set" the values. Figure 6.14 shows the portion of the RPG program that performs this work.

```
// Set the publicly accessible field values
// using JNI, then retrieve them.
setIntField(JNIEnv_P:dim:widthId:1);
setIntField(JNIEnv_P:dim:heightId:2);
widthAfter = getIntField(JNIEnv_P:dim:widthId);
heightAfter = getIntField(JNIEnv_P:dim:heightId);
// Display the results
displayString = 'Before: '
             + 'Width = '
             + %trim(%editc(widthBefore:'3'))
             + ' Height = '
             + %trim(%editc(heightBefore:'3'));
dsply displayString;
displayString = 'After: '
             + 'Width = '
             + %trim(%editc(widthAfter:'3'))
             + ' Height = '
             + %trim(%editc(heightAfter:'3'));
dsply displayString;
// Clean Up
Air_closeConverter(cd);
freeLocalRef(dim);
freeLocalRef(dimClass);
*inlr = *ON;
/end-free
```

Figure 6.14: RPG program directly accessing java.awt.Dimension variables (part 4 of 4)

The **setIntField** procedure reuses the field IDs that were retrieved earlier in the program and sets the values of the fields. The program then executes standard **DSPLY** statements to display the results to the screen. Last, it performs some cleanup to close the CCSID conversion descriptor and release the objects in the JVM. Figure 6.5 shows the program output.

```
DSPLY   Before: Width = 0 Height = 0
DSPLY   After: Width = 1 Height = 2
```

Figure 6.15: Output of RPG program directly accessing java.awt.Dimension variables

In most situations, publicly accessible variables are constants that are marked as **public static final**. For constants, you could avoid going through all this trouble by looking at the JavaDoc for the class you're working with to find out what the constant values are; then, you could create a **COPY** file to contain all the constant values. This technique is a common practice that we'll use for constants.

Some classes have changing instance variables that are publicly accessible, but they should provide getter and setter methods to be compliant with the JavaBeans specification.

Arrays of Objects

Next, let's kick it up a notch. Now that you understand the ins and outs of a single object, we can take things a step further by tackling an array of objects. For object arrays, we'll use several of the previously defined procedures, plus a few new array-specific procedures that have prototypes in the **QSYSINC/QRPGLESRC,JNI** file.

The **NewObjectArray** function (Figure 6.16) creates an array of specified objects. You must specify the size when you create the array. The function allocates the memory for the array and returns a reference variable that points to the **Array** object that is created.

```
D*------------------------------------------------------------------
D*      jobjectArray (*NewObjectArray)
D*         (JNIEnv *env, jsize len, jclass clazz, jobject init);
D*------------------------------------------------------------------
D NewObjectArray  PR                        LIKE(jobjectArray)
D                                           EXTPROC(*CWIDEN
D                                           : JNINativeInterface.
D                                             NewObjectArray_P)
D env                                       LIKE(JNIEnv_P) VALUE
D len                                       LIKE(jsize) VALUE
D clazz                                     LIKE(jclass) VALUE
D init                                      LIKE(jobject) VALUE
```

Figure 6.16: NewObjectArray function prototype in QSYSINC/QRPGLESRC,JNI

The **SetObjectArrayElement** function (Figure 6.17) assigns an object to the specified index of the object array.

```
D*-----------------------------------------------------------------
D*      void (*SetObjectArrayElement)
D*         (JNIEnv *env, jobjectArray array, jsize index, jobject val);
D*-----------------------------------------------------------------
D SetObjectArrayElement...
D                 PR             EXTPROC(*CWIDEN
D                                : JNINativeInterface.
D                                  SetObjectArrayElement_P)
D env                            LIKE(JNIEnv_P) VALUE
D array                          LIKE(jobjectArray) VALUE
D index                          LIKE(jsize) VALUE
D val                            LIKE(jobject) VALUE
```

Figure 6.17: SetObjectArrayElement function prototype in QSYSINC/QRPGLESRC,JNI

The **GetObjectArrayElement** function (Figure 6.18) retrieves the object at the specified array index.

```
D*-----------------------------------------------------------------
D*      jobject (*GetObjectArrayElement)
D*         (JNIEnv *env, jobjectArray array, jsize index);
D*-----------------------------------------------------------------
D GetObjectArrayElement...
D                 PR             LIKE(jobject)
D                                EXTPROC(*CWIDEN
D                                : JNINativeInterface.
D                                  GetObjectArrayElement_P)
D env                            LIKE(JNIEnv_P) VALUE
D array                          LIKE(jobjectArray) VALUE
D index                          LIKE(jsize) VALUE
```

Figure 6.18: GetObjectArrayElement function prototype in QSYSINC/QRPGLESRC,JNI

Let's try out these new capabilities by building a program that creates an array of strings. We'll assign a unique value to each of ten **String** objects and store them into the array of objects. After the initialization of all the array elements is complete, we'll loop through the elements and display them.

First, using the code shown in Figure 6.19, we convert the EBCDIC characters to ASCII for the communications with JNI. Then, we find the class for the objects that will be populated in the **Array**. We can verify whether the class is found by checking to see whether the result is null.

```
H THREAD(*SERIALIZE)
D cd              DS                    likeDs(iconv_t)
D toCCSID         S              10I 0
D size            S              10I 0
D i               S              10I 0
D displayString   S              52A
D ebcdicString    S            1024A
D asciiStrArray   S            1024A
D stringClass     S                    LIKE(jclass)
D stringObject    S                    LIKE(jstring)
D stringArray     S                    LIKE(jobjectArray)
D*****************************************************************
D/DEFINE OS400_JVM_12
D/DEFINE JNI_COPY_ARRAY_FUNCTIONS
D/COPY QSYSINC/QRPGLESRC,JNI
D/COPY AIRLIB/AIRSRC,SPAIRFUNC
D/COPY AIRLIB/AIRSRC,SPAIRJAVA
C/EJECT
 /free
   // Create/Attach to JVM
   CallP JavaServiceProgram();
   JNIEnv_P = getJNIEnv();
   // Create Conversion Descriptor for CCSID conversions
   toCCSID = 1208;
   size = 10;
   cd = Air_openConverter(toCCSID);
   ebcdicString = 'java/lang/String';
   asciiStrArray = Air_convert(cd: %trim(ebcdicString));
   // Get the Class
   stringClass = FindClass(JNIEnv_P:
                        %trim(asciiStrArray));
   if (stringClass = *null);
     displayString = 'FindClass Error';
     dsply displayString;
   else;
   endif;
```

Figure 6.19: RPG program using JNI to create an array of String objects (part 1 of 4)

Once we have the results of the **FindClass** function, we can create a reference variable that points to the **Array** of **String** objects created (Figure 6.20).

```
// Get the Object Array
stringArray = NewObjectArray(JNIEnv_P:
                             size:
                             stringClass:
                             *null);
if (stringArray = *null);
  displayString = 'NewObjectArray Error';
  dsply displayString;
else;
endif;
```

Figure 6.20: RPG program using JNI to create an array of String objects (part 2 of 4)

The **NewObjectArray** function creates an array with ten elements, as specified by the **size** variable. The type of the objects will be determined using the **string-Class** results from the **FindClass** function. The function allocates the memory for the array and returns the reference variable for the array.

Now, we loop through the array and set the elements (Figure 6.21). In RPG, we're used to using one (**1**) as the starting index of an array, but in Java you will have zero (**0**) as the first index.

```
// Initialize ten string array objects
for i = 0 to 9;
  stringObject = new_String('String ' + %trim(%editc(i:'3')));
  SetObjectArrayElement(JNIEnv_P:stringArray
                        :i:stringObject);
  if (Air_isJVMError());
    leave;
  else;
  endif;
endFor;
```

Figure 6.21: RPG program using JNI to create an array of String objects (part 3 of 4)

In each iteration of the loop, we first create a new **String** object using the constructor method with an initial value to be assigned to the **String** object. The created object is assigned to an element of the array.

In the loop, the program uses the **Air_isJVMError** procedure to check for an exception after setting each **Array** element. We'll discuss this procedure in the next section, which covers exception handling. If an exception is found, the procedure returns a value of *ON; otherwise, the result is *OFF.

The final segment of code (Figure 6.22) goes through each element of the **Array** and retrieves the contents of each **String** object to display the results. The program then cleans up by closing the CCSID converter and freeing the Java objects.

```
// Loop and display results
for i = 0 to 9;
   stringObject = GetObjectArrayElement(JNIEnv_P
                                :stringArray:i);
   if (Air_isJVMError());
     leave;
   else;
     displayString = String_getBytes(stringObject);
     dsply displayString;
   endif;
endFor;
// Clean Up
Air_closeConverter(cd);
freeLocalRef(stringClass);
freeLocalRef(stringObject);
freeLocalRef(stringArray);
*inlr = *ON;
/end-free
```

Figure 6.22: RPG program using JNI to create an array of String objects (part 4 of 4)

Figure 6.23 shows the output produced by the sample program.

```
DSPLY   String 0
DSPLY   String 1
DSPLY   String 2
DSPLY   String 3
DSPLY   String 4
DSPLY   String 5
DSPLY   String 6
DSPLY   String 7
DSPLY   String 8
DSPLY   String 9
```

Figure 6.23: Output of RPG program using JNI to create an array of String objects

Exception Handling

When you access Java using RPG, any exceptions that occur are passed to RPG and an RPG message is thrown. But when you use JNI, you can retrieve the exception from the JVM using the **ExceptionOccurred** procedure provided in the **QSYSINC/QRPGLESRC,JNI** file. This exception must be retrieved before another JNI operation is performed, or the exception will be overwritten.

Figure 6.24 shows the **ExceptionOccurred** procedure prototype.

```
D*-----------------------------------------------------------------
D*       jthrowable (*ExceptionOccurred)
D*         (JNIEnv *env);
D*-----------------------------------------------------------------
D ExceptionOccurred...
D                    PR                    LIKE(jthrowable)
D                                          EXTPROC(*CWIDEN
D                                          : JNINativeInterface.
D                                            ExceptionOccurred_P)
D env                                      LIKE(JNIEnv_P) VALUE
```

Figure 6.24: ExceptionOccurred function prototype in QSYSINC/QRPGLESRC,JNI

The procedure returns an object of type **Throwable**, which is a super class of **Exception**. If an exception occurred, the return value will contain a reference to a **Throwable** object. If no exception occurred, the return value will be null.

If you determine that an exception has been thrown, you may want to clear the exception to make future JNI calls. You can do so using the **ExceptionClear** procedure (Figure 6.25).

```
D*-----------------------------------------------------------------
D*       void (*ExceptionClear)
D*         (JNIEnv *env);
D*-----------------------------------------------------------------
D ExceptionClear   PR                      EXTPROC(*CWIDEN
D                                          : JNINativeInterface.
D                                            ExceptionClear_P)
D env                                      LIKE(JNIEnv_P) VALUE
```

Figure 6.25: ExceptionClear function prototype in QSYSINC/QRPGLESRC,JNI

You can use the exception-handling procedures directly in your programs or create a custom procedure to handle the details for you. Figure 6.26 shows a simple procedure to identify when an exception has occurred, display the exception to the job, and then clear the exception. To indicate whether an exception was found, the procedure returns a **boolean** value to be used for possible logic redirection in the calling program.

```
P*******************************************************************
P* Air_isJVMError(): Indicates Throwable Exception Found
P*******************************************************************
P Air_isJVMError   B                    EXPORT
D Air_isJVMError   PI            1N
D svReturn         S             1N
D svThrowable      S                    like(jthrowable)
D svString         S                    like(jstring)
D svMessage        S            52A
 /free
  svReturn = *OFF;
  if (JNIEnv_P = *NULL);
    JNIEnv_P = getJNIEnv();
  else;
  endif;
  svThrowable = ExceptionOccurred(JNIEnv_P);
  if (svThrowable = *NULL);
  else;
    svReturn = *ON;
    svString = Exception_toString(svThrowable);
    svMessage = String_getBytes(svString);
    dsply svMessage;
    ExceptionClear(JNIEnv_P);
  endif;
  freeLocalRef(svThrowable);
  freeLocalRef(svString);
  return svReturn;
 /end-free
P                        E
```

Figure 6.26: Air_isJVMError prototype in AIRLIB/AIRSRC,SPAIRJAVA

This procedure will clear the exception, so you most likely will want to have your program use the results to determine any additional steps to take in the case of an exception. The **QSYSINC/QRPGLESRC,JNI** file does contain a lot of essential

JNI prototypes. For this example, we have retrieved the text associated with the exception using the **Exception_toString** prototype (Figure 6.27), which accesses the **toString** method of the **Throwable** class.

```
D Exception_toString...
D                    PR                      ExtProc(*JAVA
D                                            :'java.lang.Throwable'
D                                            :'toString')
D                                            like(jstring)
```

Figure 6.27: Exception_toString prototype in AIRLIB/AIRSRC,SPAIRJAVA

We could have named this procedure **Throwable_toString**, but I wanted to keep the association with the **ExceptionOccurred** prototype from the JNI file provided by IBM, which returns a **Throwable** object. **Throwable** is the parent class of the **Exception** class.

The **Exception_toString** prototype will be placed into the **SPAIRJAVA** prototype file for future use.

Let's wrap up the chapter now with a sample program that demonstrates the behaviors of an exception for a common programming error that I typically encounter when I forget to replace the periods with slashes when accessing a new class using JNI.

In this example, we'll try to use the **FindClass** function in two different ways. The first way will use periods, deliberately causing an exception. Then, we'll access the function a second time using the correct characters. The program shown in Figure 6.28 performs both attempts.

```
H THREAD(*SERIALIZE)
D*
D cd              DS                      likeDs(iconv_t)
D toCCSID         S              10I 0
D displayString   S              52A
D ebcdicString    S            1024A
D errorString     S            1024A
D correctString   S            1024A
D stringClass     S                      LIKE(jclass)
```

```
D****************************************************************************
D/DEFINE OS400_JVM_12
D/COPY QSYSINC/QRPGLESRC,JNI
D/COPY AIRLIB/AIRSRC,SPAIRFUNC
D/COPY AIRLIB/AIRSRC,SPAIRJAVA
C/EJECT
 /free
  // Create/Attach to JVM
  CallP JavaServiceProgram();
  JNIEnv_P = getJNIEnv();
  // Create Conversion Descriptor for CCSID conversions
  toCCSID = 1208;
  cd = Air_openConverter(toCCSID);
  // Force an exception by using '.' instead of '/'
  ebcdicString = 'java.lang.String';
  errorString = Air_convert(cd: %trim(ebcdicString));
  // This is the correct way, replacing the '.' with '/'
  ebcdicString = 'java/lang/String';
  correctString = Air_convert(cd: %trim(ebcdicString));
  // This will cause an exception
  stringClass = FindClass(JNIEnv_P:
                 %trim(errorString));
  if (Air_isJVMError());
  else;
    displayString = 'First Attempt Success!';
    dsply displayString;
  endif;
  // This will Succeed
  stringClass = FindClass(JNIEnv_P:
                 %trim(correctString));
  if (Air_isJVMError());
  else;
    displayString = 'Second Attempt Success!';
    dsply displayString;
  endif;
  // Clean Up
  Air_closeConverter(cd);
  freeLocalRef(stringClass);
  *inlr = *ON;
 /end-free
```

Figure 6.28: RPG program demonstrating JNI exception handling

When the **FindClass** function is called the first time, it will generate an exception. The text associated with the exception will be retrieved and displayed within the **Air_isJVMError** procedure. The exception will then be cleared.

On the second **FindClass** attempt, the program will access the **String** class using the correct format for JNI and therefore will be executed successfully. Figure 6.29 shows the output generated when calling the sample program.

```
DSPLY   java.lang.NoClassDefFoundError: java.lang.String
DSPLY   Second Attempt Success!
```

Figure 6.29: Output of RPG program demonstrating JNI exception handling

On to the Fun Stuff

After reviewing the JNI code, you can see how easy it would be to make minor mistakes that could cause your program to fail — which is why it's worth the time to put your code into procedures after testing it thoroughly. That way, you can work through the details once and reuse them easily.

Well, that was the thick of it. Now, we can move on to the fun stuff and start working with the open-source projects to provide some great capabilities to your RPG programs!

7

Excel Basics

In this chapter, we discuss how to create spreadsheets in the Microsoft Excel format using RPG. We'll accomplish this task by integrating RPG with Java to access the Apache POI project.

Creating Excel Spreadsheets Using Apache POI

The Apache POI project supports various file formats based on the Microsoft Object Linking and Embedding (OLE) 2 Compound Document format. This support means you can create documents for different components of the Microsoft Office product suite, including Microsoft Excel, Microsoft PowerPoint, and Microsoft Word. POI (which stands for Poor Obfuscation Implementation) provides APIs you can use to create Excel spreadsheets using POI's Horrible Spreadsheet Format (HSSF) component.

Table 7.1 lists the components of the Apache POI package.

Table 7.1: Components of the POI project	
Component	**Description**
HSSF	Microsoft Excel
XSSF	Microsoft Excel XML
HPSF	Document Properties
HLSF	Microsoft PowerPoint
HWPF	Microsoft Word
HDGF	Microsoft Visio
HPBF	Microsoft Publisher
HSMF	Microsoft Outlook
POIFS	OLE 2 Compound Document Format

The core component of the POI project is the POIFS component, which is used by all the other components. You can use the POIFS component to work directly with an OLE 2 Compound Document, but in this book we'll use the higher-level functionality of the HSSF component to create and modify Excel spreadsheets.

We'll be using Apache POI solely to create Excel spreadsheets, but POI supports other Microsoft format files. You may want to keep that point in mind after you master the creation of Excel spreadsheets and decide to expand your service program to support PowerPoint or Word.

Installing POI

The first step in using POI is to download, from the Apache POI Web site (*http://poi.apache.org*), the latest Jar file supported by the Java Runtime Environment (JRE) installed on your IBM i system. You'll want to download the binary file. You can choose either the ***.zip** file or the ***.tar.gz** file.

Extract the downloaded file, and retrieve the **poi-<Version>-FINAL-<Date>.jar** file. (The version and date in the file name will vary depending on which version you download.)

Copy the POI Jar file into your publicly accessible Jar file directory. Then, add the file to your environment variable before starting your Java Virtual Machine.

We'll specify the location of the POI Jar file in the main procedure of the **SVAIRJAVA** service program (Figure 7.1).

```
//-----------------------------------
//---        POI for Excel        ---
//-----------------------------------
localPath = %trim(localPath)
          + ':/Public/Java/Excel_POI'
          + '/poi-3.0.2-FINAL-20080204.jar';
```

Figure 7.1: Setting the location of the POI Jar file in the SVAIRJAVA main procedure

Then, we'll use the location to set the environment variable to make the POI package visible to the JVM using the class path (Figure 7.2).

```
//------------------------------------------------------
// Put the entire class path together and implement.
//------------------------------------------------------
commandString = 'ADDENVVAR ENVVAR(CLASSPATH) '
              + 'VALUE(''.:'
              + %TRIM(localPath)
              + ''') REPLACE(*YES)';
monitor;
  ExecuteCommand(%trim(commandString):%len(%trim(commandString)));
on-error;
  displayBytes = 'ERROR occurred on Class Path!';
  DSPLY displayBytes;
endmon;
```

Figure 7.2: Setting the CLASSPATH environment variable in the SVAIRJAVA main procedure

The **ADDENVVAR** command will be executed when we call the main procedure of **SVAIRJAVA** using the **CallP JavaServiceProgram();** prototyped call.

POI Version Compatibility

The version of POI used in this book is 3.0.2. If you choose to use a newer version, make sure it will work with your JVM. On my V5R4 system, the JVM version is 1.4.2.

One of the most noticeable differences in POI versions newer than 3.0.2 is that many of the **jShort** parameters have been changed to **jInt**. This update is a welcome change because you won't have to cast your variables to **jShort**, but it does require some programming changes. Be sure to prepare for the required changes when updating your JRE and POI files.

Common Code

The RPG code samples we'll develop in this chapter (and the next two) all have the code shown in Figure 7.3 in common. In the interests of space, you won't see this code repeated in subsequent figures. These opening specifications establish the **THREAD(*SERIALIZE)** recommendation for all RPG programs that use Java and then copy in the following from the AIR service program source files:

- The generic prototypes and constants from **SPAIRFUNC**
- The standard Java prototypes from **SPAIRJAVA**
- Specialized POI HSSF Excel prototypes from **SPAIREXCEL**

```
H THREAD(*SERIALIZE)
F************************************************************************
F*    HOW TO COMPILE:
F*
F*    (1. CREATE THE MODULE)
F*    CRTRPGMOD MODULE(AIRLIB/AIR07_xx) SRCFILE(AIRLIB/AIRSRC) +
F*              DBGVIEW(*ALL) INDENT('.')
F*
F*    (2. CREATE THE PROGRAM)
F*    CRTPGM PGM(AIRLIB/AIR07_xx)
F*      BNDSRVPGM(SVAIRJAVA SVAIREXCEL) ACTGRP(AIR07_xx)
D************************************************************************
D/DEFINE OS400_JVM_12
D/COPY QSYSINC/QRPGLESRC,JNI
D/COPY AIRLIB/AIRSRC,SPAIRFUNC
D/COPY AIRLIB/AIRSRC,SPAIRJAVA
D/COPY AIRLIB/AIRSRC,SPAIREXCEL
D  declare variables...
 /free
   CallP JavaServiceProgram();
```

Figure 7.3: Common code used in the Excel RPG code samples

SPAIREXCEL and SVAIREXCEL

So far in previous chapters, we've created the **SPAIRFUNC/SVAIRFUNC** pair with some generic procedures (including EBCDIC-to-ASCII procedures) that can be used anywhere. We also have the **SPAIRJAVA/SVAIRJAVA** prototypes and procedures, which include prototypes and procedures for generic use with Java.

In this chapter, we'll create a service program for the purpose of supporting the development of programs using the Apache POI project to create and modify Excel spreadsheets. As we prototype POI classes and build custom procedures, we'll add them to the **SPAIREXCEL** and **SVAIREXCEL** prototypes and procedures.

Whenever you develop an RPG program that will work with Excel files, you'll want to provide access to the **SVAIRJAVA** and **SVAIREXCEL** service programs by copying the prototypes into the source code and binding the service programs to the program.

Apache POI and Java JavaDocs

The JavaDocs for the Apache POI project are available online at *http://poi. apache.org/apidocs/index.html*. We'll be working primarily with the **org. apache.poi.hssf.usermodel** package, which you'll find in the HSSF section of the JavaDocs. The documentation lists all the classes that are available for the package and lets you drill down through the different options you have.

For this book, all Java references will be to Version 1.4.2 of Java. You'll find the relevant JavaDocs for this version of Java at *http://java.sun.com/j2se/1.4.2/docs/api*.

Constants

Java projects typically define constants as **public static final** variables within the classes. Because the variables are **final**, they cannot be changed, so you don't need to worry about creating set or get methods to access them; you just access the variables directly from the class.

You could write JNI code with RPG, as we discussed in Chapter 6, to determine the value of the constants from the Java classes, or you could define the constants within your RPG code, which is what we'll do throughout this book.

Let's review the constant values for the **Cell** class, which we'll be using later in this chapter. Figure 7.4 shows part of the JavaDoc for the **Cell** constants. You can find this list of constants in the Apache POI JavaDocs.

org.apache.poi.ss.usermodel.Cell		
public static final int	CELL_TYPE_BLANK	3
public static final int	CELL_TYPE_BOOLEAN	4
public static final int	CELL_TYPE_ERROR	5
public static final int	CELL_TYPE_FORMULA	2
public static final int	CELL_TYPE_NUMERIC	0
public static final int	CELL_TYPE_STRING	1

Figure 7.4: Partial JavaDoc for Cell constants

We're going to take these constants and hard-code them into the **SPAIREXCEL** source file with the prototypes to makes them easily reusable. We are already including this file to provide access to the procedures, so now the constants will be available as well without any additional coding.

Figure 7.5 shows the constants after they've been hard-coded in RPG and placed into the **SPAIREXCEL** file.

```
D*************************************************************************
D* org.apache.poi.hssf.usermodel.Cell Constant Field Values
D*************************************************************************
D POI_CELL_TYPE_BLANK...
D                   C                   3
D POI_CELL_TYPE_BOOLEAN...
D                   C                   4
```

```
D POI_CELL_TYPE_ERROR...
D                  C                5
D POI_CELL_TYPE_FORMULA...
D                  C                2
D POI_CELL_TYPE_NUMERIC...
D                  C                0
D POI_CELL_TYPE_STRING...
D                  C                1
```

Figure 7.5: RPG Cell constants in SPAIREXCEL

The Java naming standard for constants uses all upper case, with underscores for spaces, so we'll propagate this standard for use with our RPG constants.

For ease of reference, the comments preceding the constant declarations name the class that contains the constants. We'll use many constants in the following chapters, applying the same approach that is illustrated here.

Excel Components

The **org.apache.poi.hssf.usermodel** package maps low-level HSSF structures to familiar elements of Microsoft Excel. In the model perspective used by this package, the spreadsheet that is built in the application is referred to as a *Workbook*. The Workbook is the object that contains all the parts that make up the spreadsheet.

Workbook

Figure 7.6 shows the RPG object code for the **HSSFWorkbook** class. You can see that it is contained in the **usermodel** package.

```
D HSSFWorkbook    S             O    CLASS(*JAVA
D                                     :'org.apache.poi.hssf.usermodel-
D                                     .HSSFWorkbook')
```

Figure 7.6: HSSFWorkbook RPG object reference in SPAIREXCEL

Several constructors are available for the **HSSFWorkbook** class. We'll start with the default constructor, which is shown in Figure 7.7.

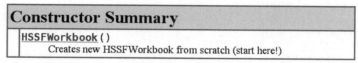

Constructor Summary
HSSFWorkbook()   Creates new HSSFWorkbook from scratch (start here!)

Figure 7.7: Partial JavaDoc for HSSFWorkbook default constructor

The **new_HSSFWorkbook** RPG procedure accesses the constructor method. Figure 7.8 shows this procedure's prototype, which will be included in the **SPAIREXCEL** source file.

```
D new_HSSFWorkbook...
D                    PR                    like(HSSFWorkbook)
D                                          ExtProc(*JAVA:
D                                          'org.apache.poi.hssf.usermodel-
D                                          .HSSFWorkbook':
D                                          *CONSTRUCTOR)
```

Figure 7.8: HSSFWorkbook constructor method prototype in SPAIREXCEL

Sheet

The simplest Workbook should contain at least one *Sheet*. The Sheet contains the grid that will hold the data. The Sheet is created from the Workbook and has a name that is displayed on the tab that references the Sheet. You can have multiple Sheets within a Workbook.

Figure 7.9 shows the RPG object reference variable for the **HSSFSheet** class.

```
D HSSFSheet          S              O    CLASS(*JAVA
D                                        :'org.apache.poi.hssf.usermodel-
D                                        .HSSFSheet')
```

Figure 7.9: HSSFSheet RPG object reference in SPAIREXCEL

We'll be creating and retrieving Sheets using the methods available from the **HSSFWorkbook** class. Figure 7.10 shows the JavaDoc method summary for the **HSSFWorkbook** methods.

Method Summary	
HSSFSheet	**createSheet**() create an HSSFSheet for this HSSFWorkbook, adds it to the sheets and returns the high level representation.
HSSFSheet	**createSheet**(java.lang.String sheetname) create an HSSFSheet for this HSSFWorkbook, adds it to the sheets and returns the high level representation.
HSSFSheet	**getSheet**(java.lang.String name) Get sheet with the given name (case insensitive match)
HSSFSheet	**getSheetAt**(int index) Get the HSSFSheet object at the given index.

Figure 7.10: Partial JavaDoc for HSSFWorkbook methods

The **HSSFWorkbook_createSheet** procedure (Figure 7.11) creates a new Sheet of the specified name for the Workbook.

```
D HSSFWorkbook_createSheet...
D                    PR                      like(HSSFSheet)
D                                            EXTPROC(*JAVA
D                                            :'org.apache.poi.hssf.usermodel-
D                                            .HSSFWorkbook'
D                                            :'createSheet')
D   argSheetName                             like(jString)
```

Figure 7.11: HSSFWorkbook createSheet method prototype in SPAIREXCEL

The **HSSFWorkbook_getSheet** procedure (Figure 7.12) returns the Sheet of the specified name from the Workbook if it already exists. If no Sheet with that name exists, the procedure returns null.

```
D HSSFWorkbook_getSheet...
D                    PR                      like(HSSFSheet)
D                                            ExtProc(*JAVA
D                                            :'org.apache.poi.hssf-
D                                            .usermodel.HSSFWorkbook'
D                                            :'getSheet')
D   argSheetName                             like(jString)
```

Figure 7.12: HSSFWorkbook getSheet method prototype in SPAIREXCEL

To simplify the creation and retrieval of a Sheet from a Workbook, we'll create a custom procedure that tries to retrieve the Sheet if it exists and creates a new one if it does not. The Sheet will be identified by using the name that is displayed on the tab in the Workbook. Figure 7.13 shows the custom procedure, **AirExcel_getSheet**.

```
P AirExcel_getSheet...
P                       B                   EXPORT
D AirExcel_getSheet...
D                       PI                  like(HSSFSheet)
D   argWorkBook                             like(HSSFWorkbook)
D   argSheetName                  1024A     varying const
D svString            S                     like(jString)
D svSheet             S                     like(HSSFSheet)
D                                           inz(*NULL)
 /free
   svString = new_String(argSheetName);
   svSheet = HSSFWorkbook_getSheet(argWorkBook: svString);
   if svSheet = *NULL;
     svSheet = HSSFWorkbook_createSheet(argWorkBook: svString);
   else;
   endif;
   freeLocalRef(svString);
   return svSheet;
 /end-free
P                       E
```

Figure 7.13: Custom AirExcel_getSheet procedure in SVAIREXCEL

The components that make up the spreadsheet use a hierarchy of parent–child relationships to identify the component with which you're working. So, when you create a sheet, you reference the Workbook that contains it. You could then identify the Sheet using the name. You could also use index references to Sheets using the **getSheetAt** method of the **HSSFWorkbook** class.

Row

Rows represent the horizontal references on the Excel grid that are contained on a Sheet. You populate the data in the Sheet by creating Rows.

Figure 7.14 shows the RPG object reference variable.

```
D HSSFRow             S               O    CLASS(*JAVA
D                                           :'org.apache.poi.hssf.usermodel-
D                                           .HSSFRow')
```

Figure 7.14: HSSFRow RPG object reference in SPAIREXCEL

Figure 7.15 shows the methods available from the **HSSFSheet** class that we'll use to create and retrieve Rows.

Method Summary	
HSSFRow	`createRow`(int rownum) Create a new row within the sheet and return the high level representation
HSSFRow	`getRow`(int rowIndex) Returns the logical row (not physical) 0-based.

Figure 7.15: Partial JavaDoc for HSSFSheet methods

The **createRow** method of **HSSFSheet** (Figure 7.16) creates a new **HSSFRow** with the specified index.

```
D HSSFSheet_createRow...
D                   PR                    like(HSSFRow)
D                                         EXTPROC(*JAVA
D                                         :'org.apache.poi.hssf.usermodel-
D                                         .HSSFSheet'
D                                         :'createRow')
D   argRow                                like(jint) value
```

Figure 7.16: HSSFSheet createRow method prototype in SPAIREXCEL

The **getRow** method of **HSSFSheet** (Figure 7.17) returns the **HSSFRow** if it already exists; otherwise, the method returns null.

```
D HSSFSheet_getRow...
D                   PR                    like(HSSFRow)
D                                         ExtProc(*JAVA
D                                         :'org.apache.poi.hssf-
D                                         .usermodel.HSSFSheet'
D                                         :'getRow')
D   argRow                                like(jInt) value
```

Figure 7.17: HSSFSheet getRowMethod prototype in SPAIREXCEL

We'll create a custom row-handling procedure that is similar to the procedure we created for Sheets. The exception handling is minimal so that we can stay focused on the functionality and also because you may want the program to bomb during development to see where the bugs are.

The **AirExcel_getRow** procedure (Figure 7.18) returns the specified Row if it exists or creates a new one.

```
D*************************************************************************
D*  AirExcel_getRow(): Retrieves the HSSFRow
D*                           with the specified index.
D*************************************************************************
P AirExcel_getRow...
P                   B                   EXPORT
D AirExcel_getRow...
D                   PI                  like(HSSFRow)
D  argSheet                            like(HSSFSheet)
D  argIndex                            like(jInt) value
D svRow             S                   like(HSSFRow)
D                                       inz(*NULL)
 /free
  svRow = HSSFSheet_getRow(argSheet: argIndex);
  if svRow = *NULL;
    svRow = HSSFSheet_createRow(argSheet: argIndex);
  else;
  endif;
  return svRow;
 /end-free
P                   E
```

Figure 7.18: Custom AirExcel_getRow procedure in SVAIREXCEL

Cell

Cells represent the vertical references on the Excel grid. This is where you store the data contents of the spreadsheet. Each Cell is contained within a Row. Figure 7.19 shows the RPG object reference variable.

```
D HSSFCell          S                 O   CLASS(*JAVA
D                                         :'org.apache.poi.hssf.usermodel-
D                                         .HSSFCell')
```

Figure 7.19: HSSFCell RPG object reference in SPAIREXCEL

We will create and retrieve Cells using the methods available from the **HSSFRow** class (Figure 7.20).

Method Summary	
HSSFCell	**createCell**(int column) Use this to create new cells within the row and return it.
HSSFCell	**createCell**(short columnIndex) **Deprecated.** *(Aug 2008) use createCell(int)*
HSSFCell	**getCell**(int cellnum) Get the hssfcell representing a given column (logical cell) 0-based.
HSSFCell	**getCell**(short cellnum) **Deprecated.** *(Aug 2008) use getCell(int)*

Figure 7.20: Partial JavaDoc for HSSFRow methods

Note that two of the methods are marked as deprecated. This is because newer versions of these methods have been made available with the latest versions of POI, and the developers recommend the use of these new methods over the older ones. If you're using an older version of POI to support an older JVM, as we are in this book, you won't have access to these newer methods, so you'll have to use the older version of the methods. Because this book is intended to support the widest audience of developers, many of whom may not have the latest version of Java on their IBM i systems, we are not discussing the latest version of the POI package. But its features are something to keep in mind when you update your version of POI.

The **createCell** method of **HSSFRow** (Figure 7.21) creates a new **HSSFCell**.

```
D HSSFRow_createCell...
D                 PR              like(HSSFCell)
D                                 EXTPROC(*JAVA
D                                 :'org.apache.poi.hssf.usermodel-
D                                 .HSSFRow'
D                                 :'createCell')
D   argColumn                     like(jshort) value
```

Figure 7.21: HSSFRow createCell method prototype in SPAIREXCEL

The **getCell** method (Figure 7.22) returns the **HSSFCell** if it already exists; otherwise, it returns null.

```
D HSSFRow_getCell...
D                    PR                      like(HSSFCell)
D                                            ExtProc(*JAVA
D                                            :'org.apache.poi.hssf-
D                                            .usermodel.HSSFRow'
D                                            :'getCell')
D  argColumn                                 like(jShort) value
```

Figure 7.22: HSSFRow getCell method prototype in SPAIREXCEL

The custom **AirExcel_getCell** method (Figure 7.23) returns the specified Cell if it exists or creates a new one otherwise.

```
D********************************************************************
D*  AirExcel_getCell(): Retrieves the HSSFCell from the Row
D*                      with the specified index.
D********************************************************************
P AirExcel_getCell...
P                    B                       EXPORT
D AirExcel_getCell...
D                    PI                      like(HSSFCell)
D  argRow                                    like(HSSFRow)
D  argIndex                                  like(jInt) value
D svCell             S                       like(HSSFCell)
D                                            inz(*NULL)
 /free
  svCell = HSSFRow_getCell(argRow: argIndex);
  if (svCell = *NULL);
    svCell = HSSFRow_createCell(argRow: argIndex);
  else;
  endif;
  return svCell;
 /end-free
P                    E
```

Figure 7.23: Custom AirExcel_getRow procedure in SVAIREXCEL

If you are creating a new spreadsheet and you know that the cells don't already exist, you may want to use the **createCell** method directly, instead of using the custom procedure, to reduce overhead.

The custom procedures simplify the implementation of the new capabilities for basic programs and will become very useful when you modify existing spreadsheets because you may be updating existing information or adding more cells than originally existed, which would require you to create new Sheets, Rows, and/or Cells.

Assigning a String Value to a Cell

Once you have a Cell to work with, you can put your text into it. The **HSSFCell setCellValue** method is overridden to accept several different parameter types, so we would want to create a different procedure for each version we want to use. The object that is used as the argument will determine the correct signature for the method.

Figure 7.24 shows the **setCellValueString** procedure, which assigns a **String** value to a Cell.

```
D HSSFCell_setCellValueString...
D                  PR            EXTPROC(*JAVA
D                                :'org.apache.poi.hssf.usermodel-
D                                .HSSFCell'
D                                :'setCellValue')
D   argValue                     like(jString)
```

Figure 7.24: HSSFCell setCellValueString method prototype in SPAIREXCEL

Figure 7.25 lists several of the **setCellValue** methods of the **HSSFCell** class. This is only a partial list of the methods that are available for the class.

Method Summary	
void	setCellValue(boolean value) set a boolean value for the cell
void	setCellValue(java.util.Calendar value) set a date value for the cell.
void	setCellValue(java.util.Date value) set a date value for the cell.
void	setCellValue(double value) set a numeric value for the cell
void	setCellValue(RichTextString value) Set a string value for the cell.
void	setCellValue(java.lang.String value) set a string value for the cell.

Figure 7.25: Partial JavaDoc for HSSFCell methods

Figure 7.26 shows a custom procedure, **AirExcel_setCellValueString**, that accepts our RPG character bytes and automatically creates and releases a **String** object that will be usable with the method of the **HSSFCell** class.

```
P AirExcel_setCellValueString...
P                     B                    EXPORT
D AirExcel_setCellValueString...
D                     PI
D   argCell                                like(HSSFCell)
D   argBytes                    65535A     varying const
D   argStyle                               like(HSSFCellStyle)
D                                          options(*nopass)
D svString         s                       like(jString)
 /free
  svString = new_String(argBytes);
  HSSFCell_setCellValueString(argCell: svString);
  if %parms > 2;
    HSSFCell_setCellStyle(argCell: argStyle);
  else;
  endif;
  freeLocalRef(svString);
  return;
 /end-free
P                     E
```

Figure 7.26: Custom AirExcel_setCellValueString procedure in SVAIREXCEL

Here, you can see that we use our familiar **String** class constructor to create a new **String** object. The procedure also initializes the string to contain the text that is contained in the bytes that are sent in as the argument to the procedure. We don't need to worry about the EBCDIC-to-ASCII translation here because we're not using JNI directly; we'll let RPG do all that extra work.

The procedure uses the **setCellValueString** method from the **HSSFCell** class to set the contents of the cell to the **String** object. The procedure also specifies an optional parameter that can be used to change the style of the cell, a topic we'll get into in more detail in the next chapter.

Assigning a Numeric Value to a Cell

You could pass a number into a Cell as a string, but then the spreadsheet would not use it properly as a numeric value. You therefore will want to assign numeric values using the correct type. We'll use the **jDouble** Java type to assign the numbers using the overridden **setCellValue** method of **HSSFCell** (Figure 7.27).

```
D HSSFCell_setCellValueNumeric...
D                      PR                  EXTPROC(*JAVA
D                                          :'org.apache.poi.hssf.usermodel-
D                                          .HSSFCell'
D                                          :'setCellValue')
D   argValue                               like(jdouble) value
```

Figure 7.27: HSSFCell setCellValueNumeric method prototype in SPAIREXCEL

Saving the Workbook

After you have populated the spreadsheet with all your data, you will create a new output file using the **FileOutputStream** class and save your Workbook to it. Make sure you close the output file when you're finished to free up resources and release any file locks.

Figure 7.28 shows the JavaDoc for the **write** method of the **HSSFWorkbook** class. This is just one of the methods that are available.

Method Summary	
void	**write**(java.io.OutputStream stream)
	Method write - write out this workbook to an Outputstream.

Figure 7.28: Partial JavaDoc for HSSFWorkbook methods

Figure 7.29 shows the RPG prototype to access the **write** method of the **HSSFWorkbook** class.

```
D HSSFWorkbook_write...
D                      PR                  EXTPROC(*JAVA
D                                          :'org.apache.poi.hssf.usermodel-
D                                          .HSSFWorkbook'
D                                          :'write')
D   argStream                              like(OutputStream)
```

Figure 7.29: HSSFWorkbook write method prototype in SPAIREXCEL

And Figure 7.30 shows the custom procedure we'll use to save the Workbook. You simply pass in the Workbook object, and the procedure takes care of all the details with the output stream.

```
P AirExcel_write...
P                      B                    EXPORT
D AirExcel_write...
D                      PI
D    argWorkBook                            like(HSSFWorkbook)
D    argFileName                  1024A     const varying
D svString            s                     like(jString)
D svOutFile           s                     like(FileOutputStream)
 /free
   svString = new_String(argFileName);
   svOutFile = new_FileOutputStream(svString);
   HSSFWorkbook_write(argWorkBook: svOutFile);
   FileOutputStream_close(svOutFile);
   freeLocalRef(svOutFile);
   freeLocalRef(svString);
   return;
 /end-free
P                      E
```

Figure 7.30: Custom AirExcel_write procedure in SVAIREXCEL

You may be looking at this and thinking, how can we pass a **FileOutputStream** as a parameter to the **HSSFWorkbook_write** procedure when the second parameter is declared as type **OutputStream** (without the "File")? This is where the inheritance and polymorphism concepts of Chapter 4 come into action. Because **FileOutputStream** is a subclass of **OutputStream**, we can pass **OutputStream**, **FileOutputStream**, and any other subclass of **OutputStream** as a parameter. But, we must use the correct class in the inheritance chain when defining the prototype because the signature needs to match so that the JVM can find the method.

FileOutputStream

The **FileOutputStream** class is not specific to the POI project. It is part of the standard Java classes, so we'll define its prototype in the **SPAIRJAVA** prototype file. Figure 7.31 shows the RPG object reference variable.

```
D FileOutputStream...
D                    S              O    CLASS(*JAVA
D                                         :'java.io.FileOutputStream')
```

Figure 7.31: FileOutputStream RPG object reference in SPAIRJAVA

The **FileOutputStream** class is located in the **java.io** package, so you can look in that package to determine the methods that are available.

The **new_FileOutputStream** procedure (Figure 7.32) accesses the default constructor method of the **FileOutputStream** class.

```
D new_FileOutputStream...
D                    PR              like(FileOutputStream)
D                                    EXTPROC(*JAVA
D                                     :'java.io.FileOutputStream'
D                                     :*CONSTRUCTOR)
D  argString                         like(jstring)
```

Figure 7.32: FileOutputStream constructor method prototype in SPAIRJAVA

Figure 7.33 shows the JavaDoc for the **close** method of the **FileOutputStream** class. This is only one of the methods available for the class.

Method Summary	
void	close() Closes this file output stream and releases any system resources associated with this stream.

Figure 7.33: Partial JavaDoc for FileOutputStream methods

The **FileOutputStream_close** procedure (Figure 7.34) accesses the **close** method of the **FileOutputStream** class.

```
D FileOutputStream_close...
D                    PR              EXTPROC(*JAVA
D                                     :'java.io.FileOutputStream'
D                                     :'close')
```

Figure 7.34: FileOutputStream close method prototype in SPAIRJAVA

Hello World

It's about time for a working example. To illustrate the concepts in action, we'll create a new Workbook with a Cell to contain the "Hello World" text string. Figure 7.35 shows the sample spreadsheet.

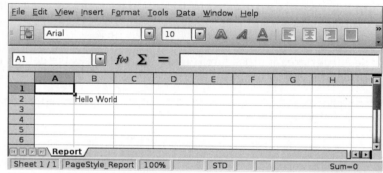

Figure 7.35: Hello World spreadsheet

Figure 7.36 shows our Hello World Excel application in RPG.

```
D  airWorkbook     S                    LIKE(HSSFWorkbook)
D  airSheet        S                    LIKE(HSSFSheet)
D  airRow          S                    LIKE(HSSFRow)
D  airCell         S                    LIKE(HSSFCell)
C/EJECT
/free
CallP JavaServiceProgram();
JNIEnv_P = getJNIEnv();
airWorkbook = new_HSSFWorkbook();
airSheet = AirExcel_getSheet(airWorkbook: 'Report');
airRow = AirExcel_getRow(airSheet:1);
airCell = AirExcel_getCell(airRow:1);
AirExcel_setCellValueString(airCell:'Hello World');
//*** Close the Spreadsheet and Reclaim Resources
AirExcel_write(airWorkbook: '/Public/air07_01.xls');
// Clean Up
freeLocalRef(airCell);
freeLocalRef(airRow);
freeLocalRef(airSheet);
freeLocalRef(airWorkbook);
*inlr = *ON;
/end-free
```

Figure 7.36: RPG code to produce Hello World spreadsheet

Once all the prototypes and procedures are built, we can create the Hello World spreadsheet with a minimal amount of code, thanks to all the modular coding of the prototypes, procedures, and most important, all the dedicated people who have contributed to the POI project!

To get to the Cell, we need to create all the other components within which the Cell is contained. We start at the top with the Workbook and work our way down to the cell.

You can see the parent–child relationship with each new component that is created:

- The Sheet is created from the Workbook.
- The Row is created from the Sheet.
- The Cell is created from the Row.

If you refer back to the sample spreadsheet screen shot, you can see that the Row and Cell references begin at index 0. Because we used Row 1 and Cell 1, the results are contained in Cell B2. You can also see that the tab on the bottom of the sheet says "Report" — the name we assigned to the Sheet. (You may also notice that I used OpenOffice Calc to view the spreadsheet; your application screen shots may look slightly different if you use Microsoft Excel to view the documents.)

Once you have the Hello World example working, you've accomplished a lot. That's because when you have this working, you know that you have your Apache POI project Jar file correctly installed in your file structure, and you know that you've set up your environment variable properly to make it visible. You've either downloaded the sample code or entered it yourself and have all the details of the Apache POI prototypes and the Java prototypes worked out.

So, congratulations! You've just written your first useful RPG–Java program to generate Excel spreadsheets. I'm sure you can see the potential from here!

Excel Formatting and Properties

Now that you know how to create spreadsheets, the next step is to pretty them up with some different types of lettering and colors. You can do this using a combination of fonts and cell styles.

Figure 8.1 shows a sample spreadsheet that uses color to make the cells in the header stand out.

Figure 8.1: Spreadsheet with fonts and colors

Because the figure is printed in black and white, you can't see the actual background color in the header cells of the spreadsheet, but when you run the program, you'll be able to see the results. The background color of the header cells will be blue, and the header characters themselves will be white.

Fonts and Colors

You use fonts to determine the way characters will be presented. You can specify many different characteristics with fonts. As a starting point, we'll use size, weight, and color.

Figure 8.2 shows the RPG object reference variable for the font class, **HSSFFont**.

```
D HSSFFont       S          O   CLASS(*JAVA
D                                :'org.apache.poi.hssf.usermodel-
D                                .HSSFFont')
```

Figure 8.2: RPG object variable for reference to HSSFFont object

Figure 8.3 lists some of the **HSSFFont** methods we'll use to specify the attributes of fonts.

Method Summary		
void	setBoldweight(short boldweight) set the boldness to use	
void	setColor(short color) set the color for the font	
void	setFontHeightInPoints(short height) set the font height	

Figure 8.3: Partial JavaDoc for HSSFFont methods

The first method, **setBoldweight**, sets the boldness of the font. Figure 8.4 shows the RPG procedure prototype for this method, which (along with the other prototypes used in this chapter) we'll add to the **SPAIREXCEL** source file.

```
D HSSFFont_setBoldweight...
D                     PR              EXTPROC(*JAVA
D                                     :'org.apache.poi.hssf.usermodel-
D                                     .HSSFFont'
D                                     :'setBoldweight')
D  argWeight                          like(jshort) value
```

Figure 8.4: Prototype for setBoldweight method of HSSFFont class

The values you can specify to determine the weight of the font are defined as
constants in the **org.apache.poi.hssf.usermodel.Font** class. We'll place these
constants, shown in Figure 8.5, into the **SPAIREXCEL** file.

```
D*******************************************************************
D* org.apache.poi.hssf.usermodel.Font Constant Field Values
D*******************************************************************
D POI_FONT_ANSI...
D               C              0
D POI_FONT_BOLD_BOLD...
D               C              700
D POI_FONT_BOLD_NORMAL...
D               C              400
D POI_FONT_COLOR_NORMAL...
D               C              32767
D POI_FONT_COLOR_RED...
D               C              10
D POI_FONT_DEFAULT_CHARSET...
D               C              1
D POI_FONT_SS_NONE...
D               C              0
D POI_FONT_SS_SUB...
D               C              2
D POI_FONT_SS_SUPER...
D               C              1
D POI_FONT_SYMBOL_CHARSET...
D               C              2
D POI_FONT_U_DOUBLE...
D               C              2
D POI_FONT_U_DOUBLE_ACCOUNTING...
D               C              34
D POI_FONT_U_NONE...
D               C              0
D POI_FONT_U_SINGLE...
D               C              1
D POI_FONT_U_SINGLE_ACCOUNTING...
D               C              33
```

Figure 8.5: Partial list of constants for Font class

The **setColor** method of the **HSSFFont** class, shown in Figure 8.6, sets the color of the font.

```
D HSSFFont_setColor...
D                  PR                    extproc(*JAVA:
D                                        'org.apache.poi.hssf.-
D                                        usermodel.HSSFFont'
D                                        :'setColor')
D  argColor                   5I 0 value
```

Figure 8.6: Prototype for setColor method of HSSFFont class

The colors are indexes into the color palette that is used in Microsoft Excel. The indexes are constant values that are defined for the **HSSFColor** class and placed in the **SPAIREXCEL** file. Figure 8.7 lists some of the available palette indexes.

```
D******************************************************************
D* org.apache.poi.hssf.util.HSSFColor Constant Field Values
D******************************************************************
D* INDEXES INTO THE EXCEL STANDARD COLOR PALETTE
D POI_AUTO...
D                  C                     64
D POI_AQUA...
D                  C                     49
D POI_BLACK...
D                  C                     8
```

Figure 8.7: Partial list of palette index constants for HSSFColor class

When you use a spreadsheet application, such as Excel or OpenOffice Calc, you can choose a font color from a grid of available colors; this grid is the color palette we'll use when setting the colors. The JavaDocs define the complete list of constants.

The third font-related method we'll look at, **setFontHeightInPoints**, sets the size of the font using points as the unit of measurement. There are 72 points per inch. Figure 8.8 shows the procedure prototype for the **setFontHeightInPoints** method.

```
D HSSFFont_setFontHeightInPoints...
D                  PR                    EXTPROC(*JAVA
D                                        :'org.apache.poi.hssf.usermodel-
D                                        .HSSFFont'
```

```
D                                          :'setFontHeightInPoints')
D   argHeightPts                           like(jshort) value
```

Figure 8.8: Prototype for setFontHeightInPoints method of HSSFFont class

Cell Styles

The cell style determines the characteristics of the cell, letting you specify cell attributes such as font, alignment, and color. Figure 8.9 shows the RPG object reference variable for the **HSSFCellStyle** object.

```
D HSSFCellStyle   S            O   CLASS(*JAVA
D                                  :'org.apache.poi.hssf.usermodel-
D                                  .HSSFCellStyle')
```

Figure 8.9: RPG object variable for reference to HSSFCellStyle object

Figure 8.10 shows a partial JavaDoc that documents some of the **HSSFCellStyle** methods we'll be using to specify our cell styles.

Method Summary	
void	**setAlignment**(short align) set the type of horizontal alignment for the cell
void	**setFillForegroundColor**(short bg) set the foreground fill color *Note: Ensure Foreground color is set prior to background color.*
void	**setFillPattern**(short fp) setting to one fills the cell with the foreground color...
void	**setFont**(HSSFFont font)

Figure 8.10: Partial JavaDoc for HSSFCellStyle methods

The **setAlignment** method of the **HSSFCellStyle** class (Figure 8.11) specifies the alignment of the contents of the cell to be displayed.

```
D HSSFCellStyle_setAlignment...
D                    PR          EXTPROC(*JAVA
D                                :'org.apache.poi.hssf.usermodel-
D                                .HSSFCellStyle'
D                                :'setAlignment')
D   argAlignment                 like(jshort) value
```

Figure 8.11: Prototype for setAlignment method of HSSFCellStyle class

The constants used to determine the alignment can be found in the
HSSFCellStyle JavaDocs. We'll place these constants, shown in Figure 8.12, into
the **SPAIREXCEL** file.

```
D***********************************************************************
D* org.apache.poi.hssf.usermodel.HSSFCellStyle Constant Field Values
D***********************************************************************
D POI_ALIGN_CENTER...
D                    C               2
D POI_ALIGN_CENTER_SELECTION...
D                    C               6
D POI_ALIGN_FILL...
D                    C               4
D POI_ALIGN_GENERAL...
D                    C               0
D POI_ALIGN_JUSTIFY...
D                    C               5
D POI_ALIGN_LEFT...
D                    C               1
D POI_ALIGN_RIGHT...
D                    C               3
```

Figure 8.12: Partial list of alignment constants in HSSFCellStyle class

The **setFillForegroundColor** method of the **HSSFCellStyle** class (Figure 8.13) sets
the foreground color using the constants defined for the **HSSFColor** class (shown
earlier in Figure 8.7).

```
D HSSFCellStyle_setFillForegroundColor...
D                    PR              EXTPROC(*JAVA
D                                    :'org.apache.poi.hssf.-
D                                    usermodel.HSSFCellStyle'
D                                    :'setFillForegroundColor')
D   argColor                         like(jShort) value
```

Figure 8.13: Prototype for setFillForegroundColor method of HSSFCellStyle class

The **setFillPattern** method of the **HSSFCellStyle** class (Figure 8.14) determines
the pattern to be used to fill the cell.

```
D HSSFCellStyle_setFillPattern...
D                    PR              EXTPROC(*JAVA
D                                    :'org.apache.poi.hssf.-
```

```
D                                       usermodel.HSSFCellStyle'
D                                       :'setFillPattern')
D    argPattern                         like(jShort) value
```

Figure 8.14: Prototype for setFillPattern method of HSSFCellStyle class

The fill patterns use constant values that we'll place into the **SPAIREXCEL** file. Figure 8.15 lists a few of these constants. The JavaDocs for the **HSSFCellStyle** class provide a complete list of the constants used with the fill patterns.

```
D**********************************************************************
D* org.apache.poi.hssf.usermodel.HSSFCellStyle Constant Field Values
D**********************************************************************
D POI_SOLID_FOREGROUND...
D                   C                   1
D POI_SPARSE_DOTS...
D                   C                   4
D POI_SQUARES...
D                   C                   15
```

Figure 8.15: Partial list of fill pattern constants in HSSFCellStyle class

You assign the font to the cell style using the **setFont** method of the **HSSFCellStyle** class (Figure 8.16).

```
D HSSFCellStyle_setFont...
D                   PR                  EXTPROC(*JAVA
D                                       :'org.apache.poi.hssf.usermodel-
D                                       .HSSFCellStyle'
D                                       :'setFont')
D    argFont                            like(HSSFFont)
```

Figure 8.16: Prototype for setFont method of HSSFCellStyle class

With the exception of the constructor methods, which we'll discuss next, we have now defined all the font and cell style methods to set the colors and fonts used to generate the sample spreadsheet.

Font and Cell Style Constructors

We will use the methods available from the **HSSFWorkbook** class to create the new cell styles and fonts. Figure 8.17 presents a partial method summary for this class.

Method Summary	
HSSFCellStyle	**createCellStyle**() create a new Cell style and add it to the workbook's style table
HSSFFont	**createFont**() create a new Font and add it to the workbook's font table

Figure 8.17: Partial JavaDoc for HSSFWorkbook methods

To create the new font, we'll use the **createFont** method of the **HSSFWorkbook** class (Figure 8.18).

```
D HSSFWorkbook_createFont...
D                 PR                    like(HSSFFont)
D                                       EXTPROC(*JAVA
D                                       :'org.apache.poi.hssf.usermodel-
D                                       .HSSFWorkbook'
D                                       :'createFont')
```

Figure 8.18: Prototype for createFont method of HSSFWorkbook class

We'll also create the cell style using a method available from the **HSSFWorkbook** class (Figure 8.19).

```
D HSSFWorkbook_createCellStyle...
D                 PR                    like(HSSFCellStyle)
D                                       EXTPROC(*JAVA
D                                       :'org.apache.poi.hssf.usermodel-
D                                       .HSSFWorkbook'
D                                       :'createCellStyle')
```

Figure 8.19: Prototype for createCellStyle method of HSSFWorkbook class

RPG Program Using Colors and Fonts

With that, we've completed all the front-end work and prepared our prototypes and constants in the **SPAIREXCEL** file, so let's write the code to create the spreadsheet that you saw at the beginning of the chapter. Figure 8.20 shows the first part of the RPG program to use colors and fonts in Excel. (As noted in the figure, the common opening code from Chapter 7 is part of this chapter's RPG code samples, too.)

```
     .
     . <Insert common header code here (Figure 7.3)>
     .
D   airWorkBook     S                      LIKE(HSSFWorkbook)
D   airSheet        S                      LIKE(HSSFSheet)
D   airRow          S                      LIKE(HSSFRow)
D   airCell         S                      LIKE(HSSFCell)
D   airFontHeight   S                      LIKE(jShort)
D   airFontNorm     S                      LIKE(HSSFFont)
D   airFontWhite    S                      LIKE(HSSFFont)
D   airStyleNorm    S                      LIKE(HSSFCellStyle)
D   airStyleBW      S                      LIKE(HSSFCellStyle)
C/EJECT
 /free
  CallP JavaServiceProgram();
  JNIEnv_P = getJNIEnv();
  airWorkbook = new_HSSFWorkbook();
  airSheet = AirExcel_getSheet(airWorkbook: 'Report');
  // Create Fonts
  airFontHeight = 8;
  // Normal Font
  airFontNorm = HSSFWorkbook_createFont(airWorkbook);
  HSSFFont_setFontHeightInPoints(airFontNorm: airFontHeight);
  // White, Bold Font
  airFontWhite = HSSFWorkbook_createFont(airWorkbook);
  HSSFFont_setFontHeightInPoints(airFontWhite: airFontHeight);
  HSSFFont_setBoldWeight(airFontWhite: POI_FONT_BOLD_BOLD);
  HSSFFont_setColor(airFontWhite: POI_WHITE);
```

Figure 8.20: RPG program using colors and fonts in Excel (part 1 of 3)

For the spreadsheet, we want to have a consistent font size for all the cells, so we'll create a normal font called **airFontNorm**. For the headers, we'll create another font called **airFontWhite**, which will be the same size in the different color white.

The program defines the **airFontHeight** variable to make changing the font size easy. I have found that once you start making spreadsheets available, users will have lots of input on formatting, so it's better to make everything as easy to change as possible. With one change of the **airFontHeight** variable and a quick recompile, you have a happy user — for a while, anyway.

The **airFontNorm** and **airFontWhite** methods both set the size of the fonts using the **setFontHeightInPoints** method. The **airFontWhite** font will also be white and set to bold.

Once we have the fonts all set up, we can use them with the cell styles. We'll create two cell styles for the sample spreadsheet: **airStyleNorm** and **airStyleBW**. The **airStyleNorm** cell style will be used for the data, and the **airStyleBW** cell style will be used for the blue and white headers. Figure 8.21 shows the next section of the RPG program, where these styles are created.

```
// Create Styles
airStyleNorm = HSSFWorkbook_createCellStyle(airWorkbook);
HSSFCellStyle_setFont(airStyleNorm: airFontNorm);
HSSFCellStyle_setAlignment(airStyleNorm: POI_ALIGN_LEFT);
//
airStyleBW = HSSFWorkbook_createCellStyle(airWorkbook);
HSSFCellStyle_setFont(airStyleBW: airFontWhite);
HSSFCellStyle_setFillForegroundColor(airStyleBW:
                    POI_BLUE);
HSSFCellStyle_setFillPattern(airStyleBW:
                    POI_SOLID_FOREGROUND);
```

Figure 8.21: RPG program using colors and fonts in Excel (part 2 of 3)

The fonts we created are assigned to the cell styles using the **setFont** method of the **HSSFCellStyle** class.

When you enter data into the cells of a spreadsheet, numeric values default to being right-justified, and character values default to left-justified. To get all the data to be left-justified in the spreadsheet, we'll use the **setAlignment** method of the **HSSFCellStyle** class to force all data using **airStyleNorm** to be left-justified, regardless of type.

The foreground color and fill pattern are set using the **setFillForegroundColor** and **setFillPattern** methods of the **HSSFCellStyle** class, respectively. These methods will use the constants that are listed in Figures 8.7 and 8.15.

Once you have the fonts and cell styles set to the values you want, you can reuse them throughout the spreadsheet, and they can be easily changed once initialized to modify the look of the entire spreadsheet.

The cell styles will be applied to the cells when the contents are assigned using the optional cell style parameter of our custom procedures.

In this example, the header cells will use the **airStyleBW** cell style and the data will use the **airStyleNorm** cell style. We'll list the user-friendly text in the first column and display the constant value in the second column. Figure 8.22 show this last portion of the RPG program.

```
// Create Cells
  airRow = AirExcel_getRow(airSheet:0);
  airCell = AirExcel_getCell(airRow:0);
  AirExcel_setCellValueString(airCell:'Color': airStyleBW);
  airCell = AirExcel_getCell(airRow:1);
  AirExcel_setCellValueString(airCell:'Code': airStyleBW);
  //
  airRow = AirExcel_getRow(airSheet:1);
  airCell = AirExcel_getCell(airRow:0);
  AirExcel_setCellValueString(airCell:'Automatic': airStyleNorm);
  airCell = AirExcel_getCell(airRow:1);
  AirExcel_setCellValueNumeric(airCell:POI_AUTO: airStyleNorm);
  //
  airRow = AirExcel_getRow(airSheet:2);
  airCell = AirExcel_getCell(airRow:0);
  AirExcel_setCellValueString(airCell:'Aqua':airStyleNorm);
  airCell = AirExcel_getCell(airRow:1);
  AirExcel_setCellValueNumeric(airCell:POI_AQUA:airStyleNorm);
  //
  airRow = AirExcel_getRow(airSheet:3);
  airCell = AirExcel_getCell(airRow:0);
  AirExcel_setCellValueString(airCell:'Black':airStyleNorm);
  airCell = AirExcel_getCell(airRow:1);
  AirExcel_setCellValueNumeric(airCell:POI_BLACK:airStyleNorm);
  //*** Save the Spreadsheet and Reclaim Resources
  AirExcel_write(airWorkbook:
                 '/Public/Air08_01.xls');
  // Clean Up
  .
  . <Insert cleanup code here>
  .
  *inlr = *ON;
 /end-free
```

Figure 8.22: RPG program using colors and fonts in Excel (part 3 of 3)

After populating all the data and setting the colors and formatting, the program saves the file and cleans up any Java objects before exiting.

AirExcel_setCellValue*Xxx* Revisited

In Chapter 7, we created a custom procedure to assign a value to a cell. We discussed the **setCellValueString** method of the **HSSFCell class**, but we skipped over the **setCellStyle** method (Figure 8.23) until now.

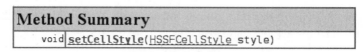

Figure 8.23: Partial JavaDoc for HSSFCell setCellStyle method

There is a custom **AirExcel_setCellValue*Xxx*** method for each type of data we'll be assigning to cells, and each of those methods has an optional parameter that lets you assign a cell style to the cell.

Figure 8.24 shows the RPG prototype for the **setCellStyle** method of **HSSFCell**.

```
D HSSFCell_setCellStyle...
D                 PR                      EXTPROC(*JAVA
D                                         :'org.apache.poi.hssf.usermodel-
D                                         .HSSFCell'
D                                         :'setCellStyle')
D   argCellStyle                          like(HSSFCellStyle)
```

Figure 8.24: Prototype for setCellStyle method of HSSFCell class

We discussed the **String** data type in Chapter 7. Let's look at the numeric value here. Figure 8.25 shows the **AirExcel_setCellValueNumeric** procedure, which we'll place in the **SVAIREXCEL** file.

```
P AirExcel_setCellValueNumeric...
P                 B                       EXPORT
D AirExcel_setCellValueNumeric...
D                 PI
D   argCell                               like(HSSFCell)
```

```
D   argNumber                           like(jDouble) value
D   argStyle                            like(HSSFCellStyle)
D                                       options(*nopass)
 /free
   HSSFCell_setCellValueNumeric(argCell: argNumber);
   if %parms > 2;
     HSSFCell_setCellStyle(argCell: argStyle);
   else;
   endif;
   return;
 /end-free
P                       E
```

Figure 8.25: Custom AirExcel_setCellValueNumeric procedure in SVAIREXCEL

The string version of **AirExcel_setCellValue*Xxx*** is a little bit more interesting because it converts the bytes to a **String** object to be assigned to the cell, but the two methods provide the same basic functionality. After the cell value is set, the method checks to see whether the cell style parameter has been passed. If the cell style has been specified, the method assigns the cell style to the cell using the **setCellStyle** method of the **HSSFCell** class.

Data Formatting

An important part of the presentation of reports is the formatting of the numbers in the report. In a spool file, you can use edit codes or edit words to format the data in a desired manner on your reports. In an Excel spreadsheet, you could set the data format of the cell to present the data in a multitude of different ways.

In the spreadsheet shown in Figure 8.26, we have a few cells that use some kind of special formatting. The date and time are formatted, and the money value includes a dollar sign (**$**) before the number. In addition, although you can't see this in the figure, the negative number (and accompanying dollar sign) appears in red with surrounding parentheses.

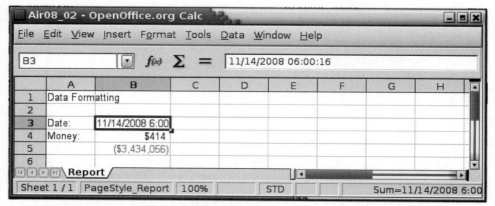

Figure 8.26: *Spreadsheet with data formatting*

The date and time values for this example use the **Date** class that is provided with Java. The name **Date** is a pretty generic name that is known to be reused in different packages, such as **java.sql.Date**, so we'll give the name **JavaDate** to the object reference defined in **SPAIRJAVA** (Figure 8.27).

```
D JavaDate...
D                S              O    CLASS(*JAVA
D                                    :'java.util.Date')
```

Figure 8.27: *RPG object variable for reference to java.util.Date object*

The default constructor method of the **Date** class, which is summarized in Figure 8.28, initializes the object to represent the date and time of the object's creation.

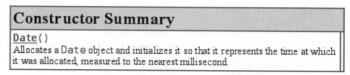

Figure 8.28: *JavaDoc for default constructor of java.util.Date class*

Figure 8.29 shows the **Date** constructor method that will be placed into
SPAIRJAVA.

```
D new_Date...
D                     PR                      like(JavaDate)
D                                             ExtProc(*JAVA
D                                             :'java.util.Date'
D                                             :*CONSTRUCTOR)
```

Figure 8.29: Prototype for default constructor of java.util.Date class

You can assign a data format to a cell style using the **setDataFormat** method of
the **HSSFCellStyle** class (Figure 8.30).

Method Summary	
void	setDataFormat(short fmt) set the data format (must be a valid format)

Figure 8.30: Partial JavaDoc for setDataFormat method of HSSFCellStyle class

Setting the data format in a cell is like using the **EDTWRD** keyword in RPG.
You specify the way that the characters should be displayed and pass in the
information, and the data format does the work for you. Figure 8.31 shows the
RPG prototype for the **setDataFormat** method.

```
D HSSFCellStyle_setDataFormat...
D                     PR                      EXTPROC(*JAVA
D                                             :'org.apache.poi.hssf.usermodel-
D                                             .HSSFCellStyle'
D                                             :'setDataFormat')
D   argFormat                                 like(jshort) value
```

Figure 8.31: Prototype for setDataFormat method of HSSFCellStyle class

Table 8.1 provides a partial list of indexes for the built-in formats that are available.

Table 8.1: Partial list of indexes for built-in formats of the HSSFDataFormat class

Index	Format string	Sample data	Result
0	General	12082008	12082008
1	0	12082008	12082008
2	0.00	12082008	12082008.00
3	#,##0	12082008	12,082,008
4	#,##0.00	1208200.8	1,208,200.80
5	($#,##0_);($#,##0)	12082008	($12,082,008
6	($#,##0_);[Red]($#,##0)	12082008	($12,082,008
7	($#,##0.00);($#,##0.00)	12082008	($12,082,008.00)
8	($#,##0.00_);[Red]($#,##0.00)	12082008	($12,082,008.00
9	0%	0.8	80%
0xe	m/d/yy	12/08/2008	12/8/08
0x16	m/d/yy h:mm	12/08/2008	12/8/08 0:00
0x25	(#,##0_);(#,##0)	12082008	(12,082,008
0x26	(#,##0_);[Red](#,##0)	12082008	(12,082,008
0x27	(#,##0.00_);(#,##0.00)	12082008	(12,082,008.00
0x28	(#,##0.00_);[Red](#,##0.00)	12082008	(12,082,008.00

You could use one of these indexes to specify the built-in format to use, or you could be more friendly to the next programmer (and yourself) for future maintenance by using the format string with the **getBuiltInFormat** method (Figure 8.32) to determine the code to be used.

Method Summary	
Static short	**getBuiltinFormat**(java.lang.String format) get the format index that matches the given format string

Figure 8.32: Partial JavaDoc for getBuiltinFormat method of HSSFDataFormat class

With the **getBuiltInFormat** method of the **HSSFDataFormat** class, you pass in a string that represents the format you want to use, and the **getBuiltInFormat** method returns the code to be used with the **setDataFormat** method of the **HSSFCellStyle** class. Figure 8.33 shows the prototype for the **getBuiltInFormat** method.

```
D HSSFDataFormat_getBuiltinFormat...
D                   PR              like(jshort)
D                                   EXTPROC(*JAVA
D                                   :'org.apache.poi.hssf.usermodel-
D                                   .HSSFDataFormat'
D                                   :'getBuiltinFormat')
D                                   static
D   argFormat                       like(jString)
```

Figure 8.33: Prototype for getBuiltinFormat method of HSSFDataFormat class

To further assist with the use of these formatting capabilities, we'll create a custom procedure that will do all the work for us so that we don't have to remember all of this. All you have to know is the format string you want to use. Appendix B provides a complete list of formats; this information is also available in the comments of the JavaDocs for the **HSSFDataFormat** class.

Figure 8.34 shows the custom procedure, **AirExcel_setCellStyleDataFormat**.

```
P AirExcel_setCellStyleDataFormat...
P                   B               EXPORT
D AirExcel_setCellStyleDataFormat...
D                   PI
D   argCellStyle                    like(HSSFCellStyle)
D   argBytes                512A    const varying options(*varsize)
D svString        S               like(jString)
 /free
   svString = new_String(%trim(argBytes));
   HSSFCellStyle_setDataFormat(argCellStyle:
     HSSFDataFormat_getBuiltinFormat(svString));
   return;
 /end-free
P                   E
```

Figure 8.34: AirExcel_setCellStyleDataFormat custom procedure

The **HSSFDataFormat_getBuiltinFormat** procedure is the second parameter to the **HSSFCellStyle_setDataFormat** procedure. This will convert the format string to the value that will be used to set the data format.

RPG Data-Formatting Program

We now have all the formatting procedures and prototypes defined and are ready to use them in our program to generate the spreadsheet shown in Figure 8.26. Figure 8.35 shows the first part of the RPG program to format data in Excel.

```
      .
      .  <Insert common header code here (Figure 7.3)>
      .
  D  airDate          S                  LIKE(JavaDate)
  D  airWorkBook      S                  LIKE(HSSFWorkbook)
  D  airSheet         S                  LIKE(HSSFSheet)
  D  airRow           S                  LIKE(HSSFRow)
  D  airCell          S                  LIKE(HSSFCell)
  D  airStyleDate     S                  LIKE(HSSFCellStyle)
  D  airStyleMoney    S                  LIKE(HSSFCellStyle)
  C/EJECT
   /free
     CallP JavaServiceProgram();
     JNIEnv_P = getJNIEnv();
     airWorkbook = new_HSSFWorkbook();
     airSheet = AirExcel_getSheet(airWorkbook: 'Report');
     // Cell Style for Date Formatting
     airDate = new_Date();
     airStyleDate = HSSFWorkbook_createCellStyle(airWorkbook);
     AirExcel_setCellStyleDataFormat(airStyleDate:'m/d/yy h:mm');
```

Figure 8.35: RPG program using data formatting in Excel (part 1 of 3)

Here, the **airStyleDate** cell style is set to format the date using the **'m/d/yy h:mm'** format, which will display the date as 11/14/2008 6:00 even though the actual data contained in the cell is **11/14/2008 06:00:16**. Notice that there is still some room left in the cell, so the data wasn't truncated. The seconds are not shown because they are not specified in the cell style.

Now, let's show the money! Figure 8.36 shows the next couple lines of the RPG program, which format the dollar figures.

```
     airStyleMoney = HSSFWorkbook_createCellStyle(airWorkbook);
     AirExcel_setCellStyleDataFormat(airStyleMoney:
                        '($#,##0_);[Red]($#,##0)');
```

Figure 8.36: RPG program using data formatting in Excel (part 2 of 3)

This formatting of monetary values specifies the use of parentheses for negative numbers as well as the use of a dollar sign. An additional format, the color red, is to be used for negative values. The semicolon (;) identifies a condition for using the second format. The first part of the parameter value, before the semicolon, applies to positive numbers; the second part is optional and indicates the format for negative numbers.

The rest of the program, shown in Figure 8.37, populates the data and uses the new cell styles on the appropriate cells.

```
// Create Cells
airRow = AirExcel_getRow(airSheet:0);
airCell = AirExcel_getCell(airRow:0);
AirExcel_setCellValueString(airCell:'Data Formatting');
// Date
airRow = AirExcel_getRow(airSheet:2);
airCell = AirExcel_getCell(airRow:0);
AirExcel_setCellValueString(airCell:'Date:');
airCell = AirExcel_getCell(airRow:1);
HSSFCell_setCellValueDate(airCell: airDate);
HSSFCell_setCellStyle(airCell: airStyleDate);
// Money
airRow = AirExcel_getRow(airSheet:3);
airCell = AirExcel_getCell(airRow:0);
AirExcel_setCellValueString(airCell:'Money:');
airCell = AirExcel_getCell(airRow:1);
HSSFCell_setCellValueNumeric(airCell: 414);
HSSFCell_setCellStyle(airCell: airStyleMoney);
airRow = AirExcel_getRow(airSheet:4);
airCell = AirExcel_getCell(airRow:1);
HSSFCell_setCellValueNumeric(airCell: -3434056);
HSSFCell_setCellStyle(airCell: airStyleMoney);
//*** Close the Spreadsheet and Reclaim Resources
AirExcel_write(airWorkbook:
                '/Public/Air08_02.xls');

 .
 . <Insert cleanup code here>
 .
*inlr = *ON;
/end-free
```

Figure 8.37: RPG program using data formatting in Excel (part 3 of 3)

Date Formatting

In Figure 8.35, we used the built-in formats available for use from the **HSSFData-Format** class with the **HSSFCellStyle** class to format the date. But there will be times when the dates you're using are not the only data in the cell, or the dates may not be contained within a cell at all. In such cases, you cannot take advantage of the cell style formatting to format the date.

In such situations, you could just use the date and time information accessible through RPG, or you could decide to use the **Date** class available in Java. As you start integrating your RPG programs with Java, you will find the need to work with the **Date** class.

To support this capability, we'll create a procedure to take care of these details for us by converting the **Date** information to bytes. You could also use this next procedure for other purposes when integrating the two languages together. For example, if you were debugging a **Date** object within an RPG program, you could use this procedure to easily convert the values into something you could view in the RPG debugger.

Figure 8.38 shows the custom procedure to convert a Java **Date** object into bytes.

```
P Air_getDateBytes...
P                 B                    EXPORT
D Air_getDateBytes...
D                 PI           512A    varying
D   argDate                            like(JavaDate)
D   argDateFormat                      like(jInt) value
D   argTimeFormat                      like(jInt) value
D svDateFormat    S                    like(DateFormat)
D svString        S                    like(jString)
D svBytes         S            512A    varying
 /free
   svDateFormat = DateFormat_getDateTimeInstance(
                  argDateFormat: argTimeFormat);
   svString = DateFormat_format(svDateFormat: argDate);
   svBytes = String_getBytes(svString);
   freeLocalRef(svDateFormat);
   freeLocalRef(svString);
   return svBytes;
 /end-free
P                 E
```

Figure 8.38: Custom procedure to convert Java Date object into bytes

The procedure formats the date and time by taking advantage of the methods available in the **DateFormat** class provided with Java. Figure 8.39 shows the constructor method for this class.

Constructor Summary	
protected	DateFormat() Create a new date format.

Figure 8.39: JavaDoc for protected DateFormat constructor

The constructor method for the **DateFormat** class is protected, so we will create an instance of this class using one of the static methods that are provided to return a **DateFormat** object (Figure 8.40).

Method Summary	
Static DateFormat	getDateTimeInstance(int dateStyle, int timeStyle) Gets the date/time formatter with the given date and time formatting styles for the default locale.
String	format(Date date) Formats a Date into a date/time string.

Figure 8.40: Partial JavaDoc for methods of DateFormat class

Several static methods are available to construct a **DateFormat** instance. We will use the version that accepts the date and time formatting styles. This will create the **DateFormat** class with the expected formatting. Figure 8.41 shows the prototype for the **getDateTimeInstance** method of the **DateFormat** class.

```
D DateFormat_getDateTimeInstance...
D                    PR             like(DateFormat)
D                                   ExtProc(*JAVA
D                                   :'java.text.DateFormat'
D                                   :'getDateTimeInstance')
D                                   static
D   argDateCode                     like(jInt) value
D   argTimeCode                     like(jInt) value
```

Figure 8.41: Prototype for getDateTimeInstance method of DateFormat class

The **DateFormat** class includes a **format** method (Figure 8.42) that converts a **Date** object value into a **String**. The resulting **String** is determined by the **DateFormat** object that is passed into the **format** method with the **Date** object.

```
D DateFormat_format...
D                    PR                    like(jString)
D                                          ExtProc(*JAVA
D                                          :'java.text.DateFormat'
D                                          :'format')
D   argDate                                like(JavaDate)
```

Figure 8.42: Prototype for format method of DateFormat class

The JavaDocs for the **DateFormat** class document the codes used to determine the format of the date and time. Figure 8.43 provides a partial list of the constants we'll be using.

```
D**********************************************************************
D* java.text.DateFormat Constant Field Values
D**********************************************************************
D DATE_FORMAT_LONG...
D                    C                     1
D DATE_FORMAT_MEDIUM...
D                    C                     2
D DATE_FORMAT_SHORT...
D                    C                     3
```

Figure 8.43: Partial list of date format constants in DateFormat class

Table 8.2 lists what the date and time values would look like for different combinations of June 21, 2009 at 9:44 PM.

Table 8.2: Date and time formatting options using DateFormat class		
Date	**Time**	**Results**
LONG	LONG	June 21, 2009 9:44:05 PM GMT-04:00
MEDIUM	MEDIUM	21-June-09 9:44:05 PM
SHORT	SHORT	06/21/2009 9:44 PM

Column Width and Text Wrap

The sample data-formatting spreadsheet illustrated in Figure 8.26 doesn't show it, but when viewing these results initially, the user has to expand the column to see them. To eliminate the need for users to manually adjust the column width for each new spreadsheet, you can set the width of the columns during the creation of the spreadsheet. You can also specify text wrapping to display the entire results of the cell, even if the results don't fit within the width of the cell using text wrap.

Figure 8.44 shows a spreadsheet that features both a customized column width and wrapped text.

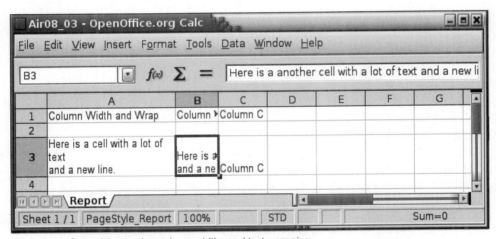

Figure 8.44: Spreadsheet using column widths and text wrapping

You want to make a good impression when you release your first program that provides Excel spreadsheets in place of a previous greenbar report. And although this enhancement may seem minor, you don't want your users to have to make any adjustments to the results, if possible. They should be able to just receive the spreadsheet and print it. If you can set the column width to an adequate size, you should be able to achieve this goal.

Figure 8.45 lists the column width methods of the **HSSFSheet** class.

Method Summary	
void	<u>setColumnWidth</u>(int <u>columnIndex</u>, int width) Set the width (in units of 1/256th of a character width)
void	<u>setColumnWidth</u>(short <u>columnIndex</u>, short width) **Deprecated.** *(Sep 2008)* use <u>setColumnWidth(int, int)</u>

Figure 8.45: Partial JavaDoc for HSSFSheet column width methods

The **setColumnWidth** method whose parameter list contains the **short** parameter is deprecated, but because we're not using the latest version of the POI package, we'll be using the **short** parameter in our prototypes. Figure 8.46 shows the prototype for this version of the **setColumnWidth** method.

```
D HSSFSheet_setColumnWidth...
D                     PR                    EXTPROC(*JAVA
D                                           :'org.apache.poi.hssf.usermodel-
D                                           .HSSFSheet'
D                                           :'setColumnWidth')
D  argColumn                                like(jshort) value
D  argWidth                                 like(jshort) value
```

Figure 8.46: Prototype for setColumnWidth method of HSSFSheet class

We'll use the **setWrapText** method of the **HSSFCellStyle** class (Figure 8.47) to provide the text-wrapping capability of the cells in our spreadsheets.

Method Summary	
void	<u>setWrapText</u>(boolean wrapped) set whether the text should be wrapped

Figure 8.47: Partial JavaDoc for HSSFCellStyle text wrap method

Figure 8.48 shows the RPG prototype for the **setWrapText** method of the **HSSFCellStyle** class.

```
D HSSFCellStyle_setWrapText...
D                     PR                    EXTPROC(*JAVA
D                                           :'org.apache.poi.hssf.usermodel-
D                                           .HSSFCellStyle'
D                                           :'setWrapText')
D   argBoolean                       1N     value
```

Figure 8.48: Prototype for setWrapText method of HSSFCellStyle class

Column Width and Text Wrap RPG Program

The sample spreadsheet illustrated in Figure 8.44 has the first column set up with appropriate column widths and text wrapping to properly display the entire values in the cells. The second column is deliberately set to show the results that you *don't* want to see on your final product.

Figure 8.49 presents the first section of the RPG code to generate the spreadsheet example.

```
 .
 . <Insert common header code here (Figure 7.3)>
 .
D  airWorkBook     S                     LIKE(HSSFWorkbook)
D  airSheet        S                     LIKE(HSSFSheet)
D  airRow          S                     LIKE(HSSFRow)
D  airCell         S                     LIKE(HSSFCell)
D  airStyleWrap    S                     LIKE(HSSFCellStyle)
 /free
  CallP JavaServiceProgram();
  JNIEnv_P = getJNIEnv();
  airWorkbook = new_HSSFWorkbook();
  airSheet = AirExcel_getSheet(airWorkbook: 'Report');
  // Set Column Widths
  HSSFSheet_setColumnWidth(airSheet: 0: 6000);
  HSSFSheet_setColumnWidth(airSheet: 1: 2000);
```

Figure 8.49: RPG program using column widths and text wrapping in Excel (part 1 of 3)

The **HSSFSheet_setColumnWidth** prototyped methods set the width of the columns. The first column is column 0, which will be set to 6,000 units, and the second column will be set to 2,000 units. The units are measured in 1/256th of a character. The remaining columns will just use the default column size that is assigned. The maximum column width using the standard font size is 255 characters.

The next part of the program (Figure 8.50) turns on text wrapping for the A3 cell in the sample spreadsheet.

```
// Cell Style for Date Formatting
airStyleWrap = HSSFWorkbook_createCellStyle(airWorkbook);
HSSFCellStyle_setWrapText(airStyleWrap: *ON);
```

Figure 8.50: *RPG program using column widths and text wrapping in Excel (part 2 of 3)*

The **HSSFCellStyle_setWrapText** prototyped method lets you turn on text wrapping for the cell. If you don't set the text wrapping on, it defaults to being turned off.

With all the formatting established, we can now populate the cell contents (Figure 8.51).

```
// Create Cells
airRow = AirExcel_getRow(airSheet:0);
airCell = AirExcel_getCell(airRow:0);
AirExcel_setCellValueString(airCell:'Column Width and Wrap');
airCell = AirExcel_getCell(airRow:1);
AirExcel_setCellValueString(airCell:'Column Width and Wrap');
airCell = AirExcel_getCell(airRow:2);
AirExcel_setCellValueString(airCell:'Column C');
// Word Wrapping
airRow = AirExcel_getRow(airSheet:2);
airCell = AirExcel_getCell(airRow:0);
HSSFCell_setCellStyle(airCell: airStyleWrap);
AirExcel_setCellValueString(airCell:
  'Here is a cell with a lot of text' +
  EBCDIC_LF + 'and a new line.');
// Second Column without wrap
airCell = AirExcel_getCell(airRow:1);
AirExcel_setCellValueString(airCell:
  'Here is a another cell with a lot of text' +
  EBCDIC_LF + 'and a new line.');
airCell = AirExcel_getCell(airRow:2);
AirExcel_setCellValueString(airCell:'Column C');
//*** Close the Spreadsheet and Reclaim Resources
AirExcel_write(airWorkbook:
```

```
                    '/Public/Air08_03.xls');
// Clean Up
    .
    . <Insert cleanup code here>
    .
*inlr = *ON;
/end-free
```

Figure 8.51: RPG program using column widths and text wrapping in Excel (part 3 of 3)

If you refer back to Figure 8.44, you can see that the first column is wider than the standard column width and the second column is slightly narrower than the standard columns. Even with the first column set at a larger width, the data in the third row (Cell A3) still does not fit in the cell, but because we have text wrapping turned on, you can see all the data that is contained within that cell.

In the third row of the second column (Cell B3), text wrapping is not turned on, so you do not see all the data. However, you can tell that there is a line feed in there because the first few characters of the second line are visible in that cell.

Setting Print and Display Properties

Another way to make your spreadsheets more desirable to users is made possible with methods in POI that help you make spreadsheets easier to read and print. In the next example, shown in Figure 8.52, we'll zoom in to make the spreadsheet easy to read.

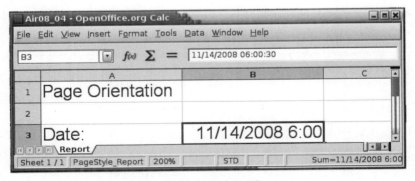

Figure 8.52: Spreadsheet using display and print settings

We will also change the page orientation to landscape and turn on the grid lines to be visible when the spreadsheet is printed. Figure 8.53 summarizes the methods of the **HSSFSheet** class that we'll use to make our spreadsheet more user-friendly.

Method Summary	
void	**setPrintGridlines**(boolean newPrintGridlines) Turns on or off the printing of gridlines.
void	**setZoom**(int numerator, int denominator) Sets the zoom magnification for the sheet.
HSSFPrintSetup	**getPrintSetup**() Gets the print setup object.

Figure 8.53: Partial JavaDoc for HSSFSheet print orientation methods

The **setPrintGridLines** method (Figure 8.54) determines whether the grid lines should be displayed on the spreadsheet when it is printed.

```
D HSSFSheet_setPrintGridLines...
D                   PR            EXTPROC(*JAVA
D                                 :'org.apache.poi.hssf.usermodel-
D                                 .HSSFSheet'
D                                 :'setPrintGridlines')
D  argSetting              1N     value
```

Figure 8.54: Prototype for setPrintGridLines method of HSSFSheet class

The **setZoom** method (Figure 8.55) sets the zoom amount, determined by the ratio of the numerator divided by the denominator.

```
D HSSFSheet_setZoom...
D                   PR            EXTPROC(*JAVA
D                                 :'org.apache.poi.hssf.usermodel-
D                                 .HSSFSheet'
D                                 :'setZoom')
D  argNumerator...
D                                 like(jInt) value
D  argDenominator...
D                                 like(jInt) value
```

Figure 8.55: Prototype for setZoom method of HSSFSheet class

To change the orientation of the page, we need to get the **HSSFPrintSetup** objectfrom the **HSSFSheet** object. Figure 8.56 shows the prototype to accomplish this task.

```
D HSSFSheet_getPrintSetup...
D                    PR                  like(HSSFPrintSetup)
D                                        extproc(*JAVA
D                                        :'org.apache.poi.hssf.usermodel-
D                                        .HSSFSheet'
D                                        :'getPrintSetup')
```

Figure 8.56: Prototype for getPrintSetup method of HSSFSheet class

The **HSSFPrintSetup** class has a **setLandscape** method (Figure 8.57) that we'll use to set the orientation of the page to be printed in landscape mode.

Method Summary		
void	setLandscape(boolean ls) Set whether to print in landscape	

Figure 8.57: Partial JavaDoc for HSSFPrintSetup setLandscape method

Figure 8.58 shows the RPG prototype for the **setLandscape** method of the **HSSFPrintSetup** class.

```
D HSSFPrintSetup_setLandscape...
D                    PR                  extproc(*JAVA
D                                        :'org.apache.poi.hssf-
D                                        .usermodel.HSSFPrintSetup'
D                                        :'setLandscape')
D    argSetting              1N          value
```

Figure 8.58: Prototype for setLandscape method of HSSFPrintSetup class

RPG Program Using Display and Print Settings

We are now ready to put together the RPG program to generate the sample spreadsheet. Figure 8.59 shows the first part of the program to work with the display and print settings. To display the grid lines on the spreadsheet when it is printed, we pass the *ON value to the **setPrintGridLines** method of **HSSFSheet**.

```
  .
  . <Insert common header code here (Figure 7.3)>
  .
D  airDate         S                      LIKE(JavaDate)
D  airWorkBook     S                      LIKE(HSSFWorkbook)
D  airSheet        S                      LIKE(HSSFSheet)
D  airRow          S                      LIKE(HSSFRow)
D  airCell         S                      LIKE(HSSFCell)
D  airStyleDate    S                      LIKE(HSSFCellStyle)
D  airPrintSetup   S                      LIKE(HSSFPrintSetup)
 /free
  CallP JavaServiceProgram();
  JNIEnv_P = getJNIEnv();
  airWorkbook = new_HSSFWorkbook();
  airSheet = AirExcel_getSheet(airWorkbook: 'Report');
  // Set Column Widths
  HSSFSheet_setColumnWidth(airSheet: 0: 4000);
  HSSFSheet_setColumnWidth(airSheet: 1: 4000);
  // Print Gridlines
  HSSFSheet_setPrintGridlines(airSheet: *ON);
```

Figure 8.59: *RPG program using display and print settings in Excel (part 1 of 4)*

Next, in Figure 8.60, the program sets the initial zoom level of the spreadsheet to 200 percent. The **setZoom** method of **HSSFSheet** sets the numerator value to 2 and the denominator to 1. The initial zoom value is therefore 2 / 1 * 100, or 200.

```
  // Zoom in to 200%
  HSSFSheet_setZoom(airSheet: 2: 1);
```

Figure 8.60: *RPG program using display and print settings in Excel (part 2 of 4)*

The page orientation isn't set on the sheet; it is set on the print setup. So, to specify page orientation, we need to retrieve the **HSSFPrintSetup** object from the **HSSFSheet**. Once we have the **HSSFPrintSetup** object, we can set the orientation to landscape using the **setLandscape** method (Figure 8.61).

```
// Set to Landscape
airPrintSetup = HSSFSheet_getPrintSetup(airSheet);
HSSFPrintSetup_setLandscape(airPrintSetup: *ON);
```

Figure 8.61: RPG program using display and print settings in Excel (part 3 of 4)

The remainder of the program (Figure 8.62) populates the data, saves the file, and reclaims the resources.

```
// Cell Style for Date Formatting
airDate = new_Date();
airStyleDate = HSSFWorkbook_createCellStyle(airWorkbook);
AirExcel_setCellStyleDataFormat(airStyleDate:'m/d/yy h:mm');
// Create Cells
airRow = AirExcel_getRow(airSheet:0);
airCell = AirExcel_getCell(airRow:0);
AirExcel_setCellValueString(airCell:'Page Orientation');
// Date
airRow = AirExcel_getRow(airSheet:2);
airCell = AirExcel_getCell(airRow:0);
AirExcel_setCellValueString(airCell:'Date:');
airCell = AirExcel_getCell(airRow:1);
HSSFCell_setCellValueDate(airCell: airDate);
HSSFCell_setCellStyle(airCell: airStyleDate);
//*** Close the Spreadsheet and Reclaim Resources
AirExcel_write(airWorkbook:
               '/Public/Air08_04.xls');
// Clean Up
 .
 . <Insert cleanup code here>
 .
*inlr = *ON;
/end-free
```

Figure 8.62: RPG program using display and print settings in Excel (part 4 of 4)

Headers and Footers

Certain pieces of information can greatly assist you in providing technical support to your users when dealing with spreadsheets, or with any report for that matter. A unique identifier for each report is a great way to expedite the process of determining which actual report the user is talking about. It is also important to have information about who ran the report and when. And when the report is being printed, the page number helps to keep everything in order.

In a typical situation, this information may not be the most important content, so it need not be at the forefront of the report, but it will be important when you troubleshoot potential problems or review archived documents. These characteristics make such information a prime candidate for header and footer content because headers and footers are visible only when you print the spreadsheet or view it using the print preview function.

Figure 8.63 shows the sample header we'll create to illustrate these capabilities.

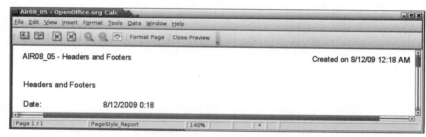

Figure 8.63: Spreadsheet header view using print preview

In this example, the left header is set to a constant value that contains a unique name for the spreadsheet, making it easily identified when a user calls with issues. We'll determine the date and time using the **Date** class that we've been using throughout the chapter. **Date** is a very useful class that helps you take advantage of formatting capabilities with minimal work to produce nice results.

For the footer, shown in Figure 8.64, we'll record the user who ran the report and provide the page number.

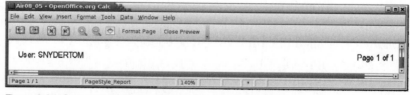

Figure 8.64: Spreadsheet footer view using print preview

You could change the headers and footers around or populate them with completely different data, but I have found the preceding format to be extremely useful.

The **HSSFHeader** and **HSSFFooter** objects are retrieved from the **HSSFSheet** object. Figure 8.65 shows the constructor methods for these classes.

Method Summary	
HSSFHeader	**getHeader**() Gets the user model for the document header.
HSSFFooter	**getFooter**() Gets the user model for the document footer.

Figure 8.65: Partial JavaDoc for HSSFSheet header and footer constructor methods

We'll use the **HSSFHeader** class to set the header elements in the spreadsheet (Figure 8.66).

```
D HSSFSheet_getHeader...
D                 PR              like(HSSFHeader)
D                                 EXTPROC(*JAVA
D                                 :'org.apache.poi.hssf.usermodel-
D                                 .HSSFSheet'
D                                 :'getHeader')
```

Figure 8.66: Prototype for getHeader method of HSSFSheet class

The **HSSFFooter** class will be used to set the footers in the spreadsheet (Figure 8.67).

```
D HSSFSheet_getFooter...
D                 PR              like(HSSFFooter)
D                                 EXTPROC(*JAVA
D                                 :'org.apache.poi.hssf.usermodel-
D                                 .HSSFSheet'
D                                 :'getFooter')
```

Figure 8.67: Prototype for getFooter method of HSSFSheet class

The **HSSFHeader** and **HSSFFooter** classes do not have a generic **setAlignment** method. Instead, they have three separate methods to set each of the three available alignments (Figure 8.68).

Method Summary	
void	setCenter(java.lang.String newCenter) Sets the center string.
void	setLeft(java.lang.String newLeft) Sets the left string.
void	setRight(java.lang.String newRight) Sets the right string.

Figure 8.68: Partial JavaDoc for HSSFHeader and HSSFFooter alignment methods

HSSFHeader_setCenter (Figure 8.69) sets the center header value.

```
D HSSFHeader_setCenter...
D                   PR                    extproc(*JAVA:
D                                         'org.apache.poi.hssf.-
D                                         usermodel.HSSFHeader'
D                                         :'setCenter')
D  argString                             like(jString)
```

Figure 8.69: Prototype for setCenter method of HSSFHeader class

HSSFHeader_setLeft (Figure 8.70) sets the left header value.

```
D HSSFHeader_setLeft...
D                   PR                    extproc(*JAVA:
D                                         'org.apache.poi.hssf.-
D                                         usermodel.HSSFHeader'
D                                         :'setLeft')
D  argString                             like(jString)
```

Figure 8.70: Prototype for setLeft method of HSSFHeader class

HSSFHeader_setRight (Figure 8.71) sets the right header value.

```
D HSSFHeader_setRight...
D                   PR                    extproc(*JAVA:
D                                         'org.apache.poi.hssf.-
D                                         usermodel.HSSFHeader'
D                                         :'setRight')
D  argString                             like(jString)
```

Figure 8.71: Prototype for setRight method of HSSFHeader class

The **HSSFFooter** class also has the same three alignment methods as **HSSFHeader**, as illustrated in Figure 8.68.

To simplify the header and footer creation and alignment, we'll create an **AirExcel_setHeader** and an **AirExcel_setFooter** procedure to handle all the details. Figure 8.72 shows the custom procedure to set the header.

```
P AirExcel_setHeader...
P                   B                    EXPORT
D AirExcel_setHeader...
D                   PI
D   argSheet                             like(HSSFSheet) const
D   argBytes                   1024A     const varying options(*varsize)
D   argAlignment                         like(jShort)
options(*noPass:*omit)
D svHeader         S                     like(HSSFHeader)
D svString         S                     like(jString)
D svAlignment      S                     like(jShort)
 /free
  // Default Alignment: Center
  if %parms < 3;
    svAlignment = POI_ALIGN_CENTER;
  else;
    svAlignment = argAlignment;
  endif;
  svString = new_String(argBytes);
  svHeader = HSSFSheet_getHeader(argSheet);
  select;
    when svAlignment = POI_ALIGN_LEFT;
      HSSFHeader_setLeft(svHeader: svString);
    when svAlignment = POI_ALIGN_RIGHT;
      HSSFHeader_setRight(svHeader: svString);
    other;
      HSSFHeader_setCenter(svHeader: svString);
  endsl;
  freelocalref(svString);
  freelocalref(svHeader);
  return;
 /end-free
P                   E
```

Figure 8.72: Custom procedure to set the header

Instead of making a separate procedure for each alignment setting, we'll create our procedures with a parameter to specify which alignment to use. To avoid the creation of redundant constants to identify the alignment, we'll reuse the constants that are defined for alignment in the **HSSFCellStyle** class. You saw a partial list of these constants in Figure 8.12.

Figure 8.73 shows the custom procedure for use with the **HSSFFooter**. If you do not specify an alignment to use, the alignment defaults to be in the center.

```
P AirExcel_setFooter...
P                    B                    EXPORT
D AirExcel_setFooter...
D                    PI
D  argSheet                               like(HSSFSheet) const
D  argBytes                      1024A    const varying options(*varsize)
D  argAlignment                           like(jShort)
options(*noPass:*omit)
D svFooter          S                     like(HSSFFooter)
D svString          S                     like(jString)
D svAlignment       S                     like(jShort)
 /free
   // Default Alignment: Center
   if %parms < 3;
     svAlignment = POI_ALIGN_CENTER;
   else;
     svAlignment = argAlignment;
   endif;
   svString = new_String(argBytes);
   svFooter = HSSFSheet_getFooter(argSheet);
   select;
     when svAlignment = POI_ALIGN_LEFT;
       HSSFFooter_setLeft(svFooter: svString);
     when svAlignment = POI_ALIGN_RIGHT;
       HSSFFooter_setRight(svFooter: svString);
     other;
       HSSFFooter_setCenter(svFooter: svString);
   endsl;
   freelocalref(svString);
   freelocalref(svFooter);
   return;
 /end-free
 P                    E
```

Figure 8.73: Custom procedure to set the footer

RPG Program to Set Header and Footer

Time to dig into the code! Figure 8.74 shows the first part of the RPG program that sets the header and footer for our sample spreadsheet.

```
    .
    .  <Insert common header code here (Figure 7.3)>
    .
D                   SDS
D  QPGM                       1    10
D  QUSER                    254   263
D  QDATE                    276   281
D  QTIME                    282   287  0
D  QCUSER                   358   367
D*
D  airAlign         S                    like(jShort)
D  airDateBytes     S              256A  varying
D  airPageBytes     S              256A  varying
D  airNumPageBytes...
D                   S              256A  varying
D  airString        S                    like(jString)
D  airDate          S                    like(JavaDate)
D  airWorkBook      S                    like(HSSFWorkbook)
D  airSheet         S                    like(HSSFSheet)
D  airRow           S                    like(HSSFRow)
D  airCell          S                    like(HSSFCell)
D  airStyleDate     S                    like(HSSFCellStyle)
C/EJECT
 /free
  CallP JavaServiceProgram();
  JNIEnv_P = getJNIEnv();
  airWorkbook = new_HSSFWorkbook();
  airSheet = AirExcel_getSheet(airWorkbook: 'Report');
  // Set Column Widths
  HSSFSheet_setColumnWidth(airSheet: 0: 4000);
  HSSFSheet_setColumnWidth(airSheet: 1: 4000);
  // Cell Style for Date Formatting
  airDate = new_Date();
  airStyleDate = HSSFWorkbook_createCellStyle(airWorkbook);
  AirExcel_setCellStyleDataFormat(airStyleDate:'m/d/yy h:mm');
  airDateBytes = Air_getDateBytes(airDate:
                      DATE_FORMAT_SHORT:
                      DATE_FORMAT_SHORT);
```

Figure 8.74: RPG program using headers and footers in Excel (part 1 of 5)

The **AirExcel_setCellStyleDataFormat** sets the cell style for the date cell. The **airDateBytes** variable contains the bytes for the date and time to be used in the header. The date is formatted using the **DATE_FORMAT_SHORT** version, which is returned from the **Air_getDateBytes** procedure described in Figure 8.38.

To set the header, the program uses the code shown in Figure 8.75.

```
// Create Headers
airAlign = POI_ALIGN_LEFT;
AirExcel_setHeader(airSheet:
                   %trim(QPGM) + ' - Headers and Footers':
                   airAlign);
airAlign = POI_ALIGN_RIGHT;
AirExcel_setHeader(airSheet:
                   'Created on ' + airDateBytes:
                   airAlign);
```

Figure 8.75: RPG program using headers and footers in Excel (part 2 of 5)

The first **AirExcel_setHeader** call sets the constant value to the header to uniquely identify the report when it is being referenced for technical support or for matching against previously run reports. This constant will be placed into the left header, as indicated by the use of the **POI_ALIGN_LEFT** constant value.

The second **AirExcel_setHeader** call creates the right header, which will contain the date on which the report was run. Because we're not using a cell, we can't use the cell style to format the date. This is why we used the **Air_getDateBytes** procedure to format the contents of the **Date** object into bytes that could be used for the header.

Next, we set the footer values. The left footer (Figure 8.76) will contain the name of the user profile that generated the spreadsheet. The program retrieves this information from the program status data structure.

```
// Create Footers
airAlign = POI_ALIGN_LEFT;
AirExcel_setFooter(airSheet:
                   'User: ' + %trim(QCUSER):
                   airAlign);
```

Figure 8.76: RPG program using headers and footers in Excel (part 3 of 5)

The right footer (Figure 8.77) will contain a format that is recognized by the spreadsheet to change depending on the page being printed. This logic will automatically set the correct page number on each printed page.

```
airAlign = POI_ALIGN_RIGHT;
airString = HSSFFooter_page();
airPageBytes = String_getBytes(airString);
airString = HSSFFooter_numPages();
airNumPageBytes = String_getBytes(airString);
AirExcel_setFooter(airSheet:
                   'Page ' + %trim(airPageBytes) +
                   ' of '  + %trim(airNumPageBytes):
                   airAlign);
```

Figure 8.77: RPG program using headers and footers in Excel (part 4 of 5)

The program finishes by populating the data into the spreadsheet, saving it, and reclaiming resources (Figure 8.78).

```
// Create Cells
airRow = AirExcel_getRow(airSheet:0);
airCell = AirExcel_getCell(airRow:0);
AirExcel_setCellValueString(airCell:'Headers and Footers');
// Date
airRow = AirExcel_getRow(airSheet:2);
airCell = AirExcel_getCell(airRow:0);
AirExcel_setCellValueString(airCell:'Date:');
airCell = AirExcel_getCell(airRow:1);
HSSFCell_setCellValueDate(airCell: airDate);
HSSFCell_setCellStyle(airCell: airStyleDate);
//*** Close the Spreadsheet and Reclaim Resources
AirExcel_write(airWorkbook:
               '/Public/Air08_05.xls');
// Clean Up
  .
  . <Insert cleanup code here>
  .
*inlr = *ON;
/end-free
```

Figure 8.78: RPG program using headers and footers in Excel (part 5 of 5)

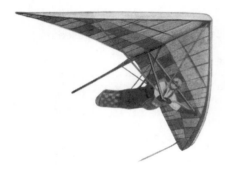

9

Excel Formulas and Charts

With a good grasp of the spreadsheet creation process and the formatting capabilities supported by the POI project, you're ready to move on to more powerful aspects of spreadsheets. In this chapter, we discuss how to use RPG and Java to define formulas and charts in your Excel spreadsheets.

Formulas

A formula lets you represent a computed value in a spreadsheet. Using formulas, you can provide computed data that relies on data from other cells in the spreadsheet. Formulas can include operators, functions, constants, and references to other cells.

The sample spreadsheet shown in Figure 9.1 uses several different types of formulas:

- Cell B7 computes the sum of the cells in the range of B3 through B6 using the **SUM** function with references to the cell range.

- Cell B9 uses the **MAX** function to determine the largest value that is contained in the data range of B3 through B6.

- Cells C7 and C9 use a conditional **IF** operation to display text based on the value in the corresponding B column.

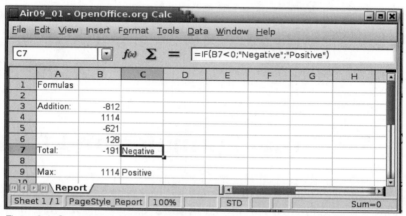

Figure 9.1: Spreadsheet containing a formula cell

The setCellFormula Method

To assign a formula to a cell, you use the **setCellFormula** method of the **HSSFCell** class (Figure 9.2). The formula is assigned to the cell using the method's string parameter.

Method Summary		
void	**setLandscape**(boolean ls)	
	Set whether to print in landscape	

Figure 9.2: Partial JavaDoc for setCellFormula method of HSSFCell class

Figure 9.3 shows the prototype for the **setCellFormula** method.

```
D HSSFCell_setCellFormula...
D                   PR               EXTPROC(*JAVA
D                                    :'org.apache.poi.hssf.usermodel-
D                                    .HSSFCell'
D                                    :'setCellFormula')
D   argValue                         like(jString) const
```

Figure 9.3: Prototype for setCellFormula method of HSSFCell class

Formulas start with an equals sign (=) at the beginning of the string, but you don't specify this symbol when using **setCellFormula**; the method does that for you.

Program Example Using Formulas

Using the **setCellFormula** method of the **HSSFCell** class, we can write the RPG program to generate the sample spreadsheet.

Figure 9.4 shows the first part of the program. This code populates the cells with constant values so that we have some data to work with.

```
     .
     . <Insert common header code here (Figure 7.3)>
     .
D   airWorkbook   S               LIKE(HSSFWorkbook)
D   airSheet      S               LIKE(HSSFSheet)
D   airRow        S               LIKE(HSSFRow)
D   airCell       S               LIKE(HSSFCell)
 /free
   CallP JavaServiceProgram();
   airWorkbook = new_HSSFWorkbook();
   airSheet = AirExcel_getSheet(airWorkbook: 'Report');
   // Create Cells
   airRow = AirExcel_getRow(airSheet:0);
   airCell = AirExcel_getCell(airRow:0);
   AirExcel_setCellValueString(airCell:'Formulas');
   // Assign Numeric Values
   airRow = AirExcel_getRow(airSheet:2);
   airCell = AirExcel_getCell(airRow:0);
   AirExcel_setCellValueString(airCell:'Addition:');
```

```
airCell = AirExcel_getCell(airRow:1);
HSSFCell_setCellValueNumeric(airCell: -812);
//
airRow = AirExcel_getRow(airSheet:3);
airCell = AirExcel_getCell(airRow:1);
HSSFCell_setCellValueNumeric(airCell: 1114);
//
airRow = AirExcel_getRow(airSheet:4);
airCell = AirExcel_getCell(airRow:1);
HSSFCell_setCellValueNumeric(airCell: -621);
//
airRow = AirExcel_getRow(airSheet:5);
airCell = AirExcel_getCell(airRow:1);
HSSFCell_setCellValueNumeric(airCell: 128);
```

Figure 9.4: RPG program using formulas in Excel (part 1 of 3)

Figure 9.5 shows the next section of RPG code.

```
// Create Sum Formula
airRow = AirExcel_getRow(airSheet:6);
airCell = AirExcel_getCell(airRow:0);
AirExcel_setCellValueString(airCell:'Total:');
airCell = AirExcel_getCell(airRow:1);
HSSFCell_setCellFormula(airCell:
          new_String('SUM(B3:B6)'));
airCell = AirExcel_getCell(airRow:2);
HSSFCell_setCellFormula(airCell:
          new_String('IF(B7<0;"Negative";"Positive")'));
```

Figure 9.5: RPG program using formulas in Excel (part 2 of 3)

For row number 6 in our program, which is row 7 when you view the spreadsheet, we set the "Total:" string in the first cell. (Remember that Java starts at row 0, while the spreadsheet starts at row 1.)

For the second cell of the row (**airRow:1**), we use the **SUM** formula to compute the sum of the data in cells B3 through B6. Notice that we don't include the equals sign in the cell assignment. When you view the cell in your spreadsheet application, this formula will be represented as **=SUM(B3:B6)**.

Instead of **SUM**, we could have used arithmetic operators to perform the same operation by setting the formula to **B3+B4+B5+B6**.

In the third cell of the row, we use the **IF** function to determine whether the number in the preceding cell is negative or positive.

Next, in Figure 9.6, the program creates row number 8, which implements the **MAX** function.

```
// Create Max Formula
airRow = AirExcel_getRow(airSheet:8);
airCell = AirExcel_getCell(airRow:0);
AirExcel_setCellValueString(airCell:'Max:');
airCell = AirExcel_getCell(airRow:1);
HSSFCell_setCellFormula(airCell:
        new_String('MAX(B3:B6)'));
airCell = AirExcel_getCell(airRow:2);
HSSFCell_setCellFormula(airCell:
        new_String('IF(B9<0;"Negative";"Positive")'));
//*** Close the Spreadsheet and Reclaim Resources
AirExcel_write(airWorkbook:
                '/Public/Air09_01.xls');
// Clean Up
   .
   . <Insert cleanup code here>
   .
*inlr = *ON;
/end-free
```

Figure 9.6: RPG program using formulas in Excel (part 3 of 3)

The **MAX** function returns the largest value found in the specified range of cells. To prove out the logic in the conditional function, you can see in Figure 9.1 that the string displayed in the cell is "Positive".

The syntax for the **IF** function is as follows:

```
IF(logical test, TRUE, [FALSE])
```

The function's first parameter must return a logical true or false value to determine which condition to implement for the cell. The second parameter is required and will indicate the results to use in the cell if the logical test returns the true value. The third parameter is optional and will indicate the results to use in the cell if the logical test returns the false value.

I have found that Microsoft Excel wants to use the comma between the parameters, while OpenOffice Calc wants to use semicolons. I use OpenOffice throughout this book, so you may have to change the formulas in this example to support Excel if that is the software you're using.

The Java Iterator Class

For previous examples, we have created new spreadsheets, but for the rest of this chapter we'll be discussing the use of existing spreadsheets.

When you work with an existing spreadsheet, you may or may not know how many rows or cells it contains. You may also have cells that are not initialized, so there could be null cells in between the valid cells. For situations such as these, you can take advantage of the **Iterator** class in Java. The **Iterator** class is a part of the **java.util** package, so the object reference will be defined in the **SPAIRJAVA** file (Figure 9.7).

```
D Iterator...
D                 S           O    CLASS(*JAVA
D                                  :'java.util.Iterator')
```

Figure 9.7: RPG object variable for reference to the java.util.Iterator object

We will use two methods available from the **Iterator** class, **hasNext** and **next**, to loop through the rows and cells. Figure 9.8 shows the JavaDoc for these methods.

Method Summary	
boolean	**hasNext**() Returns true if the iteration has more elements.
Object	**next**() Returns the next element in the iteration.

Figure 9.8: Partial JavaDoc for java.util.Iterator methods

The **hasNext** method (Figure 9.9) can be used to control the loop by determining whether another **Iterator** is available.

```
D Iterator_hasNext...
D                 PR            1N
D                               ExtProc(*JAVA
D                               :'java.util.Iterator'
D                               :'hasNext')
```

Figure 9.9: Prototype for hasNext method of java.util.Iterator class

The **next** method (Figure 9.10) retrieves the next **Iterator** from the list.

```
D Iterator_next...
D                 PR            like(jObject)
D                               ExtProc(*JAVA
D                               :'java.util.Iterator'
D                               :'next')
```

Figure 9.10: Prototype for next method of java.util.Iterator class

You use the **Iterator** class with a collection of data. The data in the collection will be in some kind of order that you can loop through until you get to the end. When you create an **Iterator**, it is positioned at the beginning of the collection, and you can loop through the elements until reaching the end.

Using Sheet Indexes

So far, we've been retrieving our sheets using the name of the sheet as the identifier of the sheet that we're interested in. You can also reference a sheet by its index using the **getSheetAt** method of the **HSSFWorkbook** class. If want to determine the name of a sheet at a particular index, you can obtain the name using the **getSheetName** method of the **HSSFWorkbook** class.

> **RPG Note**
> When you read through a file in RPG, you can use an indicator on the read statement to determine when the end of the file is encountered, or you can use a built-in function. These techniques are similar to using the **hasNext** method of the **Iterator** class to determine when the end of a collection is encountered.

Figure 9.11 shows the JavaDoc for **getSheetAt** and **getSheetName** methods of
the **HSSFWorkbook** class.

Method Summary	
HSSFSheet	**getSheetAt**(int index) Get the HSSFSheet object at the given index.
java.lang.String	**getSheetName**(int sheetIndex) Set the sheet name

Figure 9.11: Partial JavaDoc for HSSFWorkbook methods

The **getSheetAt** method, whose prototype appears in Figure 9.12, returns the
sheet at the specified index. The first sheet index is **0** (zero).

```
D HSSFWorkbook_getSheetAt...
D                     PR                    like(HSSFSheet)
D                                           ExtProc(*JAVA
D                                           :'org.apache.poi.hssf-
D                                           .usermodel.HSSFWorkbook'
D                                           :'getSheetAt')
D   argIndex                                like(jInt) value
```

Figure 9.12: Prototype for getSheetAt method of HSSFSheet class

The **getSheetName** method (Figure 9.13) retrieves the name of the sheet at a
specified index.

```
D HSSFWorkbook_getSheetName...
D                     PR                    like(jString)
D                                           ExtProc(*JAVA
D                                           :'org.apache.poi.hssf-
D                                           .usermodel.HSSFWorkbook'
D                                           :'getSheetName')
D   argIndex                                like(jInt) value
```

Figure 9.13: Prototype for getSheetAt method of HSSFSheet class

Working with Rows Within Sheets

When you work with existing spreadsheets, you need to open the workbook and
get the sheet. The next level into the data is the rows that are contained in the sheet.

Figure 9.14 lists a few of the **HSSFSheet** methods available for working with rows within a sheet.

Method Summary	
int	**getLastRowNum**() Gets the number last row on the sheet.
int	**getPhysicalNumberOfRows**() Returns the number of physically defined rows (NOT the number of rows in the sheet)
java.util.Iterator<Row>	**rowIterator**() Returns an iterator of the physical rows

Figure 9.14: Partial JavaDoc for HSSFSheet methods

The **getLastRowNum** method (Figure 9.15) gets the row number that identifies the last row that contains data.

```
D HSSFSheet_getLastRowNum...
D                 PR                 like(jInt)
D                                    ExtProc(*JAVA
D                                    :'org.apache.poi.hssf-
D                                    .usermodel.HSSFSheet'
D                                    :'getLastRowNum')
```

Figure 9.15: Prototype for getLastRowNum method of HSSFSheet class

The **getPhysicalNumberOfRows** method (Figure 9.16) returns the number of defined rows in the sheet. This number does not include null rows.

```
D HSSFSheet_getPhysicalNumberOfRows...
D                 PR                 like(jInt)
D                                    ExtProc(*JAVA
D                                    :'org.apache.poi.hssf-
D                                    .usermodel.HSSFSheet'
D                                    :'getPhysicalNumberOfRows')
```

Figure 9.16: Prototype for getPhysicalNumberOfRows method of HSSFSheet class

The **rowIterator** method (Figure 9.17) returns an object of type **Iterator** that you can use to go through the rows of the sheet.

```
D HSSFSheet_rowIterator...
D                  PR                      like(Iterator)
D                                          ExtProc(*JAVA
D                                          :'org.apache.poi.hssf-
D                                          .usermodel.HSSFSheet'
D                                          :'rowIterator')
```

Figure 9.17: Prototype for rowIterator method of HSSFSheet class

Working with Cells Within Rows

Figure 9.18 lists a few of the methods available in the **HSSFRow** class to work with existing cells within the rows.

Method Summary	
java.util. Iterator<Cell>	cellIterator()
int	getPhysicalNumberOfCells() gets the number of defined cells (NOT number of cells in the actual row!).
int	getRowNum() get row number this row represents

Figure 9.18: Partial JavaDoc for HSSFRow methods

The **cellIterator** method of the **HSSFRow** class (Figure 9.19) returns an object of type **Iterator** that can be used to go through the cells of the row. So, you could anticipate a nested loop coming up; the outer loop would go through the rows, and the inner loop would go through the cells of the row using the iterators.

```
D HSSFRow_cellIterator...
D                  PR                      like(Iterator)
D                                          ExtProc(*JAVA
D                                          :'org.apache.poi.hssf-
D                                          .usermodel.HSSFRow'
D                                          :'cellIterator')
```

Figure 9.19: Prototype for cellIterator method of HSSFRow class

The **getPhysicalNumberOfCells** method (Figure 9.20) returns the number of cells defined within the row.

```
D HSSFRow_getPhysicalNumberOfCells...
D                   PR                  like(jInt)
D                                       ExtProc(*JAVA
D                                       :'org.apache.poi.hssf-
D                                       .usermodel.HSSFRow'
D                                       :'getPhysicalNumberOfCells')
```

Figure 9.20: Prototype for getPhysicalNumberOfCells method of HSSFRow class

And the **getRowNum** method (Figure 9.21) returns the row number of the **HSSFRow** instance.

```
D HSSFRow_getRowNum...
D                   PR                  like(jInt)
D                                       ExtProc(*JAVA
D                                       :'org.apache.poi.hssf-
D                                       .usermodel.HSSFRow'
D                                       :'getRowNum')
```

Figure 9.21: Prototype for getRowNum method of HSSFRow class

Working with Cell Types and Values

Down at the cell level, we'll use a variety of methods to retrieve our information. Figure 9.22 provides the method summary for these **HSSFCell** methods.

Method Summary	
int	**getCellType**() get the cells type (numeric, formula or string)
boolean	**getBooleanCellValue**() get the value of the cell as a boolean.
java.lang.String	**getCellFormula**() Return a formula for the cell, for example, SUM(C4:E4)
short	**getCellNum**() **Deprecated.** *(Oct 2008) use getColumnIndex()*
int	**getColumnIndex**() Returns column index of this cell
double	**getNumericCellValue**() Get the value of the cell as a number.
java.lang.String	**getStringCellValue**() get the value of the cell as a string - for numeric cells we throw an exception.

Figure 9.22: Partial JavaDoc for HSSFCell methods

When reading through the cells, we can identify the type of data that is contained within the cell by using the **getCellType** method of the **HSSFCell** class (Figure 9.23).

```
D HSSFCell_getCellType...
D                    PR                      like(jInt)
D                                            ExtProc(*JAVA
D                                            :'org.apache.poi.hssf-
D                                            .usermodel.HSSFCell'
D                                            :'getCellType')
```

Figure 9.23: Prototype for getCellType method of HSSFCell class

The cell type values that the **getCellType** method returns are constants that are listed in the JavaDocs and put into the **SPAIREXCEL** file. Figure 9.24 shows the constant definitions.

```
D******************************************************************
D* org.apache.poi.hssf.usermodel.Cell Constant Field Values
D******************************************************************
D POI_CELL_TYPE_BLANK...
D                    C                       3
D POI_CELL_TYPE_BOOLEAN...
D                    C                       4
D POI_CELL_TYPE_ERROR...
D                    C                       5
D POI_CELL_TYPE_FORMULA...
D                    C                       2
D POI_CELL_TYPE_NUMERIC...
D                    C                       0
D POI_CELL_TYPE_STRING...
D                    C                       1
```

Figure 9.24: List of cell type constants in the Cell class

We will use the **getBooleanCellValue** method of the **HSSFCell** class (Figure 9.25) to retrieve the contents of cells that are of type **boolean**.

```
D HSSFCell_getBooleanCellValue...
D                    PR              1N
D                                            ExtProc(*JAVA
D                                            :'org.apache.poi.hssf-
D                                            .usermodel.HSSFCell'
D                                            :'getBooleanCellValue')
```

Figure 9.25: Prototype for getBooleanCellValue method of HSSFCell class

We'll use the **getCellFormula** method (Figure 9.26) to retrieve the contents of cells of type **formula**.

```
D HSSFCell_getCellFormula...
D                    PR               like(jString)
D                                     ExtProc(*JAVA
D                                     :'org.apache.poi.hssf-
D                                     .usermodel.HSSFCell'
D                                     :'getCellFormula')
```

Figure 9.26: Prototype for getCellFormula method of HSSFCell class

The **getCellNum** method (Figure 9.27) returns the cell number of the **HSSFCell** instance.

```
D HSSFCell_getCellNum...
D                    PR               like(jShort)
D                                     ExtProc(*JAVA
D                                     :'org.apache.poi.hssf-
D                                     .usermodel.HSSFCell'
D                                     :'getCellNum')
```

Figure 9.27: Prototype for getCellNum method of HSSFCell class

The **getNumericCellValue** method (Figure 9.28) retrieves the contents of numeric cells.

```
D HSSFCell_getNumericCellValue...
D                    PR               like(jDouble)
D                                     ExtProc(*JAVA
D                                     :'org.apache.poi.hssf-
D                                     .usermodel.HSSFCell'
D                                     :'getNumericCellValue')
```

Figure 9.28: Prototype for getNumericCellValue method of HSSFCell class

Last, we'll use the **getStringCellValue** method of the **HSSFCell** class (Figure 9.29) to retrieve the contents of string-type cells, using the **String** class.

```
D HSSFCell_getStringCellValue...
D                    PR               like(jString)
D                                     ExtProc(*JAVA
D                                     :'org.apache.poi.hssf-
D                                     .usermodel.HSSFCell'
D                                     :'getStringCellValue')
```

Figure 9.29: Prototype for getStringCellValue method of HSSFCell class

Reading an Existing Spreadsheet

Our RPG program to demonstrate the read capabilities of POI will read through the formula spreadsheet that was generated from the previous example. Figure 9.30 shows the first part of the program to read an existing spreadsheet.

```
     .
     . <Insert common header code here (Figure 7.3)>
     .
D displayString    S              52A
D airBytes         S              52A
D airInt           S                      like(jInt)
D airDouble        S                      like(jDouble)
D airWorkbook      S                      like(HSSFWorkbook)
D airSheet         S                      like(HSSFSheet)
D airRow           S                      like(HSSFRow)
D airCell          S                      like(HSSFCell)
D airString        S                      like(jString)
D airNumberRows    S                      like(jInt)
D airNumberCells   S                      like(jInt)
D airLastRow       S                      like(jInt)
D airRowNum        S                      like(jInt)
D airCellNum       S                      like(jInt)
D airRowIterator...
D                  S                      like(Iterator)
D airCellIterator...
D                  S                      like(Iterator)
 /free
   CallP JavaServiceProgram();
   airWorkbook = AirExcel_getWorkbook('/Public/Air09_01.xls');
   airString = HSSFWorkbook_getSheetName(airWorkbook: 0);
   airSheet = HSSFWorkbook_getSheetAt(airWorkbook: 0);
   airNumberRows = HSSFSheet_getPhysicalNumberOfRows(airSheet);
   airLastRow = HSSFSheet_getLastRowNum(airSheet);
   displayString = 'Last Row Number: '
                 + %trim(%editc(airLastRow:'3'));
   DSPLY displayString;
```

Figure 9.30: RPG program reading an existing Excel spreadsheet (part 1 of 8)

Nothing new up to this point. But next, we'll get into the iterators to move through the rows and cells. There will be two iterators within nested loops. The iterator in the outer loop will read through the rows of the sheet. We'll use the second iterator inside the nested loop of the row iterators to go through the cells.

Both iterators use the **Iterator** class provided with Java. The row iterator is retrieved from the sheet, and the cell iterator is retrieved from the row. Figure 9.31 shows this next section of code.

```
airRowIterator = HSSFSheet_rowIterator(airSheet);
if airRowIterator = *NULL;
else;
  dow Iterator_hasNext(airRowIterator);
    airRow = Iterator_next(airRowIterator);
    airRowNum = HSSFRow_getRowNum(airRow);
    airNumberCells = HSSFRow_getPhysicalNumberOfCells(airRow);
    displayString = '----- Row: '
                    + %trim(%editc(airRowNum:'3'))
                    + ' has '
                    + %trim(%editc(airNumberCells:'3'))
                    + ' Columns -----';
    DSPLY displayString;
    airCellIterator = HSSFRow_cellIterator(airRow);
    dow Iterator_hasNext(airCellIterator);
      airCell = Iterator_next(airCellIterator);
      airCellNum = HSSFCell_getCellNum(airCell);
      airInt = HSSFCell_getCellType(airCell);
      displayString = 'Cell ('
                      + %trim(%editc(airRowNum:'3'))
                      + ', '
                      + %trim(%editc(airCellNum:'3'))
                      + ')'
                      + ' - Type: '
                      + %trim(%editc(airInt:'3'));
```

Figure 9.31: RPG program reading an existing Excel spreadsheet (part 2 of 8)

Within the cell iterator loop, we determine the type of cell using the **getCellType** method of the **HSSFCell** class. This method returns an integer value that can be translated using the constants you saw in Figure 9.24.

The first case in the **select** statement (Figure 9.32) identifies blank cells.

```
select;
//--------------------------------------------------
  when airInt = POI_CELL_TYPE_BLANK;
    displayString = %trim(displayString)
                    + ', Blank';
```

```
      DSPLY displayString;
      airString = HSSFCell_getStringCellValue(airCell);
      airBytes = String_getBytes(airString);
      displayString = %trim(airBytes);
```

Figure 9.32: RPG program reading an existing Excel spreadsheet (part 3 of 8)

The second case (Figure 9.33) identifies **boolean** cells and creates a text representation of the **boolean** value to present.

```
//--------------------------------------------------
   when airInt = POI_CELL_TYPE_BOOLEAN;
      displayString = %trim(displayString)
                     + ', Boolean';
      DSPLY displayString;
      if HSSFCell_getBooleanCellValue(airCell);
        displayString = 'True';
      else;
        displayString = 'False';
      endif;
```

Figure 9.33: RPG program reading an existing Excel spreadsheet (part 4 of 8)

The third case (Figure 9.34) identifies the formulas. When a formula is identified, the program retrieves it as a string value and displays it.

```
//--------------------------------------------------
   when airInt = POI_CELL_TYPE_FORMULA;
      displayString = %trim(displayString)
                     + ', Formula';
      DSPLY displayString;
      airString = HSSFCell_getCellFormula(airCell);
      airBytes = String_getBytes(airString);
      displayString = 'Value: ' + %trim(airBytes);
```

Figure 9.34: RPG program reading an existing Excel spreadsheet (part 5 of 8)

Then, we have the numeric cell type, which the program identifies and retrieves using the **getNumericCellValue** method of the **HSSFCell** class (Figure 9.35).

```
//--------------------------------------------------
   when airInt = POI_CELL_TYPE_NUMERIC;
      displayString = %trim(displayString)
                     + ', Numeric';
```

```
               DSPLY displayString;
               airDouble = HSSFCell_getNumericCellValue(airCell);
               airInt = airDouble;
               airBytes = %trim(%editc(airInt:'3'));
               displayString = 'Value: ' + %trim(airBytes);
```

Figure 9.35: RPG program reading an existing Excel spreadsheet (part 6 of 8)

For string cell types, we use the **getStringCellValue** method of **HSSFCell** to retrieve the value of the cell (Figure 9.36).

```
            //------------------------------------------------
            when airInt = POI_CELL_TYPE_STRING;
               displayString = %trim(displayString)
                             + ', String';
               DSPLY displayString;
               airString = HSSFCell_getStringCellValue(airCell);
               airBytes = String_getBytes(airString);
               displayString = 'Value: ' + %trim(airBytes);
```

Figure 9.36: RPG program reading an existing Excel spreadsheet (part 7 of 8)

Last, if for some reason we find a cell that is of an unknown type, the **other** case of the **select** statement (Figure 9.37) will catch it to display a cell type that is unsupported by your RPG program. This circumstance could happen if a newer version of the POI package is installed that identifies an additional new cell type (dates, for example, which are currently identified as numeric) and your program hasn't been updated to look for the new constant that is available.

```
            //------------------------------------------------
            other;
               displayString = %trim(displayString)
                             + ', Unsupported';
          endsl;
          DSPLY displayString;
        enddo;
      enddo;
   endif;
   // Clean Up
     .
     . <Insert cleanup code here>
     .
   *inlr = *ON;
   /end-free
```

Figure 9.37: RPG program reading an existing Excel spreadsheet (part 8 of 8)

This sample program evaluates the spreadsheet that is generated from the earlier example, so you'll need to either make sure you run the previous program first or change the **Air09_01.xls** file reference to point to another Excel spreadsheet that is known to exist. When you run the program, you'll see the output shown in Figure 9.38 displayed on the screen.

```
DSPLY  Last Row Number: 8
DSPLY  ----- Row: 0 has 1 Columns -----
DSPLY  Cell (0, 0) - Type: 1, String
DSPLY  Value: Formulas
DSPLY  ----- Row: 2 has 2 Columns -----
DSPLY  Cell (2, 0) - Type: 1, String
DSPLY  Value: Addition:
DSPLY  Cell (2, 1) - Type: 0, Numeric
DSPLY  Value: 812
DSPLY  ----- Row: 3 has 1 Columns -----
DSPLY  Cell (3, 1) - Type: 0, Numeric
DSPLY  Value: 1114
DSPLY  ----- Row: 4 has 1 Columns -----
DSPLY  Cell (4, 1) - Type: 0, Numeric
DSPLY  Value: 621
DSPLY  ----- Row: 5 has 1 Columns -----
DSPLY  Cell (5, 1) - Type: 0, Numeric
DSPLY  Value: 128
DSPLY  ----- Row: 6 has 3 Columns -----
DSPLY  Cell (6, 0) - Type: 1, String
DSPLY  Value: Total:
DSPLY  Cell (6, 1) - Type: 2, Formula
DSPLY  Value: SUM(B3:B6)
DSPLY  Cell (6, 2) - Type: 2, Formula
DSPLY  Value: IF(B7<0,"Negative","Positive")
DSPLY  ----- Row: 8 has 3 Columns -----
DSPLY  Cell (8, 0) - Type: 1, String
DSPLY  Value: Max:
DSPLY  Cell (8, 1) - Type: 2, Formula
DSPLY  Value: MAX(B3:B6)
DSPLY  Cell (8, 2) - Type: 2, Formula
DSPLY  Value: IF(B9<0,"Negative","Positive")
```

Figure 9.38: Output of RPG program reading an existing Excel spreadsheet

You can notice quite a few things from the output generated by this program:

- The Row and Cell indexes start at zero.

- The **Iterator** skips over any null cells, as you can see when it goes from cell (0, 0) to cell (2, 0), not even evaluating anything from row 1. You can also see this behavior in rows 3 and 4, when the **Iterator** jumps right to cell 1 and does not evaluate cells (3, 0) or (4, 0).

- The **getPhysicalNumberOfCells** method does not give you a reference to the last cell in the row; it actually gives you the number of cells that have been defined. This fact is illustrated in all the examples, but you can see that in rows 3 and 4 the results show one column even though the data is in the second column.

My point here is that the iterators and the physical rows and cells will correspond with each other and make working with the data in the spreadsheet very convenient.

Charts, Graphs, and Images

At the time of this writing, the POI project provides minimal support for charts, graphs, and images. You can work with images, but several known bugs exist when more than one image is involved, and there is no support for graphs or charts.

To overcome these obstacles, we'll place our images and create our charts and/or graphs in a template file. The charts and graphs will reference some test data in the template that our RPG programs will update. When the changes are complete, we'll save to a new spreadsheet that will become our final product.

Templates are the same as spreadsheets; the only difference is the **.xlt** extension that is used with template files instead of the usual **.xls** extension on Excel spreadsheets.

Templates are not intended to be a final product, although they could be if you chose to use them that way. The special thing about templates is that if a user changes some data in the spreadsheet and then tries to save it, the spreadsheet application assumes that the user wants to save the spreadsheet with the **.xls** extension and give it a new name.

In addition to their saving characteristics, templates can help you keep your files organized. For my reports, I've created a standard file structure on the IFS to contain all the templates, and I name them to contain the program that uses them. This approach helps me quickly find the templates associated with my programs.

To illustrate how to use templates, we'll create a spreadsheet to show the top ten searches on the MC Press Online Web site. Figure 9.39 shows the spreadsheet template, which uses a pie chart to present its data.

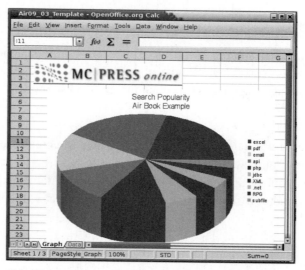

Figure 9.39: Pie chart contained in a spreadsheet template

You can see that an image, the MC Press Online logo, has also been placed into the template. This template is a simple one, but you could invest the time to create a really visually pleasing template that users would use over and over again with the daily reports you'll be generating.

We'll use two sheets in our template: Data and Graph. The Data sheet will contain the numbers that will be referenced from the Graph sheet. The Graph sheet will provide a clean display of the pie chart for a simple, one-page print.

The first step is to populate the template with test data. Using this data, we can create a graph on the Graph sheet that will reference these cells. Up to this point in our spreadsheet discussions, we have used only one sheet in our spreadsheets. To keep the chart separated from the numbers on the report, we'll put the data for this example on a separate sheet. Figure 9.40 shows the data on the Data sheet of the spreadsheet template.

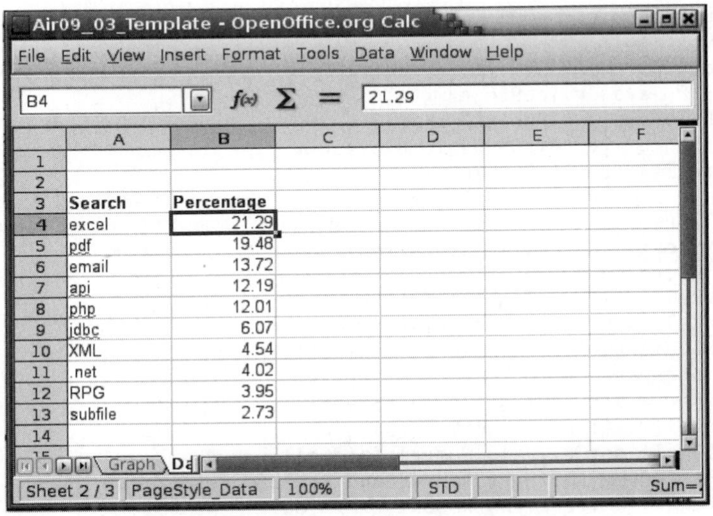

Figure 9.40: Data contained in a spreadsheet template

The graphical interface to create graphs and charts differs depending on which spreadsheet application you use and which version, but the basic process involves selecting the type of chart you want to create and assigning the range of relevant data to each axis.

Updating an Existing Spreadsheet

With our template built, we can use it from an RPG program. This program could gather the data and update the data table, which will be reflected on the pie chart. For this example, we'll update two values in the Data sheet. Then, we'll review the output to see the results.

Figure 9.41 shows the RPG program to update the existing spreadsheet.

```
  .
  . <Insert common header code here (Figure 7.3)>
  .
D   airWorkbook      S                        LIKE(HSSFWorkbook)
D   airSheet         S                        LIKE(HSSFSheet)
D   airRow           S                        LIKE(HSSFRow)
D   airCell          S                        LIKE(HSSFCell)
D   inFileName       S              2000A
D   outFileName      S              2000A
D   jvString         S                        LIKE(jString)
 /free
   CallP JavaServiceProgram();
   inFileName = '/Public/'
              + 'Air09_03_Template.xlt';
   outFileName = '/Public/'
              + 'Air09_03.xls';
   airWorkbook = AirExcel_open(%TRIM(inFileName));
   airSheet = AirExcel_getSheet(airWorkbook: 'Data');
   // Decrease by 20
   airRow = AirExcel_getRow(airSheet:3);
   airCell = AirExcel_getCell(airRow:1);
   HSSFCell_setCellValueNumeric(airCell: 1.29);
   // Increase by 20
   airRow = AirExcel_getRow(airSheet:4);
   airCell = AirExcel_getCell(airRow:1);
   HSSFCell_setCellValueNumeric(airCell: 39.48);
   //*** Close the Spreadsheet and Reclaim Resources
   AirExcel_write(airWorkbook: %TRIM(outFileName));
   // Clean Up
     .
     . <Insert cleanup code here>
     .
   *inlr = *ON;
 /end-free
```

Figure 9.41: RPG program updating an existing Excel spreadsheet

After the program is run, you can open the **Air09_03.xls** file that is generated. Figure 9.42 shows the updated Data sheet, reflecting the new percentages. You can see that the B4 value was reduced to 1.29 and the B5 value was increased to 39.48.

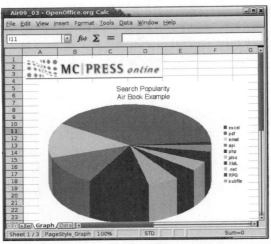

Figure 9.42: Data contained in Excel spreadsheet generated from template

Looking at the updated graph (Figure 9.43), you can see how the pie chart has changed to reflect the changes.

Figure 9.43: Pie chart contained in Excel spreadsheet generated from template

Forcing the Spreadsheet to Recalculate

When you use formulas, charts, and graphs in your templates, calculated values may not be updated to reflect the changes in the data that your program has made. This is because the changes were not made to the sheet interactively, and the sheet may not have known to recalculate the formulas, graphs, and charts.

You can force a spreadsheet to recalculate all the values each time it is opened by using Visual Basic for Applications code (VBA) that will be associated with your template. Visual Basic for Applications is similar to Visual Basic but is dependent on the application with which it is used.

In our examples, we'll only be referencing Microsoft Excel. The VBA code will be stored within the **.xlt** or **.xls** file that is generated. We will create this code in the template using Microsoft Excel to be reused with the final product, so we don't have to worry about doing this from POI.

The VBA code would then be placed into your final product to ensure that your data changes will be reflected in any formulas, graphs, or charts that your RPG program changes.

Using VBA to Force Recalculation

I know, *another* language to learn! Don't worry; this won't be too bad. We're only doing this one thing in VBA, and then we're done.

Depending on the spreadsheet software you're using and the version, there will be different ways to access the Visual Basic code of your spreadsheet. In Microsoft Excel 2003, you can right-click on the Excel icon located to the left of the **File** menu and select **View Code**. You can also go to the **Tools** menu and select **Macro** to find the Visual Basic Editor.

When you are in the Visual Basic editor of Microsoft Excel, drop-down boxes at the top of the editor window take you to the Workbook and the procedure you want to modify. We'll be working with the Workbook and the Open procedure.

When you select these options, you'll see an empty subroutine with the name **Workbook_Open()**. We will place a single statement inside the subroutine to force the entire spreadsheet to recalculate with the **Application.CalculateFullRebuild** VBA method. The final subroutine should look as shown in Figure 9.44.

```
Private Sub Workbook_Open()
Application.CalculateFullRebuild
End Sub
```

Figure 9.44: VBA code used to force cell references to recalculate

I'm sure there are dozens of different ways to accomplish this goal. There could be ways to set the client to do this without the Visual Basic code, but then you would have to configure each client and maintain that configuration when new computers are installed or rebuilt. Even then, depending on the settings and the size of the spreadsheets, you might degrade performance by having the spreadsheets recalculate more often than necessary.

With the VBA method, you force everything to be recalculated only when the spreadsheet is opened, which is exactly what you need to reflect the changes that were made when the spreadsheet was built. Another alternative would be to have the user manually recalculate the spreadsheet using the F9 key within Excel.

Using **Application.CalculateFullRebuild** is like swinging the big hammer to force all the dependencies to be rebuilt. There are other Visual Basic commands you could try, such as **CalculateFull** or just **Calculate**, and you could also work with a single sheet using **ActiveSheet**. But I've found this answer to provide the results I was looking for, so feel free to try it out and implement the methods that suit your needs.

Microsoft has dropped support for VBA in future versions of the Microsoft Office Suite to force the use of .NET for purposes such as this one. But OpenDocument Format support is coming in future versions of Microsoft products, so maybe we'll be able to do this using open document templates and not have to worry about changing it again. Until then, and until you want to force all your users to update to the latest version of Office, you can use this VBA solution.

10

PDF Basics

In this chapter, we discuss the creation of Portable Document Format (PDF) files using RPG. We'll create PDFs by integrating RPG with Java to access the iText project. iText is an open-source Java library written by Bruno Lowagie and Paul Soares for creating and manipulating PDF files.

Installing iText

To install iText, go to the download section of the iText Web site (*http://www. lowagie.com/iText*), and obtain the latest Jar file supported on the Java Runtime Environment (JRE) installed on your IBM i system. You'll want to download the current release of the iText core file, which you'll find in the "Compiled code" section of the download table.

This book uses an older version of iText that you can obtain by following a link to the iText archive on the download page. I've deliberately used the older version to set the minimum Java requirement to 1.4.2.

Copy the iText Jar file into your publicly accessible Jar file directory. Then, add the Jar file to your environment variable before starting your Java Virtual Machine.

We'll specify the **/Public/Java/PDF_iText/iText-2.1.2u.jar** location of the iText Jar file in the main procedure of the **SVAIRJAVA** service program (Figure 10.1).

```
//---------------------------------
//---        iText for PDF         ---
//---------------------------------
localPath = %TRIM(localPath)
          + ':/Public/Java'
          + '/PDF_iText/iText-2.1.2u.jar';
```

Figure 10.1: Setting the location of the iText Jar file in the SVAIRJAVA main procedure

Then, we'll use the location to set the environment variable to make the iText package visible to the JVM using the class path (Figure 10.2).

```
//----------------------------------------------------
// Put the entire class path together and implement.
//----------------------------------------------------
commandString = 'ADDENVVAR ENVVAR(CLASSPATH) '
              + 'VALUE('''.:'
              + %TRIM(localPath)
              + ''') REPLACE(*YES)';
monitor;

  ExecuteCommand(%trim(commandString):%len(%trim(commandString)));
on-error;
  displayBytes = 'ERROR occurred on Class Path!';
  DSPLY displayBytes;
endmon;
```

Figure 10.2: Setting the CLASSPATH environment variable in the SVAIRJAVA main procedure

The **ADDENVVAR** command will be executed when you call the main procedure of **SVAIRJAVA** using the **CallP JavaServiceProgram();** prototyped call.

iText Version Compatibility

The version of iText used in this book is 2.1.2u. If you choose to use a newer version, make sure that it will work with your JVM. On my V5R4 system, the JVM version is 1.4.2.

Common Code

The RPG code samples we'll develop in this series of chapters all have the code shown in Figure 10.3 in common. These opening specifications establish the **THREAD(*SERIALIZE)** recommendation for all RPG programs using Java and then copy in the generic prototypes and constants in the **SPAIRFUNC** service program source file, the standard Java prototypes in **SPAIRJAVA**, and the specialized iText PDF prototypes in **SPAIRPDF**.

```
H THREAD(*SERIALIZE)
F***************************************************************************
F*    HOW TO COMPILE:
F*
F*    (1. CREATE THE MODULE)
F*    CRTRPGMOD MODULE(AIRLIB/AIR10_xx) SRCFILE(AIRLIB/AIRSRC) +
F*              DBGVIEW(*ALL) INDENT('.')
F*
F*    (2. CREATE THE PROGRAM)
F*    CRTPGM PGM(AIRLIB/AIR10_xx)
F*      BNDSRVPGM(SVAIRJAVA SVAIRPDF) ACTGRP(AIR10_xx)
D***************************************************************************
D/DEFINE OS400_JVM_12
D/COPY QSYSINC/QRPGLESRC,JNI
D/COPY AIRLIB/AIRSRC,SPAIRFUNC
D/COPY AIRLIB/AIRSRC,SPAIRJAVA
D/COPY AIRLIB/AIRSRC,SPAIRPDF
D  declare variables...
  /free
    CallP JavaServiceProgram();
```

Figure 10.3: Common code used in the PDF RPG code samples

SPAIRPDF and SVAIRPDF

We'll be building a new prototype file (**SPAIRPDF**) and service program (**SVAIR-PDF**) for the purpose of creating PDFs using iText. As we work through the chapters that deal with PDFs, we'll add the prototypes and procedures to these files, unless otherwise specified.

Whenever you develop an RPG program that works with PDF files, you'll want to provide access to the **SVAIRJAVA** and **SVAIRPDF** service programs by copying the prototypes into the source code and binding the service programs to the program.

iText and Java JavaDocs

The JavaDocs for the iText project are available online at *http://www.1t3xt.info/api*. This documentation lists all the classes that are available for the package and lets you drill down through the different options.

For this book, all references will be to Version 1.4.2 of Java, so you'll find the relevant Java JavaDocs at *http://java.sun.com/j2se/1.4.2/docs/api*.

iText Components

A variety of iText classes support the creation of PDF files with Java. We'll start with the most fundamental one, the **Document** class.

Document

The document is where all the content is placed to create a PDF. **Document** is a very generic name for a class, so we'll call this class **ITextDocument** in our **SPAIRPDF** prototype file.

Figure 10.4 shows the RPG object reference for the **Document** class. You can see that it is contained in the **com.lowagie.text** package, which will be visible through the class path that is initialized in the main procedure of the **SVAIRJAVA** service program.

```
D ITextDocument...
D                     S              O    CLASS(*JAVA
D                                         :'com.lowagie.text-
D                                         .Document')
```

Figure 10.4: The com.lowagie.text.Document RPG object reference in SPAIRPDF

Figure 10.5 shows the JavaDoc for the two constructors we'll use to create our documents using iText.

Constructor Summary
Document()   Constructs a new Document -object.
Document(Rectangle pageSize)   Constructs a new Document -object.

Figure 10.5: Partial JavaDoc for Document default constructor

Figure 10.6 shows the prototype for the default constructor of the iText **Document** class.

```
D new_ITextDocument...
D                 PR                like(ITextDocument)
D                                   ExtProc(*JAVA:
D                                   'com.lowagie.text-
D                                   .Document':
D                                   *CONSTRUCTOR)
```

Figure 10.6: Prototype for default constructor method of Document class

The second constructor we're interested in accepts a **Rectangle** object parameter. We can use the **Rectangle** object to specify the size and orientation of the pages within the document. Figure 10.7 shows the prototype for the **Document** constructor with the **Rectangle** argument.

```
D new_ITextDocumentFromRectangle...
D                 PR                like(ITextDocument)
D                                   ExtProc(*JAVA:
D                                   'com.lowagie.text-
D                                   .Document':
D                                   *CONSTRUCTOR)
D  inRectangle                      like(ITextRectangle)
```

Figure 10.7: Prototype for Document constructor method with Rectangle argument

If you were viewing the JavaDoc shown in Figure 10.5, you could click on the **Rectangle** link of the second constructor to be taken to the **Rectangle** class. Here, you would find that this constructor is using the **Rectangle** class in the **com. lowagie.text** package.

Rectangle

The **Rectangle** class provided with iText lets us specify rectangular shapes within iText. Because the name **Rectangle** is so generic, we'll use the name **ITextRectangle** in our prototypes (Figure 10.8).

```
D ITextRectangle...
D                   S          O    CLASS(*JAVA
D                                   :'com.lowagie.text-
D                                   .Rectangle')
```

Figure 10.8: Rectangle RPG object reference

We can use the **rotate** method of the **Rectangle** class (Figure 10.9) to change the orientation of pages to landscape versus portrait.

Method Summary	
Rectangle	rotate() Rotates the rectangle.

Figure 10.9: Partial JavaDoc for Rectangle rotate method

Figure 10.10 shows the prototype for the **rotate** method of the **Rectangle** class in iText.

```
D ITextRectangle_rotate...
D                   PR                like(ITextRectangle)
D                                     EXTPROC(*JAVA
D                                     :'com.lowagie.text-
D                                     .Rectangle'
D                                     :'rotate')
```

Figure 10.10: Prototype for rotate method of Rectangle class

A **PageSize** class provided with iText assists with the use of pages in PDFs by providing a predefined set of common **Rectangle** objects that we can use to set the size of our pages. Figure 10.11 provides a partial list of some of the commonly used rectangles in the **PageSize** class of iText.

Field Summary	
static Rectangle	**11X17** This is the 11x17 format
static Rectangle	**A4** This is the a4 format
static Rectangle	**EXECUTIVE** This is the executive format
static Rectangle	**LEGAL** This is the legal format
static Rectangle	**LETTER** This is the letter format

Figure 10.11: Partial JavaDoc for Rectangle constants defined in PageSize class

Rectangle **A4** (8.26 x 11.69 inches) is the default page size that is used if no size is specified for the document.

These constants are not defined in the **SPAIRPDF** file because there is a convenient method in the **PageSize** class that we will be using. The **getRectangle** method of the **PageSize** class (Figure 10.12) retrieves the **Rectangle** object that matches the name of the **Rectangle**.

Method Summary	
static Rectangle	**getRectangle**(String name) This method returns a Rectangle based on a String.

Figure 10.12: Partial JavaDoc for PageSize getRectangle method

For the **getRectangle** method (Figure 10.13), you pass in a **String** object containing the **Rectangle** size you want to use (e.g., **"LETTER"**), and the method returns the corresponding **Rectangle** object that is defined in the **PageSize** class of iText.

```
D PageSize_getRectangle...
D                    PR               like(ITextRectangle)
D                                     ExtProc(*JAVA
D                                     :'com.lowagie.text-
D                                     .PageSize'
```

```
D                                        :'getRectangle')
D                                        static
D       argSizeName                      like(jString)
```

Figure 10.13: Prototype for rotate method of Rectangle class

Text Components

PDFs are extremely flexible, and with flexibility comes complexity. To simplify development, the iText project provides high-level text objects that automatically take care of the detailed complexities and includes some comprehensive classes to perform the task of adding Java strings to your PDF.

We'll use several different classes to add text, starting with the smaller classes and working up to the larger ones.

Chunk

Let's start with the **Chunk** object (Figure 10.14), the smallest iText text class we'll be using. A **Chunk** requires all its characters to have the same size and font.

```
D ITextChunk...
D                    S           O    CLASS(*JAVA
D                                     :'com.lowagie.text-
D                                     .Chunk')
```

Figure 10.14: Chunk RPG object reference

Figure 10.15 shows the prototype for the **Chunk** object constructor we'll use. The constructor has a **String** parameter that initializes the value of the **Chunk** when it is created.

```
D new_ITextChunk...
D                    PR          like(ITextChunk)
D                                ExtProc(*JAVA:
D                                'com.lowagie.text-
D                                .Chunk':
D                                *CONSTRUCTOR)
D   inString                     like(jString)
```

Figure 10.15: Prototype for constructor method of Chunk class

Because they are so small, chunks give you the most control over how the characters are displayed, but they do not have knowledge of line spacing. If you simply added a bunch of chunks to your document, the first line would just keep getting overwritten.

To keep things simple, we won't work with the **Chunk** class very much. But the one thing we'll want to use the **Chunk** for is new line indicators.

The **Chunk** class has a **static final** value defined as a constant for the new line, referred to as **Chunk.NEWLINE**. But because we're using the RPG version of the constructor method of the **Chunk** class instead of the Java Native Interface version, the characters will be converted from EBCDIC to ASCII automatically.

This means that the use of the constant available in the **Chunk** class will not give us the desired results. So, when we create a **Chunk**, we'll use the EBCDIC values for carriage return and line feed, as shown in Figure 10.16. The constant values for **EBCDIC_CR** and **EBCDIC_LF** are defined in the **SPAIRFUNC** prototype file.

```
airString = new_String(EBCDIC_CR + EBCDIC_LF);
airNewLine = new_ITextChunk(airString);
```

Figure 10.16: RPG equivalent of Chunk.NEWLINE using EBCDIC characters

Phrase

The **Phrase** object (Figure 10.17) is an **ArrayList** of chunks and is aware of line spacing.

```
D ITextPhrase...
D                   S              0    CLASS(*JAVA
D                                       :'com.lowagie.text-
D                                       .Phrase')
```

Figure 10.17: Phrase RPG object reference

Figure 10.18 shows the prototype for the **Phrase** object constructor we'll be using. The constructor has a **String** parameter that initializes the value of the **Phrase** when it is created.

```
D new_ITextPhrase...
D                 PR            like(ITextPhrase)
D                               ExtProc(*JAVA:
D                               'com.lowagie.text-
D                               .Phrase':
D                               *CONSTRUCTOR)
D  inString                     like(jString)
```

Figure 10.18: Prototype for constructor method of Phrase class

Phrases are useful when you want to control or reuse sections of a **Paragraph**.

Paragraph

The **Paragraph** object (Figure 10.19) is a sequence of **Phrase** objects. It is possible to construct a **Paragraph** by adding **Chunk** and **Phrase** objects to the **Paragraph**.

```
D ITextParagraph...
D                 S          O   CLASS(*JAVA
D                               :'com.lowagie.text-
D                               .Paragraph')
```

Figure 10.19: Paragraph RPG object reference

Figure 10.20 shows the prototype for the **Paragraph** object constructor we'll be using.

```
D new_ITextParagraph...
D                 PR            like(ITextParagraph)
D                               ExtProc(*JAVA:
D                               'com.lowagie.text-
D                               .Paragraph':
D                               *CONSTRUCTOR)
D  inString                     like(jString)
```

Figure 10.20: Prototype for constructor method of Paragraph class

Paragraphs automatically insert new line characters at the end of the paragraphs and let you specify the alignment of the paragraphs.

You can also specify the font with the **Paragraph** constructor (Figure 10.21).

```
D new_ITextParagraphFromFont...
D                       PR              like(ITextParagraph)
D                                       ExtProc(*JAVA:
D                                       'com.lowagie.text-
D                                       .Paragraph':
D                                       *CONSTRUCTOR)
D   inString                            like(jString)
D   inFont                              like(ITextFont)
```

Figure 10.21: Prototype for constructor method of Paragraph class with font

To make things easier, we'll create a custom procedure to take care of the bytes-to-**String** details. We'll also support both of the **Paragraph** constructors just as they were intended, by providing an optional **Font** parameter on the procedure to determine which version of the constructor to use. Figure 10.22 shows the custom procedure, **AirPdf_newParagraph**.

```
P AirPdf_newParagraph...
P                       B               EXPORT
D AirPdf_newParagraph...
D                       PI              like(ITextParagraph)
D   argBytes                    65535A  const varying
D                                       options(*varsize)
D   argFont                             like(ITextFont)
D                                       options(*nopass)
D   svString            S               like(jString)
D   svParagraph         S               like(ITextParagraph)
D                                       inz(*NULL)
  /free
    svString = new_String(argBytes);
    if (%parms > 1);
      svParagraph = new_ITextParagraphFromFont(svString: argFont);
    else;
      svParagraph = new_ITextParagraph(svString);
    endif;
    // Clean Up
    freeLocalRef(svString);
    return svParagraph;
  /end-free
P                       E
```

Figure 10.22: Custom procedure to create a new Paragraph with optional font

Adding Elements to a Document

Documents have a generic **add** method (Figure 10.23) that lets you add content to a document. All the text components we've discussed — **Chunk**, **Phrase**, and **Paragraph** — implement the **Element** interface, so they can be passed into the **add** method of the **Document** class.

Method Summary	
bool ean	**add**(Element element) Adds an Element to the Document.

Figure 10.23: Partial JavaDoc for Document add method

Figure 10.24 shows the prototype for the **add** method of the **Document** class.

```
D ITextDocument_add...
D                    PR              1N
D                                       EXTPROC(*JAVA
D                                       :'com.lowagie.text.Document'
D                                       :'add')
D   inElement                           like(ITextElement)
```

Figure 10.24: Prototype for add method of Document class

The **Element** class (Figure 10.25) is an interface that needs to be implemented by components that will use the **add** method of the **Document** class.

```
D ITextElement...
D                    S               O  CLASS(*JAVA
D                                       :'com.lowagie.text-
D                                       .Element')
```

Figure 10.25: Element RPG object reference

Saving the PDF File

iText supports the creation of PDF, Rich Text Format (RTF), and Hypertext Markup Language (HTML) documents. Which document writer you use determines the type of file that is created. Because we are creating PDFs, we'll use the **PdfWriter** class to create our documents. Figure 10.26 lists the constructor methods for this class.

Constructor Summary	
protected	PdfWriter() Constructs a PdfWriter.
protected	PdfWriter(PdfDocument document, OutputStream os) Constructs a PdfWriter.

Figure 10.26: Partial JavaDoc for PdfWriter protected constructor methods

The constructors for the **PdfWriter** class are protected, so we'll use the static **getInstance** method (Figure 10.27) to create an instance of the class.

Method Summary	
static PdfWriter	getInstance(Document document, OutputStream os) Use this method to get an instance of the PdfWriter.

Figure 10.27: Partial JavaDoc for PdfWriter getInstance static method

We'll be using JNI to implement the **getInstance** method of the **PdfWriter** class, so we'll create the custom procedure shown in Figure 10.28 to handle all the details. For more information about JNI, refer to Chapter 6.

```
P AirPdf_setPdfWriter...
P                    B               EXPORT
D AirPdf_setPdfWriter...
D                    PI              like(PdfWriter)
D   argDocument                      like(ITextDocument)
D   argOutFile                       like(FileOutputStream)
D instanceID       S                 like(jMethodId)
D writerClass      S                 like(jclass)
D                                    inz(*NULL)
D svWriter         S                 like(PdfWriter)
D                                    inz(*NULL)
D cd               DS                likeDs(iconv_t)
D ebcdicString     S        1024A
D asciiWriter      S        1024A
D asciiInit        S        1024A
D asciiInstance    S        1024A
D asciiInstanceSignature...
```

```
D                   S              1024A
D toCCSID           S              10I 0
 /free
  if (JNIEnv_P = *NULL);
    JNIEnv_P = getJNIEnv();
  else;
  endif;
  // Create Conversion Descriptor for CCSID conversions
  toCCSID = 1208;
  cd = Air_openConverter(toCCSID);
  ebcdicString = 'com/lowagie/text/pdf/PdfWriter';
  asciiWriter = Air_convert(cd: %trim(ebcdicString));
  //----------------------------------------------------------------
  // First, Find the PdfWriter Class
  //----------------------------------------------------------------
  writerClass = FindClass(JNIEnv_P:
                %trim(asciiWriter));
  if (Air_isJVMError());
    freeLocalRef(writerClass);
    Air_closeConverter(cd);
    return *NULL;
  else;
  endif;
  //----------------------------------------------------------------
  // Second, Find the MethodID for the Constructor
  //----------------------------------------------------------------
  ebcdicString = 'getInstance';
  asciiInstance = Air_convert(cd: %trim(ebcdicString));
  ebcdicString = '(Lcom/lowagie/text/Document;'
               + 'Ljava/io/OutputStream;)'
               + 'Lcom/lowagie/text/pdf/PdfWriter;';
  asciiInstanceSignature = Air_convert(cd: %trim(ebcdicString));
  InstanceID = GetStaticMethodID(JNIEnv_P:writerClass:
                  %trim(asciiInstance):
                  %trim(asciiInstanceSignature));
  if (Air_isJVMError());
    freeLocalRef(writerClass);
    Air_closeConverter(cd);
    return *NULL;
  else;
  endif;
  //----------------------------------------------------------------
  // Third, Call the getInstance method
  //----------------------------------------------------------------
  svWriter = CallWriterGetInstanceMethod(JNIEnv_P:
                    writerClass:
                    InstanceID:argDocument:
                    argOutFile);
```

```
 if (Air_isJVMError());
   freeLocalRef(writerClass);
   Air_closeConverter(cd);
   return *NULL;
 else;
 endif;
 //------------------------------------------------------------
 // Clean Up
 freeLocalRef(writerClass);
 Air_closeConverter(cd);
 return svWriter;
/end-free
P                      E
```

Figure 10.28: RPG procedure for PdfWriter getInstance method using JNI

iText provides other writers to create RTF and HTML files, but we'll limit our discussion to using of **PDFWriter** to create PDFs. To write the document, we'll employ the **PDFWriter** class using the file output stream. The details of getting the writer and the output file will be handled within a new procedure, **AirPdf_newDocumentOutput**. Figure 10.29 shows the first part of this custom procedure.

```
P AirPdf_newDocumentOutput...
P                      B                    EXPORT
D AirPdf_newDocumentOutput...
D                      PI                   like(ITextDocument)
D   argFileName                  2048A      const varying
D                                           options(*varsize)
D   argSizeName                    64A      const varying
D                                           options(*nopass: *varsize)
D   argRotate                       1N      const options(*nopass)
D   svString         S                      like(jString)
D   svDocument       S                      like(ITextDocument)
D                                           inz(*NULL)
D   svRectangle      S                      like(ITextRectangle)
D                                           inz(*NULL)
D   svOutFile        S                      like(FileOutputStream)
  /free
   if (%parms > 1);
     svString = new_String(%trim(argSizeName));
     monitor;
       svRectangle = PageSize_getRectangle(svString);
       if (%parms > 2);
         if (argRotate);
           svRectangle = ITextRectangle_Rotate(svRectangle);
```

```
        else;
          endif;
        else;
        endif;
        svDocument = new_ITextDocumentFromRectangle(svRectangle);
      on-error;
        svDocument = *NULL;
      endmon;
    else;
    endif;
```

Figure 10.29: RPG procedure to open an iText document for output (part 1 of 3)

When creating the output document, the procedure first looks to see whether a **Rectangle** object was passed to use for the page size. If a **Rectangle** was specified, the procedure then checks whether the object will be rotated to indicate landscape or portrait orientation.

If no **Rectangle** is specified, or if an error occurs upon the attempt to apply the **Rectangle**, the procedure creates the **Document** object using the default constructor. Figure 10.30 shows this portion of the RPG code.

```
if (svDocument = *NULL);
  monitor;
    svDocument = new_ITextDocument();
  on-error;
    svDocument = *NULL;
    return svDocument;
  endmon;
else;
endif;
```

Figure 10.30: RPG procedure to open an iText document for output (part 2 of 3)

After the **Document** object has been created, the procedure creates the file output stream and uses it with the **PdfWriter**. The document is then opened and returned to the calling program (Figure 10.31).

```
svString = new_String(%trim(argFileName));
monitor;
  svOutFile = new_FileOutputStream(svString);
  AirPdf_setPdfWriter(svDocument: svOutFile);
  ITextDocument_open(svDocument);
```

```
  on-error;
    svDocument = *NULL;
  endmon;
  // Clean Up
  freeLocalRef(svString);
  freeLocalRef(svOutFile);
  return svDocument;
 /end-free
P                     E
```

Figure 10.31: RPG procedure to open an iText document for output (part 3 of 3)

When you use iText, the PDF file is initialized as soon as it is opened, so you need to set the page size margins before opening the document; otherwise, the setting won't be applied to the first page. By doing it all in the **AirPdf_newDocumentOutput** procedure, we can eliminate any problems. You can see that the procedure assigns the page size, file output stream, and **PdfWriter** before opening the document using the **ITextDocument_open** procedure.

Figure 10.32 shows the JavaDoc for the **open** and **close** methods of the **Document** class.

Field Summary	
protected boolean	**open** Is the document open or not?
protected boolean	**close** Has the document already been closed?

Figure 10.32: Partial JavaDoc for open and close methods of Document class

Figure 10.33 shows the **open** method prototype for the **Document** class.

```
D ITextDocument_open...
D                 PR              EXTPROC(*JAVA
D                                 :'com.lowagie.text.Document'
D                                 :'open')
```

Figure 10.33: Prototype for open method of Document class

And Figure 10.34 shows the **close** method prototype for the **Document** class.

```
D ITextDocument_close...
D                    PR              EXTPROC(*JAVA
D                                    :'com.lowagie.text.Document'
D                                    :'close')
```

Figure 10.34: Prototype for close method of Document class

Hello World

It's time to create our first PDF from RPG! As an example, we'll create a new PDF to contain the "Hello World!" text string. Figure 10.35 shows the sample PDF.

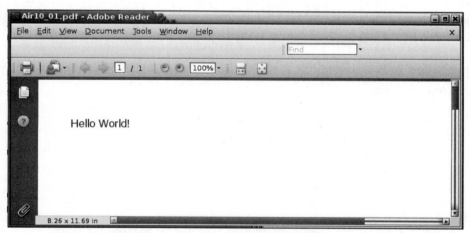

Figure 10.35: Hello World PDF

This example is a classic Hello World application, which simply puts the text into a PDF using RPG with the prototypes and service programs we've created. Figure 10.36 shows the RPG program.

```
       .
       . <Insert common header code here (Figure 10.3)>
       .
D  airDocument    S                 LIKE(ITextDocument)
D  airParagraph   S                 LIKE(ITextParagraph)
 /free
```

```
CallP JavaServiceProgram();
airDocument = AirPdf_newDocumentOutput(
                    '/Public/AIR10_01.pdf');
airParagraph = AirPdf_newParagraph('Hello World!');
ITextDocument_add(airDocument: airParagraph);
ITextDocument_close(airDocument);
// Clean Up
  .
  . <Insert cleanup code here>
  .
*inlr = *ON;
/end-free
```

Figure 10.36: RPG program for Hello World PDF

Thanks to all the front-end work done with the development of the **SPAIRPDF** and **SVAIRPDF** prototypes and service program — and, most of all, to the efforts of those who contributed to the iText project — the Hello World program is very simple. We simply open the document as an output file, create a paragraph containing the Hello World text, add the paragraph to the document, and close the document. That's the way it should be — nice and simple.

Even though this program is the simplest, it will probably be your biggest step. That's because you must have everything installed and working properly for the program to run. Once you have the Hello World program running, you know that your Jar files are installed properly and your class path is set up correctly, and you know your JVM is compatible with your Jar files. You also know that you either have coded your prototypes and procedures properly or have downloaded and properly compiled all the necessary source files.

So, even though it is a simple program, you've accomplished a lot. Not to mention that you have just gained the confidence to plow through the rest of the topics to learn how to generate high-quality electronic reports and add great value to your software in the eyes of your users. Congratulations!

PDF Metadata

Before we dive into all the different kinds of content we'll be putting into our PDFs, let's take a moment to talk about the metadata that you can assign to that content.

In iText, you can assign metadata to a file. I have found this feature useful for recording information about the users who create files. If you have a program that lets you select options during report generation, you can also store those options here to re-create the report.

You access the metadata of an existing PDF by looking at the properties, which are usually available from the **File** menu of your PDF viewer. Figure 10.37 shows the PDF properties window displaying the metadata for our sample PDF.

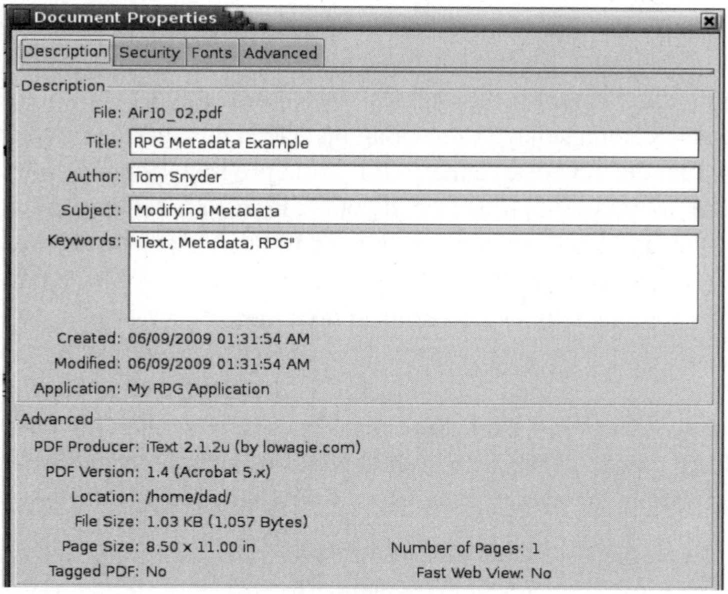

Figure 10.37: PDF properties window displaying metadata

The available methods, shown in Figure 10.38, correspond to the labels on the properties window.

Method Summary	
boolean	**addAuthor**(String author) Adds the author to a Document.
boolean	**addCreationDate**() Adds the current date and time to a Document.
boolean	**addCreator**(String creator) Adds the creator to a Document.
boolean	**addKeywords**(String keywords) Adds the keywords to a Document.
boolean	**addSubject**(String subject) Adds the subject to a Document.
boolean	**addTitle**(String title) Adds the title to a Document.

Figure 10.38: Partial JavaDoc for metadata methods of Document class

The **addAuthor** method of the **Document** class (Figure 10.39) adds the specified author value to the metadata of the PDF.

```
D ITextDocument_addAuthor...
D                    PR              1N
D                                    EXTPROC(*JAVA
D                                    :'com.lowagie.text.Document'
D                                    :'addAuthor')
D   inString                         like(jString)
```

Figure 10.39: Prototype of addAuthor method of Document class

The **addCreationDate** method (Figure 10.40) adds the created date value to the PDF's metadata. This method has no parameters; it simply uses the date and time when the method is called.

```
D ITextDocument_addCreationDate...
D                    PR              1N
D                                    EXTPROC(*JAVA
D                                    :'com.lowagie.text.Document'
D                                    :'addCreationDate')
```

Figure 10.40: Prototype of addCreationDate method of Document class

The **addCreator** method (Figure 10.41) adds the specified creator value to the PDF's metadata. I usually put the program name here so that I can identify the program that created the file.

```
D ITextDocument_addCreator...
D                    PR              1N
D                                        EXTPROC(*JAVA
D                                        :'com.lowagie.text.Document'
D                                        :'addCreator')
D   inString                             like(jString)
```

Figure 10.41: Prototype of addCreator method of Document class

The **addKeywords** method (Figure 10.42) adds the specified keyword values to the PDF's metadata.

```
D ITextDocument_addKeywords...
D                    PR              1N
D                                        EXTPROC(*JAVA
D                                        :'com.lowagie.text.Document'
D                                        :'addKeywords')
D   inString                             like(jString)
```

Figure 10.42: Prototype of addKeywords method of Document class

The **addSubject** method (Figure 10.43) adds the specified subject value to the PDF's metadata.

```
D ITextDocument_addSubject...
D                    PR              1N
D                                        EXTPROC(*JAVA
D                                        :'com.lowagie.text.Document'
D                                        :'addSubject')
D   inString                             like(jString)
```

Figure 10.43: Prototype of addSubject method of Document class

Last, the **addTitle** method (Figure 10.44) adds the specified title value to the metadata of the PDF.

```
D ITextDocument_addTitle...
D                   PR            1N
D                                      EXTPROC(*JAVA
D                                      :'com.lowagie.text.Document'
D                                      :'addTitle')
D   inString                           like(jString)
```

Figure 10.44: Prototype of addTitle method of Document class

For all but one of the metadata methods, we'll provide a custom procedure in service program **SVAIRPDF** to put the EBCDIC bytes into a **String** object to use with the method. The one exception is the creation date method, which has no parameter, so the byte processing is not necessary.

Figure 10.45 shows the custom procedure that prepares the bytes for use with the **addTitle** method of the **Document** class. The other metadata methods will have similar procedures associated with them.

```
P AirPdf_addTitle...
P                   B              EXPORT
D AirPdf_addTitle...
D                   PI
D   argDocument                    like(ITextDocument)
D   argBytes            65535A     const varying options(*varsize)
D   svString        S              like(jString)
 /free
   svString = new_String(%trim(argBytes));
   ITextDocument_addTitle(argDocument: svString);
   // Clean Up
   freeLocalRef(svString);
   return;
 /end-free
P                   E
```

Figure 10.45: AirPdf_addTitle procedure

With all the metadata prototypes and procedures out of the way, we can write the PDF metadata program in RPG (Figure 10.46). In the metadata displayed in the properties window above, you can see that the size is 8.50 x 11.00 inches, which is the page size of **LETTER**. The program sets this value during the creation of the output document using the optional parameter of the **AirPdf_newDocumentOutput** procedure.

```
       .
       . <Insert common header code here (Figure 10.3)>
       .
D  airDocument    S                LIKE(ITextDocument)
D  airParagraph   S                LIKE(ITextParagraph)
D  airMessage     S        1024A   VARYING
D  airFileName    S        1024A   VARYING
 /free
  CallP JavaServiceProgram();
  airFileName = '/Public/Air10_02.pdf';
  airDocument = AirPdf_newDocumentOutput(%trim(airFileName):'LETTER');
  airMessage = 'Look at Properties to see Metadata!';
  airParagraph = AirPdf_newParagraph(airMessage);
  ITextDocument_add(airDocument: airParagraph);
  AirPdf_addTitle(airDocument: 'RPG Metadata Example');
  AirPdf_addSubject(airDocument: 'Modifying Metadata');
  AirPdf_addKeywords(airDocument: 'iText, Metadata, RPG');
  AirPdf_addCreator(airDocument: 'My RPG Application');
  AirPdf_addAuthor(airDocument: 'Tom Snyder');
  ITextDocument_addCreationDate(airDocument);
  ITextDocument_close(airDocument);
  // Clean Up
       .
       . <Insert cleanup code here>
       .
  *inlr = *ON;
 /end-free
```

Figure 10.46: RPG program using metadata in a PDF

Here we have another simple RPG program to generate a PDF file. The text in the document will tell the user to look at the properties to find the metadata. When the user opens the properties window, something similar to what you saw in Figure 10.35 will be displayed.

At this point, you have enough information to convert your existing spool file reports using simple text into PDF format. In the next chapter, we'll explore some of the formatting options that are available with iText to really make your reports look good.

11

PDF Formatting

Colors and fonts will be our first step in PDF formatting.

Figure 11.1 shows the sample PDF we'll create in this chapter, which features colored text of varied size and font style. If you were to view this image in color, the first line of text would be in a shade of green, and the second line would be blue.

Figure 11.1: Fonts and colors PDF

Colors

To specify colors in iText, we will use the **Color** class that is available with Java. Figure 11.2 shows the definition of the RPG object reference variable for the class.

```
D JavaColor...
D                    S              O    CLASS(*JAVA
D                                        :'java.awt.Color')
```

Figure 11.2: JavaColor RPG object reference in SPAIRJAVA

Several constructors are available for the **Color** class, but there is no default constructor. This is because when you create an instance of the **Color** class, it must know what color it is. So, this forces you to assign the color when the **Color** class is created. Figure 11.3 shows the constructor we'll use, which uses an **int** parameter to specify the color.

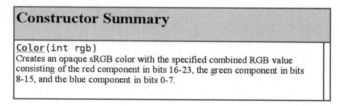

Figure 11.3: Partial JavaDoc for one of the Color constructor methods

Figure 11.4 shows the RPG prototype for this constructor.

```
D new_Color...
D                    PR             like(JavaColor)
D                                   ExtProc(*JAVA
D                                   :'java.awt.Color'
D                                   :*CONSTRUCTOR)
D   argInt                          like(jInt) value
```

Figure 11.4: Prototype for constructor method of Color class in SPAIRJAVA

If you have ever worked with colors in HTML, you are probably familiar with the hexadecimal codes used to determine the colors on a Web page. We'll be using the same hex codes within our PDFs. I am not a graphic designer, but I wanted my PDFs to look their best, so I recruited a graphic designer to help me design the templates for the reports, and speaking in hexadecimal color codes was an appreciative beginning.

Java offers tons of methods to do many things so that you don't have to reinvent the wheel; it's just a matter of learning about them. Without drifting too far from the topic of PDFs, I want to briefly discuss one such method, the **parseInt** method of the Integer class in **SPAIRJAVA** (Figure 11.5).

Method Summary	
Static int	**parseInt**(String s, int radix) Parses the string argument as a signed integer in the radix specified by the second argument.

Figure 11.5: Partial JavaDoc for parseInt method of java.lang.Integer class

The **parseInt** method will help us to use the standard HTML hexadecimal codes with our colors by accepting a **String** object that will contain the hex values extracted from the **String**. The method will then convert the value from hexadecimal to **int** by specifying a radix of 16 in the second parameter. Figure 11.6 shows the prototype for **parseInt** method of the **Integer** class in **SPAIRJAVA**.

```
D Integer_parseIntWithRadix...
D                  PR                 like(jInt)
D                                     ExtProc(*JAVA
D                                     :'java.lang.Integer'
D                                     :'parseInt')
D                                     static
D    argString                        like(jString)
D    argRadix                         like(jInt) value
```

Figure 11.6: Prototype for parseInt method of Integer class in SPAIRJAVA

For a quick refresher on radixes, integers have a number set of 0 through 9 for a total of 10 numbers, which is a radix of 10. For hexadecimal, the number set goes from 0 to 9 with the additional six characters A through F, which is a radix of 16.

To easily support the HTML hex codes, we'll create a custom procedure (Figure 11.7) to take care of all the hexadecimal-to-integer business.

```
*****************************************************************
 * Air_getColorFromHex(): Gets a Color using the HTML Hex Colors
 * Uses 6 character HTML Hex Codes, refer to CONSTANTS
*****************************************************************
P Air_getColorFromHex...
P                   B                    EXPORT
D Air_getColorFromHex...
D                   PI                   like(JavaColor)
D  argHexColor                     6A    const
D svString          S                    like(jString)
D svColor           S                    like(JavaColor)
D                                         inz(*NULL)
D svRadix           S                    like(jInt) inz(16)
 /free
   svString = new_String(%trim(argHexColor));
   svColor = new_Color(Integer_parseIntWithRadix(svString: svRadix));
   freeLocalRef(svString);
   return svColor;
 /end-free
P                   E
```

Figure 11.7: Custom procedure to convert the hexadecimal string to an integer

Now that we have a custom procedure to convert the hexadecimal codes used with HTML to create **Color** objects, you could search the Web for a plethora of available colors and their names. I have defined a small set of colors in the **SPAIRJAVA** file (Figure 11.8) that you can grow to be as large as desired.

```
D*****************************************************************
D* HTML HEX COLORS
D*****************************************************************
D COLOR_BLACK...
D                   C                    '000000'
D COLOR_RED...
D                   C                    'FF0000'
D COLOR_CRIMSON...
D                   C                    'DC143C'
D COLOR_GREEN...
D                   C                    '00FF00'
D COLOR_LIME_GREEN...
D                   C                    '32CD32'
```

```
D COLOR_SEA_GREEN...
D                 C              '2E8B57'
D COLOR_BLUE...
D                 C              '0000FF'
D COLOR_DARK_BLUE...
D                 C              '00008B'
D COLOR_CORNFLOWER_BLUE...
D                 C              '6495ED'
D COLOR_ROYAL_BLUE...
D                 C              '4169E1'
```

Figure 11.8: Partial list of hexadecimal Color constants in SPAIRJAVA

Fonts

iText provides a **Font** class, which we'll name **ITextFont** in our prototypes (Figure 11.9).

```
D ITextFont...
D              S          O    CLASS(*JAVA
D                               :'com.lowagie.text-
D                               .Font')
```

Figure 11.9: iText Font RPG object reference in SPAIRPDF

Several **Font** constructors are available in iText. To create our new font, we'll use the one that accepts the **Family**, **Size**, and **Style** parameters. Figure 11.10 shows the prototype for this constructor.

```
D new_ITextFont...
D              PR               like(ITextFont)
D                               ExtProc(*JAVA:
D                               'com.lowagie.text-
D                               .Font':
D                               *CONSTRUCTOR)
D  inFamily                     like(jInt) value
D  inSize                       like(jFloat) value
D  inStyle                      like(jInt) value
```

Figure 11.10: Prototype for constructor method of iText Font class

The size parameter will be a numeric value that determines the size. The family and style will be determined from constants we'll define in the **SPAIRPDF** file

(Figure 11.11). You can find these constants defined in the JavaDocs for the **Font** class.

```
D*********************************************************************
D* com.lowagie.text.Font Constant Field Values
D*********************************************************************
D ITEXT_FONT_BOLD...
D                      C                    1
D ITEXT_FONT_BOLD_ITALIC...
D                      C                    3
D ITEXT_FONT_HELVETICA...
D                      C                    1
D ITEXT_FONT_ITALIC...
D                      C                    2
D ITEXT_FONT_NORMAL...
D                      C                    0
```

Figure 11.11: Partial list of constants for iText Font class in SPAIRPDF

We'll set the color of the font using the **setColor** method of the **Font** class that is provided with iText (Figure 11.12).

Method Summary	
void	**setColor**(Color color) Sets the color.

Figure 11.12: Partial JavaDoc for setColor method of Font class

We'll use the **setColor** method that uses the Java **Color** class we defined in Figure 11.2 as the parameter. The **Color** object will be created using the **Air_getColorFromHex** procedure that we created in Figure 11.7. Figure 11.13 shows the prototype for the **setColor** method of the iText **Font** class.

```
D ITextFont_setColor...
D                      PR                   EXTPROC(*JAVA
D                                           :'com.lowagie.text.Font'
D                                           :'setColor')
D  inColor                                  like(JavaColor)
```

Figure 11.13: Prototype for setColor method of iText Font class

We are now ready to create the program that will generate the PDF you saw at the beginning of the chapter. Figure 11.14 shows the first part of the RPG code.

```
     .
     .  <Insert common header code here (Figure 10.3)>
     .
  D  airBytes       S           1024A    varying
  D  airFileName    S           1024A    varying
  D  airString      S                    like(jString)
  D  airDocument    S                    like(ITextDocument)
  D  airParagraph   S                    like(ITextParagraph)
  D  airFontGreen   S                    like(ITextFont)
  D  airColorGreen  S                    like(JavaColor)
  D  airFontBlue    S                    like(ITextFont)
  D  airColorBlue   S                    like(JavaColor)
   /free
    CallP JavaServiceProgram();
    airFileName = '/Public/Air11_01.pdf';
    airDocument = AirPdf_newDocumentOutput(airFileName:'LETTER':*ON);
    //
    airColorGreen = Air_getColorFromHex(COLOR_SEA_GREEN);
    airFontGreen = new_ITextFont(ITEXT_FONT_HELVETICA: 22:
                                 ITEXT_FONT_BOLD);
    ITextFont_setColor(airFontGreen: airColorGreen);
    airColorBlue = Air_getColorFromHex(COLOR_CORNFLOWER_BLUE);
    airFontBlue = new_ITextFont(ITEXT_FONT_HELVETICA: 16:
                                ITEXT_FONT_BOLD_ITALIC);
    ITextFont_setColor(airFontBlue: airColorBlue);
```

Figure 11.14: RPG program using colors and fonts in PDF (part 1 of 2)

Our document will have the **LETTER** page size, and you can also see that it will be rotated to landscape orientation through the use of the optional ***ON** parameter in the **AirPdf_newDocumentOutput** procedure.

The preceding code creates the color using the custom **Air_getColorFromHex** procedure and the **COLOR** constants defined in **SPAIRJAVA**. After creating the font, the procedure assigns the color using the **setColor** method of the **ITextFont** class.

As Figure 11.15 shows, assigning the font to the paragraph is as easy as passing the font into the **AirPdf_newParagraph** procedure as a parameter. The font is an optional parameter of this procedure, which we created in Chapter 10 (Figure 10.22).

```
//
airParagraph = AirPdf_newParagraph(
                'COLOR_SEA_GREEN, Helvetica, Bold, 22':
                airFontGreen);
ITextDocument_add(airDocument: airParagraph);
//
airParagraph = AirPdf_newParagraph(
                'COLOR_CORNFLOWER_BLUE, Helvetica, Bold/Italic, 16':
                airFontBlue);
ITextDocument_add(airDocument: airParagraph);
//
ITextDocument_close(airDocument);
// Clean Up
  .
  . <Insert cleanup code here>
  .
*inlr = *ON;
/end-free
```

Figure 11.15: RPG program using colors and fonts in PDF (part 2 of 2)

PDF Tables

In the next example, we'll create a table. I thought my kids would have a little fun with this one, so I let them choose the contents of the table. We'll be creating a simple table that will be populated with some of my kids' favorite things. Figure 11.16 shows the sample table.

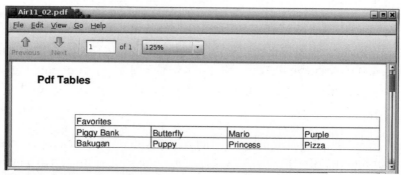

Figure 11.16: PDF with a table

We will use the iText **PdfPTable** class to create the table in the PDF. Figure 11.17 shows the prototype for the constructor method of the **PdfPTable** class.

```
D new_PdfPTable...
D                    PR                like(PdfPTable)
D                                      ExtProc(*JAVA
D                                      :'com.lowagie.text.pdf-
D                                      .PdfPTable'
D                                      :*CONSTRUCTOR)
D  inColumns                           like(jInt) value
```

Figure 11.17: Prototype for constructor method of iText PdfPTable class

Just as we added cells to sheets in the Excel chapters, we'll be adding cells to our PDF table to contain the data. Figure 11.18 shows the default constructor method of the iText **PdfPCell** class.

```
D new_PdfPCell...
D                    PR                like(PdfPCell)
D                                      ExtProc(*JAVA
D                                      :'com.lowagie.text.pdf-
D                                      .PdfPCell'
D                                      :*CONSTRUCTOR)
```

Figure 11.18: Prototype for default constructor method of iText PdfPCell class

As an alternative to using the default constructor of **PdfPCell**, you can construct cells and initialize them by passing in a **Phrase** object (Figure 11.19).

```
D new_PdfPCellFromPhrase...
D                    PR                like(PdfPCell)
D                                      ExtProc(*JAVA
D                                      :'com.lowagie.text.pdf-
D                                      .PdfPCell'
D                                      :*CONSTRUCTOR)
D  inPhrase                            like(ITextPhrase)
```

Figure 11.19: Prototype for constructor method of iText PdfPCell class with Phrase

If you've ever worked with HTML, you may be familiar with the **colspan** concept. The **colspan** attribute lets you specify a width for the table cell that is relative to the columns in the table. For example, you could make one cell as wide as several cells within a table. The **setColSpan** method of the **PdfPCell** class sets the column span property (Figure 11.20).

```
D PdfPCell_setColSpan...
D                     PR                    EXTPROC(*JAVA
D                                           :'com.lowagie.text.pdf-
D                                           .PdfPCell'
D                                           :'setColspan')
D   argColSpan                              like(jint) value
```

Figure 11.20: Prototype for setColSpan method of iText PdfPCell class

To add the cells to the table, we can use the **addCell** method of the **PdfPTable** class (Figure 11.21).

```
D PdfPTable_addCell...
D                     PR                    EXTPROC(*JAVA
D                                           :'com.lowagie.text.pdf-
D                                           .PdfPTable'
D                                           :'addCell')
D   argCell                                 like(PdfPCell)
```

Figure 11.21: Prototype for addCell method of iText PdfPTable class

When you're creating a simple text cell to add to a table, you can skip right over the creation of the cell and use the **addCell** method with a string object. This approach creates the cell, populating it with the **String**. Figure 11.22 shows the prototype for this variation of the method.

```
D PdfPTable_addStringCell...
D                     PR                    EXTPROC(*JAVA
D                                           :'com.lowagie.text.pdf-
D                                           .PdfPTable'
D                                           :'addCell')
D   argString                               like(jString)
```

Figure 11.22: Prototype for addStringCell method of iText PdfPTable class

That's all the cell stuff we need to create the sample table. Time to get coding! Figure 11.23 shows the first part of the RPG program.

```
  .
  .  <Insert common header code here (Figure 10.3)>
  .
D  airFileName    S         1024A    varying
D  airString      S                  like(jString)
D  airDocument    S                  like(ITextDocument)
D  airParagraph   S                  like(ITextParagraph)
D  airFontHead    S                  like(ITextFont)
D  airNewLine     S                  like(ITextChunk)
D  airTable       S                  like(PdfPTable)
D  airCell        S                  like(PdfPCell)
D  i              S            3S 0
C/EJECT
 /free
  CallP JavaServiceProgram();
  //
  airString = new_String(EBCDIC_CR + EBCDIC_LF);
  airNewLine = new_ITextChunk(airString);
  airFileName = '/Public/Air11_02.pdf';
  airDocument = AirPdf_newDocumentOutput(airFileName:'LETTER');
  airString = new_String(%trim(airFileName));
  //
  airFontHead = new_ITextFont(ITEXT_FONT_HELVETICA: 15:
                              ITEXT_FONT_BOLD);
  //------------------------------------------------------------
  airParagraph = AirPdf_newParagraph('Pdf Tables':
                                      airFontHead);
  ITextDocument_add(airDocument: airParagraph);
  //
  ITextDocument_add(airDocument: airNewLine);
  //
  airParagraph = AirPdf_newParagraph('Favorites');
  airTable = new_PdfPTable(4);
```

Figure 11.23: RPG program using tables in PDF (part 1 of 3)

The number of columns is specified when the **PdfPTable** object is created by passing an integer into the constructor method.

Figure 11.24 shows the next part of the program.

```
  airCell = new_PdfPCellFromPhrase(airParagraph);
  PdfPCell_setColSpan(airCell: 4);
  PdfPTable_addCell(airTable: airCell);
```

Figure 11.24: RPG program using tables in PDF (part 2 of 3)

This code sets the column span of the header cell to 4, which stretches this cell to a width equal to the width of four regular cells to create the expected header appearance for our table. Once the attributes and contents of the header cell are defined, the program adds the cell to the table using the **addCell** method of the **PdfPTable** class.

Next, the code shown in Figure 11.25 populates the contents of the cells in the table using the **AirPdf_addTableStringCell** procedure, which implements the **addCell** method of the **PdfPTable** class. At the time this book was written, the **addCell** method is overridden to accept **Image** objects, **PdfPCell** objects, **PdfPTable** objects, **Phrase** objects, and **String** objects. So, you have some flexibility with the cells in the tables.

```
AirPdf_addTableStringCell(airTable: 'Piggy Bank');
AirPdf_addTableStringCell(airTable: 'Butterfly');
AirPdf_addTableStringCell(airTable: 'Mario');
AirPdf_addTableStringCell(airTable: 'Purple');
AirPdf_addTableStringCell(airTable: 'Bakugan');
AirPdf_addTableStringCell(airTable: 'Puppy');
AirPdf_addTableStringCell(airTable: 'Princess');
AirPdf_addTableStringCell(airTable: 'Pizza');
ITextDocument_add(airDocument: airTable);
//------------------------------------------------------------
ITextDocument_close(airDocument);
// Clean Up
  .
  . <Insert cleanup code here>
  .
*inlr = *ON;
/end-free
```

Figure 11.25: RPG program using tables in PDF (part 3 of 3)

The **PdfPTable** class implements the **Element** interface, so you could add the table to the document just as you would a text element, using the add method of the **Document**.

The cells that are added to the table will start from the left and will be added to the right until the number of columns specified when the table was created is reached; then the program will automatically create a new row and start from the left again. This process will be repeated until all the cells are added to the table.

Adding a New Page

You can indicate a new document page by using the **newPage** method of the **Document** class (Figure 11.26).

```
D ITextDocument_newPage...
D                    PR           1N
D                                     EXTPROC(*JAVA
D                                     :'com.lowagie.text.Document'
D                                     :'newPage')
```

Figure 11.26: Prototype for newPage method of iText Document class

The next example, which illustrates the use of hyperlinks, will include an example of the implementation of multiple pages.

Hyperlinks

Figures 11.27 and 11.28 show the two pages of the PDF we'll construct to illustrate the use of hyperlinks. You can create hyperlinks to be internal to the PDF, or you can link to a Web site. For this example, clicking on the link that jumps to the internal label of this PDF will take you to the second page of the PDF.

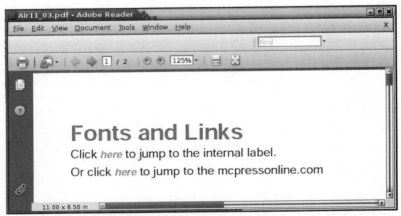

Figure 11.27: PDF with internal and external hyperlinks (page 1 of 2)

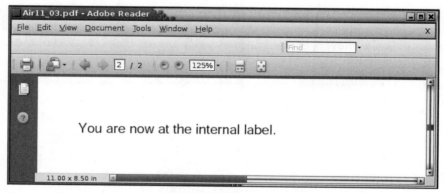

Figure 11.28: PDF with internal and external hyperlinks (page 2 of 2)

In iText, hyperlinks are created using *anchors*. We'll work with two of the constructors for the **Anchor** class. The first constructor accepts a **String** object to specify the link (Figure 11.29).

```
D new_ITextAnchor...
D                    PR                  like(ITextAnchor)
D                                        ExtProc(*JAVA:
D                                        'com.lowagie.text-
D                                        .Anchor':
D                                        *CONSTRUCTOR)
D   inString                             like(jString)
```

Figure 11.29: Prototype for constructor method of iText Anchor class

The second constructor also accepts a font to use when displaying the anchor in the PDF (Figure 11.30).

```
D new_ITextAnchorFromFont...
D                    PR                  like(ITextAnchor)
D                                        ExtProc(*JAVA:
D                                        'com.lowagie.text-
D                                        .Anchor':
D                                        *CONSTRUCTOR)
D   inString                             like(jString)
D   inFont                               like(ITextFont)
```

Figure 11.30: Prototype for constructor method of iText Anchor class using Font

We will emulate the overridden constructors and handle the conversion between bytes and Java **String** objects with a standard custom procedure (Figure 11.31). The optional font parameter will determine which constructor to use.

```
P AirPdf_newAnchor...
P                     B                    EXPORT
D AirPdf_newAnchor...
D                     PI                   like(ITextAnchor)
D   argBytes                    65535A     const varying
D                                          options(*varsize)
D   argFont                                like(ITextFont)
D                                          options(*nopass)
D   svString        S                      like(jString)
D   svAnchor        S                      like(ITextAnchor)
D                                          inz(*NULL)
 /free
   svString = new_String(argBytes);
   if (%parms > 1);
     svAnchor = new_ITextAnchorFromFont(svString: argFont);
   else;
     svAnchor = new_ITextAnchor(svString);
   endif;
   // Clean Up
   freeLocalRef(svString);
   return svAnchor;
 /end-free
P                     E
```

Figure 11.31: Custom procedure to create iText anchors

An anchor creates a distinct reference location within the PDF that can link either to an external location or to a location that is internal to the PDF with which you're working. The **setReference** method of the **Anchor** class (Figure 11.32) lets us specify the location we want to jump to when the user clicks the anchor text in the PDF.

```
D ITextAnchor_setReference...
D                     PR                   EXTPROC(*JAVA
D                                          :'com.lowagie.text.Anchor'
D                                          :'setReference')
D   inString                               like(jString)
```

Figure 11.32: Prototype for setReference method of iText Anchor class

Figure 11.33 shows the custom procedure to convert the bytes to a **String** object for use with the **setReference** method.

```
P AirPdf_setAnchorReference...
P                   B                 EXPORT
D AirPdf_setAnchorReference...
D                   PI
D   argAnchor                         like(ITextAnchor)
D   argBytes                  65535A  const varying
D                                     options(*varsize)
D   svString        S                 like(jString)
 /free
  svString = new_String(argBytes);
  ITextAnchor_setReference(argAnchor: svString);
  // Clean Up
  freeLocalRef(svString);
  return;
 /end-free
P                   E
```

Figure 11.33: Custom procedure for iText anchor references

By using anchor references within a PDF, you can create internal links in the document that let users jump from one location to another. To do this, you need to create destination markers that tell the anchor where to jump. This is done by setting a name to an anchor using the **setName** method of the **Anchor** class (Figure 11.34).

```
D ITextAnchor_setName...
D                   PR                EXTPROC(*JAVA
D                                     :'com.lowagie.text.Anchor'
D                                     :'setName')
D   inString                         like(jString)
```

Figure 11.34: Prototype for setName method of iText Anchor class

> ### RPG anchor
> A named anchor is similar to the **TAG** statement in RPG. The **TAG** statement creates a point in the program that can be jumped to during program execution through use of the **GOTO** statement. You cannot **GOTO** a location if you don't have a **TAG** for the destination location.

Figure 11.35 shows the custom procedure to set an iText anchor name.

```
P AirPdf_setAnchorName...
P                 B                        EXPORT
D AirPdf_setAnchorName...
D                 PI
D   argAnchor                              like(ITextAnchor)
D   argBytes                   65535A      const varying
D                                          options(*varsize)
D   svString       S                       like(jString)
 /free
   svString = new_String(argBytes);
   ITextAnchor_setName(argAnchor: svString);
   // Clean Up
   freeLocalRef(svString);
   return;
 /end-free
P                 E
```

Figure 11.35: Custom procedure for iText anchor names

Named anchors are needed only for internal links. When you are jumping to an external URL, you specify the URL to jump to.

The **Chunk** class offers alternatives to the anchor methods we're using that let you specify links and references. You can also use the **setRemoteGoto** method of the **Chunk** class to link to external PDFs, and you may want to extend the service program to support this functionality in the future.

For our sample program, we'll try out both the internal and external capabilities of the iText anchors. Figure 11.36 shows the first part of the RPG program.

```
   .
   . <Insert common header code here (Figure 10.3)>
   .
D   airBytes       S          1024A      varying
D   airFileName    S          1024A      varying
D   airString      S                     like(jString)
D   airDocument    S                     like(ITextDocument)
D   airParagraph   S                     like(ITextParagraph)
D   airAnchor      S                     like(ITextAnchor)
D   airFontHead    S                     like(ITextFont)
D   airColorHead   S                     like(JavaColor)
```

```
D  airFont        S                        like(ITextFont)
D  airColor       S                        like(JavaColor)
 /free
   CallP JavaServiceProgram();
   airFileName = '/Public/Air11_03.pdf';
   airDocument = AirPdf_newDocumentOutput(airFileName:'LETTER':*ON);
   //
   airColorHead = Air_getColorFromHex(COLOR_SEA_GREEN);
   airFontHead = new_ITextFont(ITEXT_FONT_HELVETICA: 22:
                               ITEXT_FONT_BOLD);
   ITextFont_setColor(airFontHead: airColorHead);
   airColor = Air_getColorFromHex(COLOR_CORNFLOWER_BLUE);
   airFont = new_ITextFont(ITEXT_FONT_HELVETICA: 10:
                           ITEXT_FONT_BOLD_ITALIC);
   ITextFont_setColor(airFont: airColor);
   //
   airParagraph = AirPdf_newParagraph('Fonts and Links':
                                      airFontHead);
   ITextDocument_add(airDocument: airParagraph);
   //
   airParagraph = AirPdf_newParagraph('Click ');
```

Figure 11.36: RPG program using hyperlinks in PDF (part 1 of 4)

At this point, we have all the content prior to our first anchor. The first word of the sentence containing the link is added to the **Paragraph** object. Next (Figure 11.37), we create the anchor and add it to the paragraph.

```
   airAnchor = AirPdf_newAnchor('here': airFont);
   AirPdf_setAnchorReference(airAnchor: '#label');
   ITextParagraph_add(airParagraph: airAnchor);
```

Figure 11.37: RPG program using hyperlinks in PDF (part 2 of 4)

When the program adds the anchor to the paragraph, it appends it to the existing text in the paragraph. The reference that is being assigned to the anchor will be an internal link, so you need to precede the anchor name with the number sign (#). So, in this example, the anchor will be looking for an anchor named **'label'**.

The rest of the sentence is completed by appending the remainder of the string to the paragraph. Then, we create another anchor to be used for the external link (Figure 11.38).

```
airString = new_String(' to jump to the internal label.');
ITextParagraph_add(airParagraph: airString);
ITextDocument_add(airDocument: airParagraph);
//
airParagraph = AirPdf_newParagraph('Or click ');
//
airAnchor = AirPdf_newAnchor('here': airFont);
airBytes = 'http://www.mcpressonline.com';
AirPdf_setAnchorReference(airAnchor: airBytes);
ITextParagraph_add(airParagraph: airAnchor);
```

Figure 11.38: RPG program using hyperlinks in PDF (part 3 of 4)

The external link will not have the number sign in the anchor reference. This link will use the same **setReference** method of the **Anchor** class as the internal link.

To clearly indicate the jump when we click on the internal link of the document, we'll create a second page in our PDF that will contain the named anchor (Figure 11.39).

```
airString = new_String(' to jump to the mcpressonline.com');
ITextParagraph_add(airParagraph: airString);
ITextDocument_add(airDocument: airParagraph);
// Create a new page
ITextDocument_newPage(airDocument);
//
airBytes = 'You are now at the internal label.';
airAnchor = AirPdf_newAnchor(airBytes);
AirPdf_setAnchorName(airAnchor: 'label');
ITextDocument_add(airDocument: airAnchor);
//
ITextDocument_close(airDocument);
// Clean Up
  .
  . <Insert cleanup code here>
  .
*inlr = *ON;
/end-free
```

Figure 11.39: RPG program using hyperlinks in PDF (part 4 of 4)

The **setAnchorName** method of the **Anchor** class is used here to assign the name to the anchor to jump to internally.

Lists

The last topic I'll touch on related to PDF formatting is lists. Lists provide an easy way to format the data in your PDF in an appealing way. Lists automatically format the items within them to be indented, with a corresponding bullet for each item in the list. Figure 11.40 shows a sample PDF with an unordered and an ordered list.

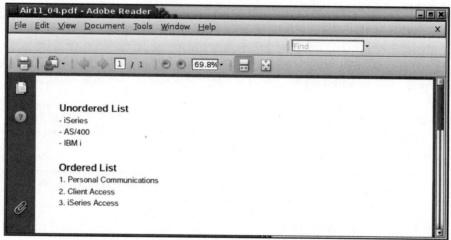

Figure 11.40: PDF with unordered and ordered lists

iText provides the **List** class (Figure 11.41) to work with the lists.

```
D ITextList...
D                    S            O    CLASS(*JAVA
D                                      :'com.lowagie.text-
D                                      .List')
```

Figure 11.41: iText List RPG object reference

When we construct the **List** objects, we'll indicate whether the list is numbered or not. Figure 11.42 shows the **List** constructor method prototype.

```
D new_ITextList...
D                     PR                    like(ITextList)
D                                           ExtProc(*JAVA:
D                                           'com.lowagie.text-
D                                           .List':
D                                           *CONSTRUCTOR)
D   inNumbered                        1N    value
```

Figure 11.42: Prototype for constructor method of iText List class

Figure 11.43 shows the constant values that can be used. These values are defined in the JavaDocs and have been placed into the **SPAIRPDF** file.

```
D*****************************************************************
D* com.lowagie.text.List Constant Field Values
D*****************************************************************
D ITEXT_LIST_ALPHABETICAL...
D                     C                     CONST(*ON)
D ITEXT_LIST_LOWERCASE...
D                     C                     CONST(*ON)
D ITEXT_LIST_NUMERICAL...
D                     C                     CONST(*OFF)
D ITEXT_LIST_ORDERED...
D                     C                     CONST(*ON)
D ITEXT_LIST_UNORDERED...
D                     C                     CONST(*OFF)
D ITEXT_LIST_UPPERCASE...
D                     C                     CONST(*OFF)
```

Figure 11.43: Partial list of constants for iText List class in SPAIRPDF

You add items to a list using the **add** method of the **List** class (Figure 11.44). The method accepts any **Object** as a parameter.

```
D ITextList_add...
D                     PR              1N
D                                           EXTPROC(*JAVA
D                                           :'com.lowagie.text.List'
D                                           :'add')
D   inObject                                like(jObject)
```

Figure 11.44: Prototype for add method of iText List class

The **jobject** reference (Figure 11.45) is defined in the JNI source member of the
QRPGLESRC file of the **QSYSINC** library.

```
D jobject          S                 O    CLASS(*JAVA
D                                         : 'java.lang.Object')
```

Figure 11.45: RPG object reference in the QSYSINC/QRPGLESRC,JNI file

And that is it for the preliminaries for our **List** program. For this example, we will
create two lists: one unordered and one ordered. Figure 11.46 shows the first part
of the RPG program.

```
.
.   <Insert common header code here (Figure 10.3)>
.
D  airFileName     S            1024A    varying
D  airString       S                     like(jString)
D  airDocument     S                     like(ITextDocument)
D  airParagraph    S                     like(ITextParagraph)
D  airList         S                     like(ITextList)
D  airFontHead     S                     like(ITextFont)
D  airNewLine      S                     like(ITextChunk)
 /free
   CallP JavaServiceProgram();
   airFileName = '/Public/Air11_04.pdf';
   airDocument = AirPdf_newDocumentOutput(airFileName:'LETTER');
   airString = new_String(EBCDIC_CR + EBCDIC_LF);
   airNewLine = new_ITextChunk(airString);
   //
   airFontHead = new_ITextFont(ITEXT_FONT_HELVETICA: 15:
                               ITEXT_FONT_BOLD);
   //
   airParagraph = AirPdf_newParagraph('Unordered List':
                                      airFontHead);
   ITextDocument_add(airDocument: airParagraph);
   //
   airList = new_ITextList(ITEXT_LIST_UNORDERED);
   airString = new_String('iSeries');
   ITextList_add(airList: airString);
   airString = new_String('AS/400');
   ITextList_add(airList: airString);
   airString = new_String('IBM i');
   ITextList_add(airList: airString);
   ITextDocument_add(airDocument: airList);
   //
   ITextDocument_add(airDocument: airNewLine);
```

Figure 11.46: RPG program using lists in PDF (part 1 of 2)

Our first list will be an unordered list, which is indicated when the **List** object is constructed using the **ITEXT_LIST_UNORDERED** constant. The **add** method of the **List** class is very versatile with respect to the **Object** parameter, so I did not create a custom procedure for this, although you could do so. I simply created the **String** objects and passed them directly to the prototyped **add** method of the **List** class (Figure 11.47).

```
airParagraph = AirPdf_newParagraph('Ordered List':
                                    airFontHead);
ITextDocument_add(airDocument: airParagraph);
//
airList = new_ITextList(ITEXT_LIST_ORDERED);
airString = new_String('Personal Communications');
ITextList_add(airList: airString);
airString = new_String('Client Access');
ITextList_add(airList: airString);
airString = new_String('iSeries Access');
ITextList_add(airList: airString);
ITextDocument_add(airDocument: airList);
//
ITextDocument_close(airDocument);
// Clean Up
  .
  . <Insert cleanup code here>
  .
*inlr = *ON;
/end-free
```

Figure 11.47: RPG program using lists in PDF (part 2 of 2)

To create the ordered list, you just specify the **ITEXT_LIST_ORDERED** constant when creating the list, and the numbering and formatting is handled automatically. You simply add the items the same way we did for the unordered list.

Well, that should be a good start for the text content in your PDF files. In the next chapter, we'll discuss images and bar codes.

12

PDF Images and Bar Codes

We have a few more topics to cover before you're through with your crash course in creating PDFs using Java and RPG. In this chapter, you'll learn how easy it is to incorporate images and bar codes into your PDF documents.

Images with Borders

Our first image example will create a PDF containing an image with a border. Figure 12.1 shows the sample document.

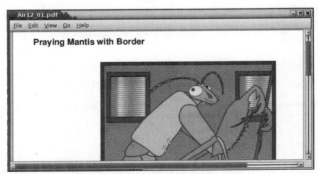

Figure 12.1: PDF containing an image with a border

We'll use the iText **Image** class (Figure 12.2) to work with images in PDF files.

```
D ITextImage...
D                 S              O    CLASS(*JAVA
D                                     :'com.lowagie.text-
D                                     .Image')
```

Figure 12.2: iText image RPG object reference in SPAIRPDF

Two methods from the **Image** class (Figure 12.3) will enable us to create and align the image shown in the PDF.

Method Summary	
static Image	getInstance(String filename) Gets an instance of an Image.
void	setAlignment(int alignment) Sets the alignment for the image.

Figure 12.3: Partial JavaDoc for iText image methods

The **getInstance** method of the **Image** class (Figure 12.4) lets us create an image by specifying the image file name and location. **getInstance** is a static method that creates an instance of the **Image** class.

```
D ITextImage_getInstance...
D                 PR             like(ITextImage)
D                                extProc(*JAVA
D                                :'com.lowagie.text.Image'
D                                :'getInstance')
D                                static
D   argImageName                 like(jString)
```

Figure 12.4: Prototype for getInstance method of iText Image class

We'll create a custom procedure (Figure 12.5) to convert our bytes into a Java **String** for use with the method and create an instance of the iText **Image** class.

```
P AirPdf_getImage...
P                 B              EXPORT
D AirPdf_getImage...
D                 PI             like(ITextImage)
D   argInFile         2048A      const varying options(*varsize)
```

```
D   svString        S                       like(jString)
D   svImage         S                       like(ITextImage)
D                                           inz(*NULL)
 /free
   // Create/Attach to JVM
   JNIEnv_P = getJNIEnv();
   svString = new_String(%trim(argInFile));
   monitor;
     svImage = ITextImage_getInstance(svString);
   on-error;
     svImage = *NULL;
   endmon;
   // Clean Up
   freeLocalRef(svString);
   return svImage;
 /end-free
P               E
```

Figure 12.5: Custom procedure to get an image

The **setAlignment** method (Figure 12.6) is used to control the horizontal alignment of the image within the document.

```
D ITextImage_setAlignment...
D                   PR                      EXTPROC(*JAVA
D                                           :'com.lowagie.text.Image'
D                                           :'setAlignment')
D   argAlign                                like(jInt) value
```

Figure 12.6: Prototype for setAlignment method of Image class

Several constants defined for the iText **Image** class let us specify alignments and other attributes. We'll define a partial list of the useful constants in the **SPAIRPDF** file (Figure 12.7).

```
D*********************************************************************
D* com.lowagie.text.Image Constant Field Values (Partial)
D*********************************************************************
D ITEXT_IMAGE_ALIGN_BASELINE...
D                   C                       7
D ITEXT_IMAGE_ALIGN_BOTTOM...
D                   C                       6
D ITEXT_IMAGE_ALIGN_CENTER...
D                   C                       1
D ITEXT_IMAGE_ALIGN_LEFT...
D                   C                       0
```

```
D ITEXT_IMAGE_ALIGN_MIDDLE...
D                        C              5
D ITEXT_IMAGE_ALIGN_RIGHT...
D                        C              2
D ITEXT_IMAGE_ALIGN_TOP...
D                        C              4
D ITEXT_IMAGE_BOTTOM...
D                        C              2
D ITEXT_IMAGE_BOX...
D                        C             15
D ITEXT_IMAGE_TOP...
D                        C              1
D ITEXT_IMAGE_TEXTWRAP...
D                        C              4
```

Figure 12.7: Partial list of iText Image constants

To create the border around the image, we'll use three methods inherited from the **Rectangle** class (Figure 12.8).

Method Summary	
void	**setBorder**(int border) Enables/Disables the border on the specified sides.
void	**setBorderColor**(Color borderColor) Sets the color of the border.
void	**setBorderWidth**(float borderWidth) Sets the borderwidth of the table.

Figure 12.8: Partial JavaDoc for iText Rectangle methods

The **Image** class of iText is a subclass of the **Rectangle** class, so the methods of **Rectangle** are inherited in the **Image** class and will be used to set the border on our image. We'll use the **setBorder** method of the **Image** class to specify the type of border to use. You indicate borders using constants that are defined in the **Rectangle** class. Figure 12.7 (above) provides a partial list of these constants. Figure 12.9 shows the prototype for the **setBorder** method.

```
D ITextImage_setBorder...
D                        PR              EXTPROC(*JAVA
D                                        :'com.lowagie.text.Image'
D                                        :'setBorder')
D   argValue                             like(jInt) value
```

Figure 12.9: Prototype for setBorder method of Image class (inherited from Rectangle)

The **setBorderWidth** method of the **Image** class controls the width of the border (Figure 12.10).

```
D ITextImage_setBorderWidth...
D                    PR                  EXTPROC(*JAVA
D                                        :'com.lowagie.text.Image'
D                                        :'setBorderWidth')
D  argWidth                              like(jFloat) value
```

Figure 12.10: Prototype for setBorderWidth method of Image class (inherited from Rectangle)

We'll specify the color of the border using the **setBorderColor** method of the **Image** class (Figure 12.11). The **java.awt.Color** class will be used to assign the color of the border.

```
D ITextImage_setBorderColor...
D                    PR                  EXTPROC(*JAVA
D                                        :'com.lowagie.text.Image'
D                                        :'setBorderColor')
D  argColor                              like(JavaColor)
```

Figure 12.11: Prototype for setBorderColor method of Image class (inherited from Rectangle)

Setting the color of the border could involve a few steps, but we'll simplify the process by creating a custom procedure (Figure 12.12) to take care of converting the hexadecimal value to a **Color** object and assigning the **Color** to the border of the image.

```
P AirPdf_setImageBorderColor...
P                    B                   EXPORT
D AirPdf_setImageBorderColor...
D                    PI
D  argImage                             like(ITextImage)
D  argColor                    6A        const
D  svColor          S                    like(JavaColor)
 /free
   svColor = Air_getColorFromHex(argColor);
   monitor;
     ITextImage_setBorderColor(argImage: svColor);
   on-error;
   endmon;
```

```
      // Clean Up
      freeLocalRef(svColor);
      return;
    /end-free
   P                        E
```

Figure 12.12: Custom procedure to set the image border color

Ah, I love using a generic procedure that was placed into a service program for a second time! Here, we are reusing the **Air_getColorFromHex(argColor)** procedure from Chapter 11 (Figure 11.7) to convert the hex string to a Java **Color** object.

Okay, enough appreciation for modular coding, and on to the sample program. We'll create the image, put a border around it, and add it to the document. Figure 12.13 shows the RPG program that does all this work.

```
      .
      .  <Insert common header code here (Figure 10.3)>
      .
   D   airFileName     S            1024A    varying
   D   airImageName    S            1024A    varying
   D   airBytes        S            1024A    varying
   D   airString       S                     like(jString)
   D   airDocument     S                     like(ITextDocument)
   D   airParagraph    S                     like(ITextParagraph)
   D   airFontHead     S                     like(ITextFont)
   D   airNewLine      S                     like(ITextChunk)
   D   airImage        S                     like(ITextImage)
   C/EJECT
    /free
     CallP JavaServiceProgram();
     airFileName = '/Public/Air12_01.pdf';
     airImageName = '/Public/mantis.png';
     airDocument = AirPdf_newDocumentOutput(airFileName:'LETTER');
     airString = new_String(EBCDIC_CR + EBCDIC_LF);
     airNewLine = new_ITextChunk(airString);
     //
     airFontHead = new_ITextFont(ITEXT_FONT_HELVETICA: 15:
                                 ITEXT_FONT_BOLD);
     //
```

```
airBytes = 'Praying Mantis with Border';
airParagraph = AirPdf_newParagraph(airBytes:
                                    airFontHead);
ITextDocument_add(airDocument: airParagraph);
//
ITextDocument_add(airDocument: airNewLine);
//
airImage = AirPdf_getImage(airImageName);
ITextImage_setAlignment(airImage: ITEXT_IMAGE_ALIGN_MIDDLE);
ITextImage_setBorder(airImage: ITEXT_IMAGE_BOX);
AirPdf_setImageBorderColor(airImage: COLOR_INDIGO);
ITextImage_setBorderWidth(airImage: 7);
ITextDocument_add(airDocument: airImage);
//
ITextDocument_close(airDocument);
// Clean Up
 .
 . <Insert cleanup code here>
 .
*inlr = *ON;
/end-free
```

Figure 12.13: RPG program using images with borders in PDF

Passing the **ITEXT_IMAGE_ALIGN_MIDDLE** constant as the argument to the **setAlignment** method of the **Image** class centers the image horizontally in the document. The border is then assigned to the image using the **setBorder** method. The border is specified to be a box, which will create the border on all four sides of the image.

The color of the border is next set to indigo using the **setImageBorderColor** method. The width of the border is set to 7 using the **setBorderWidth** method.

The iText **Image** class implements the **Element** interface, so we can add the image to the document using the **add** method of the **Document** class.

Images with Text Wrapping

When creating visually appealing reports using PDFs, it is fairly common to wrap text around images. To achieve this look, you just align the image where you want it on the page and activate the text wrap option. Figure 12.14 illustrates the text-wrapping feature of iText.

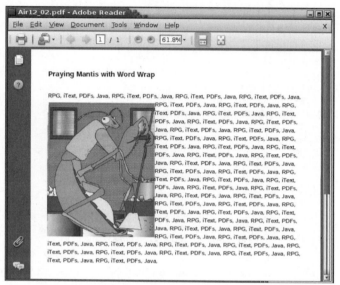

Figure 12.14: PDF containing an image with text wrapping

For this example, we'll reuse the image from the previous example and change the size of it within the document using the **scalePercent** method of the iText **Image** class (Figure 12.15).

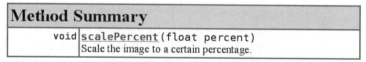

Figure 12.15: Partial JavaDoc for the scalePercent method of iText Image class

The **scalePercent** method accepts a **float** parameter to determine the percentage to resize the image when it is placed into the document. Figure 12.16 shows the prototype for the method.

```
D ITextImage_scalePercent...
D                    PR                    EXTPROC(*JAVA
D                                          :'com.lowagie.text.Image'
D                                          :'scalePercent')
D   argWidth                               like(jFloat) value
```

Figure 12.16: Prototype for scalePercent method of Image class

The rest of the procedures that we need have already been defined, so let's write the code to create the new PDF. Figure 12.17 shows the first portion of the RPG program.

```
      .
      . <Insert common header code here (Figure 10.3)>
      .
D   airFileName    S            1024A    varying
D   airImageName   S            1024A    varying
D   airBytes       S            1024A    varying
D   airString      S                     like(jString)
D   airDocument    S                     like(ITextDocument)
D   airParagraph   S                     like(ITextParagraph)
D   airPhrase      S                     like(ITextPhrase)
D   airFontHead    S                     like(ITextFont)
D   airNewLine     S                     like(ITextChunk)
D   airImage       S                     like(ITextImage)
D   airAlignment   S                     like(jInt)
D   i              S            3S 0
C/EJECT
 /free
  CallP JavaServiceProgram();
  airFileName = '/Public/Air12_02.pdf';
  airImageName = '/Public/mantis.png';
  airDocument = AirPdf_newDocumentOutput(airFileName:'LETTER');
  airString = new_String(EBCDIC_CR + EBCDIC_LF);
  airNewLine = new_ITextChunk(airString);
  //
  airFontHead = new_ITextFont(ITEXT_FONT_HELVETICA: 15:
                              ITEXT_FONT_BOLD);
  //
  airBytes = 'Praying Mantis with Word Wrap';
  airParagraph = AirPdf_newParagraph(airBytes:
                                     airFontHead);
  ITextDocument_add(airDocument: airParagraph);
```

```
//
ITextDocument_add(airDocument: airNewLine);
//
airBytes = 'RPG, iText, PDFs, Java, ';
airPhrase = AirPdf_newPhrase(airBytes);
airImage = AirPdf_getImage(airImageName);
airAlignment = %bitOR(ITEXT_IMAGE_ALIGN_LEFT: ITEXT_IMAGE_TEXTWRAP);
```

Figure 12.17: RPG program using images with text wrapping (part 1 of 3)

When specifying the alignment for the image, we can combine multiple attributes by logically **OR**ing the constant values for left alignment and text wrap together to achieve the desired results. I really like this method because it minimizes the number of parameters and also reduces the number of constants we need to define. The **%bitOR** built-in function is explained in detail in the Chapter 3.

The next part of the program (Figure 12.18) applies the alignment to the image and then scales down the image to 75 percent using the **scalePercent** method of the iText **Image** class.

```
ITextImage_setAlignment(airImage: airAlignment);
ITextImage_scalePercent(airImage: 75);
ITextDocument_add(airDocument: airImage);
```

Figure 12.18: RPG program using images with text wrapping (part 2 of 3)

The next step is to add our text to the document. We'll do this by repeatedly adding the **'RPG, iText, PDFs, Java,'** text that we assigned above to a **Phrase** object.

This is where the different text objects available with iText come in handy. The **Phrase** object is aware of font height, so the characters won't just keep overlaying themselves on the first line, as would happen if we used a **Chunk**. With a **Phrase**, the text continues to concatenate to itself to be easily reused.

If we used a **Paragraph** instead of a **Phrase**, each repetition of the text would appear on a separate line. So, the **Phrase** object is the appropriate class to use for this example.

Figure 12.19 shows the final section of the program, which performs a loop to add the desired text.

```
// Do is not allowed in free-format; use For instead.
for i=0 to 51;
   ITextDocument_add(airDocument: airPhrase);
endfor;
//
ITextDocument_close(airDocument);
// Clean Up
   .
   . <Insert cleanup code here>
   .
*inlr = *ON;
/end-free
```

Figure 12.19: RPG program using images with text wrapping (part 3 of 3)

We are writing our code in free-format RPG, so the **DO** operation code is not available. Instead, the program uses the **FOR** operation code to create a loop that repeatedly adds the **Phrase** to our document. To use the **DO** command, you would need to switch from free format to fixed format (unless, of course, you were writing the whole program in fixed-format RPG).

Bar Codes

In iText, you can easily create bar codes that can be added to your PDF documents. The bar code classes convert letters and numbers into a bar code for use as an image. Then, you simply add the image to your document. Figure 12.20 shows a sample PDF that contains bar codes.

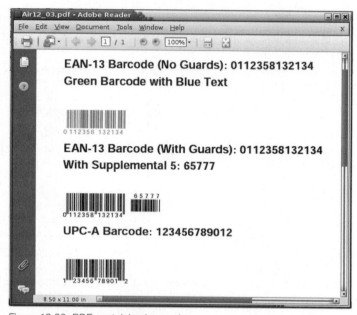

Figure 12.20: PDF containing bar codes

You can also use the iText classes to create bar code images in the form of **java. awt.Image** objects for use outside PDF files. For this chapter, we'll use the classes only for PDFs, but this capability is something to keep in mind for future possibilities.

Bar codes are optical representations of letters and numbers that can be read by a machine. They come in different flavors, and, fortunately, iText classes support the various symbologies that are available. The European Article Number (EAN) and Universal Produce Code (UPC) bar codes are pretty popular, so we'll cover a few different examples to demonstrate how to create them.

The **BarcodeEAN** class (Figure 12.21) supports both EAN and UPC bar codes.

```
D ITextBarcodeEAN...
D                 S              O    CLASS(*JAVA
D                                     :'com.lowagie.text.pdf-
D                                     .BarcodeEAN')
```

Figure 12.21: BarcodeEAN RPG object reference

We'll be using the default constructor (Figure 12.22) for our **BarcodeEAN** objects.

```
D new_ITextBarcodeEAN...
D                 PR                  like(ITextBarcodeEAN)
D                                     ExtProc(*JAVA
D                                     :'com.lowagie.text.pdf-
D                                     .BarcodeEAN'
D                                     :*CONSTRUCTOR)
```

Figure 12.22: Prototype for constructor method of BarcodeEAN class

Sometimes, bar codes have supplemental digits (typically used for suggested pricing) that are separate from the main bar code. You can see an example of this in the second bar code in Figure 12.20, which has a value of 65777. iText provides the **BarcodeEANSUPP** class (Figure 12.23) to create this type of bar code.

```
D ITextBarcodeEANSUPP...
D                 S              O    CLASS(*JAVA
D                                     :'com.lowagie.text.pdf-
D                                     .BarcodeEANSUPP')
```

Figure 12.23: BarcodeEANSUPP RPG object reference

The **BarcodeEANSUPP** object is constructed from two separate iText bar code objects: one for the main EAN/UPC bar code and one for the supplemental bar code. Figure 12.24 shows the prototype for the constructor method of the **BarcodeEANSUPP** class.

```
D new_ITextBarcodeEANSUPP...
D                 PR                  like(ITextBarcodeEANSUPP)
D                                     ExtProc(*JAVA
D                                     :'com.lowagie.text.pdf-
D                                     .BarcodeEANSUPP'
```

```
D                                         :*CONSTRUCTOR)
D    argEAN                               like(ITextBarCode)
D    argSUPP                              like(ITextBarCode)
```

Figure 12.24: Prototype for constructor method of BarcodeEANSUPP class

To create the sample EAN bar codes, we'll use several methods from the **BarcodeEAN** class. This class supports multiple symbologies, so we'll also use it to create our UPC bar codes. Figure 12.25 shows the methods available with the **Barcode** class. Because the **BarcodeEAN** class extends the **Barcode** class, these methods are also available to the **BarcodeEAN** class.

Method Summary	
Image	`createImageWithBarcode`(`PdfContentByte` cb, `Color` barColor, `Color` textColor) Creates an **Image** with the bar code.
void	`setBaseline`(float baseline) Sets the text baseline.
void	`setCode`(`String` code) Sets the code to generate.
void	`setCodeType`(int codeType) Sets the code type.
void	`setGuardBars`(boolean guardBars) Sets the property to show the guard bars for bar code EAN.

Figure 12.25: Partial JavaDoc for the Barcode methods

When you create a bar code, you can choose to display the characters that the bar code represents. You can determine whether the characters should appear above or below the bar code image and how far you want to space them from the bar code using the base line.

If the base line value is less than or equal to 0 (zero), the characters will be placed above the bar code. If the base line value is greater than 0, the characters will be placed below the bar code.

Figure 12.26 shows the prototype for the **setBaseLine** method of the **BarcodeEAN** class, which we'll use to set the baseline.

```
D ITextBarCodeEAN_setBaseline...
D                    PR             EXTPROC(*JAVA
D                                   :'com.lowagie.text.pdf-
D                                   .BarcodeEAN'
D                                   :'setBaseline')
D   inCodeType                      like(jFloat) value
```

Figure 12.26: Prototype for setBaseLine method of BarcodeEAN class

The **setCode** method of the **BarcodeEAN** class (Figure 12.27) sets the value that the bar code will represent.

```
D ITextBarCodeEAN_setCode...
D                    PR             EXTPROC(*JAVA
D                                   :'com.lowagie.text.pdf-
D                                   .BarcodeEAN'
D                                   :'setCode')
D   inCode                          like(jString)
```

Figure 12.27: Prototype for setCode method of BarcodeEAN class

The **setCodeType** method of the **BarcodeEAN** class (Figure 12.28) sets the type of bar code to generate. This is where you determine whether you are creating an EAN, a UPC, or a supplemental bar code.

```
D ITextBarCodeEAN_setCodeType...
D                    PR             EXTPROC(*JAVA
D                                   :'com.lowagie.text.pdf-
D                                   .BarcodeEAN'
D                                   :'setCodeType')
D   inCodeType                      like(jInt) value
```

Figure 12.28: Prototype for setCodeType method of BarcodeEAN class

The bar code types are determined using constants that are defined in the Java-Docs of the **Barcode** class and placed into the **SPAIRPDF** file (Figure 12.29).

```
D************************************************************************
D* com.lowagie.text.pdf.Barcode Field Values (Partial)
D************************************************************************
D ITEXT_BARCODE_CODABAR...
D                    C              12
```

```
D ITEXT_BARCODE_CODE128...
D                         C          9
D ITEXT_BARCODE_CODE128_RAW...
D                         C          11
D ITEXT_BARCODE_CODE128_UCC...
D                         C          10
D ITEXT_BARCODE_EAN13...
D                         C          1
D ITEXT_BARCODE_EAN8...
D                         C          2
D ITEXT_BARCODE_PLANET...
D                         C          8
D ITEXT_BARCODE_POSTNET...
D                         C          7
D ITEXT_BARCODE_SUPP2...
D                         C          5
D ITEXT_BARCODE_SUPP5...
D                         C          6
D ITEXT_BARCODE_UPCA...
D                         C          3
D ITEXT_BARCODE_UPCE...
D                         C          4
```

Figure 12.29: Partial list of Barcode constants

As you peruse the bar code constants, you may see other formats that spark your interest, such as the Postal Numeric Encoding Technique (POSTNET) and the Postal Alpha Numeric Encoding Technique (PLANET), which are used by the U.S. Postal Service. Wouldn't it be nice to put postal bar codes on your mail labels? That could be a fun project to practice your iText bar coding skills.

Guard bars are bars in the code that are longer than the rest to divide the symbol into two halves. The third bar code in Figure 12.20 includes a guard bar. You can specify the use of guard bars with the **setGuardBars** method of the **BarcodeEAN** class (Figure 12.30). The method accepts a **boolean** value to turn the guard bars on or off.

```
D ITextBarCodeEAN_setGuardBars...
D                    PR              EXTPROC(*JAVA
D                                    :'com.lowagie.text.pdf-
D                                    .BarcodeEAN'
D                                    :'setGuardBars')
D  inGuardBars                  1N   value
```

Figure 12.30: Prototype for setGuardBars method of BarcodeEAN class

We will create a custom procedure to perform our typical conversion from bytes to **String** and also to support the guard bars feature with an optional parameter. Figure 12.31 shows the custom procedure, **AirPdf_setBarcodeEANCode**.

```
P AirPdf_setBarcodeEANCode...
P                       B              EXPORT
D AirPdf_setBarcodeEANCode...
D                       PI
D   argBarCode                         like(ITextBarcodeEAN)
D   argBytes                    512A   const varying options(*varsize)
D   argGuardBars                 1N    value options(*nopass)
D   svString        S                  like(jString)
 /free
   JNIEnv_P = getJNIEnv();
   svString = new_String(argBytes);
   monitor;
     ITextBarcodeEAN_setCode(argBarcode: svString);
     if %parms > 2;
       ITextBarcodeEAN_setGuardBars(argBarcode: argGuardBars);
     else;
     endif;
   on-error;
   endmon;
   // Clean Up
   freeLocalRef(svString);
   return;
 /end-free
P                       E
```

Figure 12.31: Custom procedure to set the bar code

Last, we'll create an **Image** from our bar code using the **createImageWithBarcode** method of the **Barcode** class (Figure 12.32).

```
D ITextBarCode_createImageWithBarCode...
D                       PR              like(ITextImage)
D                                       EXTPROC(*JAVA
D                                       :'com.lowagie.text.pdf-
D                                       .Barcode'
D                                       :'createImageWithBarcode')
D   inContByte                          like(PdfContentByte)
D   inBarColor                          like(JavaColor)
D   inTextColor                         like(JavaColor)
```

Figure 12.32: Prototype for createImageWithBarcode method of Barcode class

When creating bar codes using the **createImageWithBarcode** method, you can specify the colors to use for both the bars and the text. A custom procedure lets us easily support this feature with the hexadecimal values we've been using so far (Figure 12.33).

```
P AirPdf_getBarcodeImage...
P                       B                EXPORT
D AirPdf_getBarcodeImage...
D                       PI               like(ITextImage)
D   argBarCode                           like(ITextBarcode)
D   argContByte                          like(PdfContentByte)
D   argBarColor                 6A       const options(*nopass)
D   argTextColor                6A       const options(*nopass)
D   svBarColor        S                  like(JavaColor)
D                                        inz(*NULL)
D   svTextColor       S                  like(JavaColor)
D                                        inz(*NULL)
D   svImage           S                  like(ITextImage)
D                                        inz(*NULL)
 /free
   JNIEnv_P = getJNIEnv();
   if %parms > 2;
     svBarColor = Air_getColorFromHex(argBarColor);
     if %parms > 3;
       svTextColor = Air_getColorFromHex(argTextColor);
     else;
     endif;
   else;
   endif;
   svImage =
     ITextBarcode_createImageWithBarCode(argBarCode:
                                         argContByte:
                                         svBarColor:
                                         svTextColor);
   // Clean Up
   freeLocalRef(svBarColor);
   freeLocalRef(svTextColor);
   return svImage;
 /end-free
P                       E
```

Figure 12.33: Custom procedure to get the bar code image

You may have noticed that the **createImageWithBarcode** method is looking for a **PdfContentByte** parameter. We'll need to retrieve this object from the **PdfWriter**, which means we'll have to do a little bit more manual work when creating our document.

The **PdfContentByte** object (Figure 12.34) lets you perform transformations to graphics and text within PDF documents.

```
D  PdfContentByte...
D                     S              O    CLASS(*JAVA
D                                          :'com.lowagie.text.pdf-
D                                          .PdfContentByte')
```

Figure 12.34: PdfContentByte RPG object reference

Normally, we would use our **AirPdf_newDocumentOutput** procedure to take care of the PDF writer and file output details, but in this case we need the **PdfWriter** object that is used in the **AirPdf_newDocumentOutput** procedure to get the **PdfContentByte** object. The **PdfContentByte** object is returned from the **getDirectContent** method of the **PdfWriter** class, so we'll put the mechanics of the **AirPdf_newDocumentOutput** procedure into our program to support this. Figure 12.35 shows the first portion of the RPG program, which gets the job done.

```
      .
      . <Insert common header code here (Figure 10.3)>
      .
D  airFileName       S          1024A    varying
D  airImageName      S          1024A    varying
D  airBytes          S          1024A    varying
D  airString         S                   like(jString)
D  airOutFile        S                   like(FileOutputStream)
D  airDocument       S                   like(ITextDocument)
D  airParagraph      S                   like(ITextParagraph)
D  airPhrase         S                   like(ITextPhrase)
D  airRectangle      S                   like(ITextRectangle)
D  airFontHead       S                   like(ITextFont)
D  airNewLine        S                   like(ITextChunk)
D  airImage          S                   like(ITextImage)
D  airBarcode        S                   like(ITextBarcodeEAN)
D  airBarSUPP5       S                   like(ITextBarcodeEAN)
D  airBarCodeTotal...
D                    S                   like(ITextBarcodeEANSUPP)
D  airWriter         S                   like(PdfWriter)
D  airContentByte...
```

```
D                   S                    like(PdfContentByte)
D  i                S              3S 0
C/EJECT
 /free
   CallP JavaServiceProgram();
   //
   airString = new_String(EBCDIC_CR + EBCDIC_LF);
   airNewLine = new_ITextChunk(airString);
   airFileName = '/Public/Air12_03.pdf';
   airImageName = '/Public/mantis.png';
   // airDocument = AirPdf_newDocumentOutput(airFileName:'LETTER');
   airString = new_String(%trim('LETTER'));
   monitor;
     airRectangle = PageSize_getRectangle(airString);
     airDocument = new_ITextDocumentFromRectangle(airRectangle);
   on-error;
     airDocument = *NULL;
   endmon;
   airString = new_String(%trim(airFileName));
   monitor;
     airOutFile = new_FileOutputStream(airString);
     // HERE is where you get the PdfWriter
     airWriter = AirPdf_setPdfWriter(airDocument: airOutFile);
     ITextDocument_open(airDocument);
     airContentByte = PdfWriter_getDirectContent(airWriter);
   on-error;
     airDocument = *NULL;
   endmon;
```

Figure 12.35: RPG program using bar codes (part 1 of 4)

I considered using a data structure as the return parameter of the **AirPdf_new-DocumentOutput** procedure to contain the **Document** object and the **PdfWriter** object, but as of V5R4 you cannot have objects as subfields of a data structure.

The object references are only references to the objects on the heap, so I suppose you could push the object references into numeric variables and place them into a data structure to support this capability. But I didn't want to get too creative, so I just put the extra code into the program to support the use of the **PdfContentByte** in the program.

Now that we have our **PdfContentByte**, we can use it to create the bar code images for our document. The first bar code uses the EAN-13 symbology with colors and without guards. Figure 12.36 shows the next section of the program, which creates this bar code according to these specifications.

```
airFontHead = new_ITextFont(ITEXT_FONT_HELVETICA: 15:
                            ITEXT_FONT_BOLD);
//-------------------------------------------------------------
//-------- EAN-13 NO GUARDS AND IN COLOR ----------------------
//-------------------------------------------------------------
airBytes = 'EAN-13 Barcode (No Guards): 0112358132134';
airParagraph = AirPdf_newParagraph(airBytes:
                                   airFontHead);
ITextDocument_add(airDocument: airParagraph);
airBytes = 'Green Barcode with Blue Text';

airParagraph = AirPdf_newParagraph(airBytes:
                                   airFontHead);
ITextDocument_add(airDocument: airParagraph);
//
ITextDocument_add(airDocument: airNewLine);
//
airBarcode = new_ITextBarcodeEAN();
AirPdf_setBarcodeEANCode(airBarcode: '0112358132134': *OFF);
// HERE is where you use the contentByte from the PdfWriter
airImage = AirPdf_getBarcodeImage(airBarCode:
                                  airContentByte:
                                  COLOR_SEA_GREEN:
                                  COLOR_CORNFLOWER_BLUE);
ITextDocument_add(airDocument: airImage);
```

Figure 12.36: RPG program using bar codes (part 2 of 4)

The second bar code (Figure 12.37) also uses the EAN-13 symbology, but it uses the default color and has guards. This example also includes a supplemental code.

```
//-------------------------------------------------------------
//-------- EAN-13 WITH GUARDS AND SUPP5 -----------------------
//-------------------------------------------------------------
airBytes = 'EAN-13 Barcode (With Guards): 0112358132134';
airParagraph = AirPdf_newParagraph(airBytes:
                                   airFontHead);
ITextDocument_add(airDocument: airParagraph);
airBytes = 'With Supplemental 5: 65777';
airParagraph = AirPdf_newParagraph(airBytes:
                                   airFontHead);
ITextDocument_add(airDocument: airParagraph);
```

```
//
ITextDocument_add(airDocument: airNewLine);
//
airBarcode = new_ITextBarcodeEAN();
AirPdf_setBarcodeEANCode(airBarcode: '0112358132134': *ON);
airBarSUPP5 = new_ITextBarcodeEAN();
ITextBarcodeEAN_setCodeType(airBarSUPP5: ITEXT_BARCODE_SUPP5);
AirPdf_setBarcodeEANCode(airBarSUPP5: '65777': *ON);
ITextBarcodeEAN_setBaseLine(airBarSUPP5: -2);
airBarCodeTotal = new_ITextBarcodeEANSUPP(airBarcode:
                                          airBarSUPP5);
airImage = AirPdf_getBarcodeImage(airBarCodeTotal:
                                  airContentByte);
ITextDocument_add(airDocument: airImage);
```

Figure 12.37: RPG program using bar codes (part 3 of 4)

To create the bar code with the supplemental code, we create two separate bar codes. One is an EAN bar code, and the other is specified as an **airBarSUPP5** type. We save the final product in the **airBarCodeTotal** variable by passing the two bar codes into the **new_ITextBarcodeEANSUPP** procedure to create the final results.

The final bar code uses the UPC-A symbology. The UPC bar code is created as an **ITextBarcodeEAN** object, but we set the code type to UPC using the **ITEXT_BARCODE_UPCA** constant with the **setCodeType** method of the iText **BarcodeEAN** class (Figure 12.38).

```
//------------------------------------------------------------
//---------------- UPC-A BARCODE -----------------------------
//------------------------------------------------------------
airBytes = 'UPC-A Barcode: 123456789012';
airParagraph = AirPdf_newParagraph(airBytes:
                                   airFontHead);
ITextDocument_add(airDocument: airParagraph);
//
ITextDocument_add(airDocument: airNewLine);
//
airBarcode = new_ITextBarcodeEAN();
AirPdf_setBarcodeEANCode(airBarcode: '123456789012');
ITextBarcodeEAN_setCodeType(airBarCode: ITEXT_BARCODE_UPCA);
airImage = AirPdf_getBarcodeImage(airBarCode:
                                  airContentByte);
ITextDocument_add(airDocument: airImage);
```

```
//-----------------------------------------------------------
ITextDocument_close(airDocument);
// Clean Up
   .
   . <Insert cleanup code here>
   .
*inlr = *ON;
/end-free
```

Figure 12.38: RPG program using bar codes (part 4 of 4)

That concludes our discussion of PDFs in this book, but there is much more you can do with iText and PDFs. I hope you have found some useful examples that you can use right away and have also seen some options to extend your service programs to support any features you'd like to provide.

In the next chapter, we'll cover a possible distribution method for your PDFs and Excel spreadsheets using e-mail.

13

Sending E-Mail

Now that you can provide your reports in electronic format, you're going to need a new distribution method for those reports. Just think of all the paper you'll save by not printing out every greenbar report, not to mention the manpower you'll conserve because no one will have to gather the reports and distribute them to the appropriate users. On top of these benefits is the dramatically improved appearance your reports will have because you've migrated them from the 132-column greenbar format.

You may be thinking about storing the electronic documents on your integrated file system (IFS) and mapping network drives from the clients, but I have found that users generally like to have the reports delivered automatically to their e-mail boxes. Here are some of the issues you would need to address if you were to provide the electronic reports via the IFS using network drives:

- The IBM i user profiles would need to be cooperative with your Microsoft Windows clients.
- Network drives would need to be mapped to the correct IFS location for each client computer.

- You would not be able to send electronic documents directly from the IBM i system to individuals who are not employees. Someone would need to retrieve such files from the network drive and e-mail or fax them to the client.

- Housekeeping would be required on the directory locations to keep old files from building up and consuming all your DASD.

- You could run into file-locking issues if a user were using a file when an application tried to re-create it.

- Security would need to be configured and administrated on the IFS folders to which you were providing the electronic documents.

- Users would become dependent on the network drives for archiving, putting more responsibility on your staff and increasing your backup time with additional files.

- You might have to support numerous client operating systems, and software requirements would need to be satisfied on all the clients.

You can eliminate these problems by distributing the electronic documents using e-mail. In this scenario, your RPG application simply sends an e-mail message to the requested e-mail address. The recipient does not need a user profile on the IBM i system, and storage housekeeping and archiving are the responsibilities of the recipient. You don't need to worry about getting those network drives to work from Macintosh clients, and numerous other administrative problems are avoided.

JavaMail

JavaMail is an API provided by Sun Microsystems that is platform-independent, easy to use, and free! The API provides a mail model that you can use to build your own custom e-mail client. Much more is possible with JavaMail, but we'll only be covering the process of sending e-mails to provide a functional conclusion for electronic document distribution.

JavaMail Implementation Requirements

The JavaMail API requires JDK/JRE 1.4 or higher. JavaMail is not included with the Java Runtime Environment, so you'll need to go to Sun Microsystems' Java Web site to download it.

You will also need the JavaBeans Activation Framework (JAF). The JAF is included with Java SE 6, but if you're using an earlier Java version, as we are throughout this book, you'll need to manually install the JAF.

Installing JavaMail

To install JavaMail, go to *http://java.sun.com/products/javamail/downloads* and download the latest Jar file that is supported on the JRE installed on your IBM i system. To obtain the JAF, go to *http://java.sun.com/javase/technologies/desktop/javabeans/jaf/downloads/index.html*.

Copy the JavaMail and JAF Jar files into your publicly accessible Jar file directory, and then add the files to your environment variable before starting the Java Virtual Machine. When you decompress the downloaded files, you need only the **mail.jar** file from JavaMail and the **activation.jar** file from JAF.

We will specify the **/Public/Java/JavaMail/** location of the **activation.jar** and **mail.jar** files in the main procedure of the **SVAIRJAVA** service program (Figure 13.1).

```
//------------------------------------------
// JAF - JavaBeans Activation Framework
// JAF and JavaMail for e-mail
//------------------------------------------
localPath = %TRIM(localPath)
           + ':/Public/Java'
           + '/JavaMail/activation.jar';
localPath = %trim(localPath)
           + ':/Public/Java'
           + '/JavaMail/mail.jar';
```

Figure 13.1: Setting the location of the JavaMail Jar files in the SVAIRJAVA main procedure

Then, we'll use the location to set the environment variable to make the JavaMail package visible to the JVM using the class path (Figure 13.2).

```
//--------------------------------------------------------
// Put the entire class path together and implement.
//--------------------------------------------------------
commandString = 'ADDENVVAR ENVVAR(CLASSPATH) '
               + 'VALUE('''.:'
               + %TRIM(localPath)
               + ''') REPLACE(*YES)';
monitor;
  ExecuteCommand(%trim(commandString):%len(%trim(commandString)));
on-error;
  displayBytes = 'ERROR occurred on Class Path!';
  DSPLY displayBytes;
endmon;
```

Figure 13.2: Setting the CLASSPATH environment variable in the SVAIRJAVA main procedure

The **ADDENVVAR** command will be executed when we call the main procedure of **SVAIRJAVA** using the **CallP JavaServiceProgram();** prototyped call.

Common Code

The RPG code samples illustrated in this and the next chapter all have code similar to that shown in Figure 13.3 in common. These opening specifications establish the **THREAD(*SERIALIZE)** recommendation for all RPG programs using Java and then copy in the generic prototypes and constants in the **SPAIRFUNC** source file, the standard Java prototypes in **SPAIRJAVA**, and the specialized JavaMail prototypes in **SPAIREMAIL**. The call to the Java service program will ensure that the JVM is initialized properly.

```
H THREAD(*SERIALIZE)
F***************************************************************************
F*   HOW TO COMPILE:
F*
F*   (1. CREATE THE MODULE)
F*   CRTRPGMOD MODULE(AIRLIB/AIR13_xx) SRCFILE(AIRLIB/AIRSRC) +
F*              DBGVIEW(*ALL) INDENT('.')
F*
F*   (2. CREATE THE PROGRAM)
F*   CRTPGM PGM(AIRLIB/AIR13_xx)
```

```
F*      BNDSRVPGM(SVAIRFUNC SVAIRJAVA SVAIREMAIL) ACTGRP(AIR13_xx)
D*********************************************************************
D/DEFINE OS400_JVM_12
D/COPY QSYSINC/QRPGLESRC,JNI
D/COPY AIRLIB/AIRSRC,SPAIRFUNC
D/COPY AIRLIB/AIRSRC,SPAIRJAVA
D/COPY AIRLIB/AIRSRC,SPAIREMAIL
D   declare variables...
 /free
   CallP JavaServiceProgram();
```

Figure 13.3: Common JavaMail code used in the RPG code

SPAIREMAIL and SVAIREMAIL

We will be providing a new prototype file (**SPAIREMAIL**) and service program (**SVAIREMAIL**) for the purpose of creating e-mails using the JavaMail API. In this chapter and the next, we'll add the prototypes and procedures to these files unless otherwise specified.

Whenever you are developing an RPG program that works with e-mail, you'll want to provide access to **SVAIRJAVA** and **SVAIREMAIL**, and sometimes to **SVAIRFUNC**, by copying the prototypes into the source code and binding the service programs to the program.

JavaMail and JAF JavaDocs

The JavaDocs for the JavaMail API are available online at *http://java.sun.com/products/javamail/javadocs/index.html*. You can find the JavaDocs for the JAF at *http://java.sun.com/javase/technologies/desktop/javabeans/glasgow/javadocs/index.html*. These JavaDocs list all the classes that are available for each package and let you drill down through the different options you have.

Sending a Text E-Mail

Our JavaMail Hello World example will send a text message containing the "Hello World!" text along with some automatically generated information about the user, date, and time. Figure 13.4 shows a sample e-mail produced by the application.

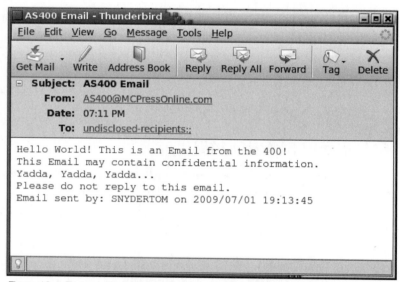

Figure 13.4: Text e-mail viewed by recipient e-mail client

In this example, we'll create an e-mail object that will be initialized with all the default settings, such as host, user, and password. You could also synchronize your IBM i users and e-mail users if you'd like to use the e-mail address of the user who sent the message.

Because you may have IBM i users who don't have an e-mail account at your company, we will set up a generic account for the system that can be used for all outgoing e-mail from applications. In the footer of the e-mails, we'll record the user information and any legal disclaimers; this information will automatically be included with each e-mail that is sent out.

Specifying the User Name and Password

For this example, we'll assume that the IBM i system will be sending all its e-mails through the same Simple Mail Transfer Protocol (SMTP) server, using the same user ID and password. This information can be set in the constructor.

This example was created for demonstration purposes to keep the code as simple as possible. In practice, you may not want to put the user name and password within your source code. In that case, you could modify the code to store the password in a more secure way or possibly prompt for the information or use the IBM i user profile information.

E-Mail Addresses

When providing e-mail capabilities, you obviously will be working with e-mail addresses to specify where the e-mails are being sent and also to indicate where the e-mails are coming from. JavaMail uses the **InternetAddress** class when dealing with e-mail addresses, so we need to provide access to this class within RPG (Figure 13.5).

```
D InternetAddress...
D                   S              O    CLASS(*JAVA
D                                       :'javax.mail.internet-
D                                       .InternetAddress')
```

Figure 13.5: InternetAddress RPG object reference in SPAIREMAIL

We will instantiate the **InternetAddress** class with a string parameter that contains the e-mail address we'll be working with. Figure 13.6 shows the prototype for the constructor method of this class.

```
D new_InternetAddress...
D                   PR             Like(InternetAddress)
D                                  ExtProc(*JAVA:
D                                  'javax.mail.internet-
D                                  .InternetAddress':
D                                  *CONSTRUCTOR)
D   argString                      Like(jstring) Const
```

Figure 13.6: Prototype for constructor method of InternetAddress class

To simplify this repeated process, we'll provide a standard procedure to use our RPG bytes and construct the **InternetAddress** class (Figure 13.7).

```
P AirEmail_newInternetAddress...
P                       B                  EXPORT
D AirEmail_newInternetAddress...
D                       PI                 like(InternetAddress)
D argAddress                     65535A    const varying
D*
D svAddress           S                    like(InternetAddress)
D                                          inz(*NULL)
D svString            S                    like(jString)
D                                          inz(*NULL)
 /free
   svString = new_String(%trim(argAddress));
   svAddress = new_InternetAddress(svString);
   freeLocalRef(svString);
   return svAddress;
 /end-free
P                       E
```

Figure 13.7: Custom procedure to create a new Internet address

The **InternetAddress** class extends the **Address** class. The **Address** class is contained in the **javax.mail** package, whereas the **InternetAddress** class is contained in the **javax.mail.internet** package. The **InternetAddress** class uses the syntax of RFC822, which is where the differences come into play for the extended class.

Even though we can take advantage of polymorphism when using the classes, we still need to define the **Address** class when defining our prototypes to have the correct signatures. Figure 13.8 shows the **Address** RPG object reference in the **SPAIREMAIL** source file.

```
D Address...
D                       S              O   CLASS(*JAVA
D                                          :'javax.mail-
D                                          .Address')
```

Figure 13.8: Address RPG object reference in SPAIREMAIL

To support the use of more than one e-mail address in our recipient list when sending e-mails, we will need to supply an array of objects. To do this, we'll

use the **jobjectArray** code provided in the **QSYSINC/QRPGLESRC,JNI** file
(Figure 13.9).

```
D jobjectArray     S              O    CLASS(*JAVA
D                                      : 'java.lang.Object')
```

Figure 13.9: RPG object reference for an Array of Objects in QSYSINC/QRPGLESRC,JNI

Figure 13.10 shows the **NewObjectArray** prototype that is contained in the
QSYSINC/QRPGLESRC,JNI file. You've seen this procedure before, in Chapter 6.

```
D*-----------------------------------------------------------------
D*      jobjectArray (*NewObjectArray)
D*         (JNIEnv *env, jsize len, jclass clazz, jobject init);
D*-----------------------------------------------------------------
D NewObjectArray   PR              LIKE(jobjectArray)
D                                  EXTPROC(*CWIDEN
D                                  : JNINativeInterface.
D                                    NewObjectArray_P)
D env                              LIKE(JNIEnv_P) VALUE
D len                              LIKE(jsize) VALUE
D clazz                            LIKE(jclass) VALUE
D init                            LIKE(jobject) VALUE
```

Figure 13.10: NewObjectArray function prototype in QSYSINC/QRPGLESRC,JNI

In the earlier chapter, we discussed how to create an array of **String** objects.
We'll use the same logic here to create an array of **InternetAddress** objects in the
AirEmail_newInternetAddressArray procedure. Figure 13.11 shows the first part
of this custom procedure.

```
P AirEmail_newInternetAddressArray...
P                   B              EXPORT
D AirEmail_newInternetAddressArray...
D                   PI             like(jobjectArray)
D argSize                          like(jsize) VALUE
D                                  options(*nopass)
D*
D size             S              like(jsize)
D addressClass     S              like(jclass)
D                                  inz(*NULL)
D addressArray     S              like(jobjectArray)
D                                  inz(*NULL)
D cd               DS             likeDs(iconv_t)
```

```
D ebcdicString    S              1024A
D asciiAddress    S              1024A
D toCCSID         S               10I 0
 /free
   if %parms < 1;
     size = 100;
   else;
     size = argSize;
   endif;
   if (JNIEnv_P = *NULL);
     JNIEnv_P = getJNIEnv();
   else;
   endif;
   // Create Conversion Descriptor for CCSID conversions
   toCCSID = 1208;
   cd = Air_openConverter(toCCSID);
   ebcdicString = 'javax/mail/internet/InternetAddress';
   asciiAddress = Air_convert(cd: %trim(ebcdicString));
   addressClass = FindClass(JNIEnv_P:
                              %trim(asciiAddress));
   if (Air_isJVMError());
     freeLocalRef(addressClass);
     Air_closeConverter(cd);
     return *NULL;
   else;
   endif;
```

Figure 13.11: Custom procedure to create a new Internet address array (part 1 of 2)

The procedure starts out with parameter validation and conversion between character sets using the **Air_convert** method in the **SVAIRFUNC** service program. Then, it gets a reference to the class using the JNI **FindClass** method from the **QSYSINC/QRPGLESRC,JNI** file.

Next (Figure 13.12), the procedure creates the object array using the **NewObjectArray** procedure; then it returns the array as type **jobjectArray**.

```
   addressArray = NewObjectArray(JNIEnv_P:
                                   size:
                                   addressClass:
                                   *NULL);
   if (Air_isJVMError());
     freeLocalRef(addressClass);
     Air_closeConverter(cd);
```

```
       return *NULL;
     else;
     endif;
     // Clean Up
     Air_closeConverter(cd);
     freeLocalRef(addressClass);
     return addressArray;
    /end-free
 P                    E
```

Figure 13.12: Custom procedure to create a new Internet address array (part 2 of 2)

To add objects to the array, we'll create a custom procedure named **AirEmail_add-InternetAddress** (Figure 13.13). This procedure first looks for an empty element in the object array by searching for a null value. When the value is found, the procedure stores the index and exits the loop.

```
 P AirEmail_addInternetAddress...
 P                       B                 EXPORT
 D AirEmail_addInternetAddress...
 D                       PI            1N
 D argObjectArray                          like(jobjectArray)
 D argAddress                    1024A     varying value
 D*
 D svReturn          S            1N
 D size              S                      like(jsize)
 D index             S                      like(jsize)
 D i                 S                      like(jsize)
 D cd                DS                     likeDs(iconv_t)
 D displayString     S            52A
 D ebcdicString      S          1024A
 D asciiAddress      S          1024A
 D toCCSID           S           10I 0
 D javaString        S                      like(jstring)
 D newElement        S                      like(InternetAddress)
 D arrayObject       S                      like(jobject)
  /free
    svReturn = *ON;
    if (JNIEnv_P = *NULL);
      JNIEnv_P = getJNIEnv();
    else;
    endif;
    if (argObjectArray = *NULL);
      return *OFF;
    else;
    endif;
    size = GetArrayLength(JNIEnv_P: argObjectArray);
```

```
// Look for next available index
index = size;
for i = 0 to size;
  arrayObject = GetObjectArrayElement(JNIEnv_P
                                    :argObjectArray:i);

  if (Air_isJVMError());
    leave;
  else;
    if (arrayObject = *NULL);
      index = i;
      leave;
    else;
    endif;
  endif;
endfor;
```

Figure 13.13: Custom procedure to add an Internet address to the array (part 1 of 2)

After an available index is found, the bytes that were sent into the procedure to represent the e-mail address are converted to a **String** and then to an **InternetAddress**, which is added to the object array (Figure 13.14).

```
if (index >= size);
  svReturn = *OFF;
else;
  javaString = new_String(%trim(argAddress));
  newElement = new_InternetAddress(javaString);
  SetObjectArrayElement(JNIEnv_P:
                        argObjectArray:
                        index:
                        newElement);
  if (Air_isJVMError());
    svReturn = *OFF;
  else;
  endif;
endif;
return svReturn;
/end-free
P                           E
```

Figure 13.14: Custom procedure to add an Internet address to the array (part 2 of 2)

This procedure favors simplicity of use over performance. To make it faster, you could store the next available index in your calling program and pass it in as a parameter to eliminate the need to loop through the array to find the next available element. I chose to take the simple route because the procedure is used only once, at the exit of the programs that generate the reports. But your situation may be better suited for performance with a little extra coding in your main program.

Creating the Session

As our next step, we need to create a **Session** object for use with the message. We can use a **Properties** file to set the **Session** configuration when the object is created.

The **Session** object (Figure 13.15) and some methods are defined in the **SPAIREMAIL** prototype file.

```
D Session...
D                      S              O    CLASS(*JAVA
D                                          :'javax.mail-
D                                          .Session')
```

Figure 13.15: Session RPG object reference in SPAIREMAIL

We'll be using two of the **Session** methods in our text e-mail example (Figure 13.16).

Method Summary	
static Session	`getDefaultInstance`(`Properties` props) Get the default Session object.
void	`setDebug`(`boolean debug`) Set the debug setting for this Session.

Figure 13.16: Partial JavaDoc for Session methods

The **getDefaultInstance** method will be used to create an instance of the **Session** class (Figure 13.17).

```
D Session_getDefaultInstance...
D                   PR                    Like(Session)
D                                         extproc(*JAVA:
D                                         'javax.mail-
D                                         .Session':
D                                         'getDefaultInstance')
D                                         static
D   argProps                              Like(Properties)
```

Figure 13.17: Prototype for getDefaultInstance method of Session class

The **getDefaultInstance** method is a static method that can be used to instantiate the **Session** class with attributes that will be specified with a **Properties** object (Figure 13.18).

```
D Properties        S             O       CLASS(*JAVA:
D                                         'java.util.Properties')
```

Figure 13.18: Properties RPG object reference in SPAIRJAVA

The **Properties** class is included with Java, so we'll place the prototypes and procedures into the **SPAIRJAVA** file (Figure 13.19).

```
D new_Properties    PR                    ExtProc(*JAVA
D                                         :'java.util.Properties'
D                                         :*CONSTRUCTOR)
D                                         like(Properties)
```

Figure 13.19: Properties default constructor method in SPAIRJAVA

To set the values of the **Properties** object, we'll use the **setProperty** method of the **Properties** class (Figure 13.20).

Method Summary
Object **setProperty**(String key, String value) Calls the Hashtable method put.

Figure 13.20: Partial JavaDoc for setProperty method of java.util.Properties class

The properties to be set will be referenced using a key. The key will identify the property that is having the value assigned. Figure 13.21 shows the prototype for the **setProperty** method of the **Properties** class.

```
D Properties_setProperty...
D                      PR              ExtProc(*JAVA
D                                      :'java.util.Properties'
D                                      :'setProperty')
D                                      like(jObject)
D   key                                like(jstring) const
D   value                              like(jstring) const
```

Figure 13.21: Prototype for setProperty method of Properties class

Table 13.1 lists a few of the properties that will be assigned to our **Session** object.

Table 13.1: Partial list of properties used by JavaMail session	
Property	**Description**
mail.user	User name on mail server
mail.password	Password on mail server
mail.transport.protocol	Default transport protocol
mail.host	Default mail server
mail.smtp.localhost	Name of local host sending e-mail
mail.smtps.auth	Using authentication

For more information about the properties used by JavaMail, see Appendix A of the JavaMail Specifications, available at *http://java.sun.com/products/javamail/ JavaMail-1.4.pdf.*

You'll find the **setDebug** method of the **Session** class (Figure 13.22) very helpful when you are first setting up your e-mail client. This method provides debugging information when you try to connect to your e-mail server.

```
D Session_setDebug...
D                      PR              extproc(*JAVA:
D                                      'javax.mail-
D                                      .Session':
D                                      'setDebug')
D   argBool             1N             VALUE
```

Figure 13.22: Prototype for setDebug method of Session class

Creating the MIME Message

Once the session has been created and configured for the SMTP e-mail server, you can create the message that will be sent using the **Session** object.

We will create a custom procedure, **AirEmail_newMessage**, to handle all the details of creating the **MimeMessage** object. We'll set the configuration to use default settings for the e-mail server that will be used to send the e-mail. Figure 13.23 shows the first section of procedure **AirEmail_newMessage**. To provide some flexibility, the procedure specifies the user, password, host, and prototype as optional parameters that will override the defaults if they are specified; otherwise, the default settings will be used.

```
 P AirEmail_newMessage...
 P                          B                    EXPORT
 D AirEmail_newMessage...
 D                          PI                   like(MimeMessage)
 D   argUser                         1024A       const varying
 D                                               options(*NoPass:*omit)
 D   argPassword                     1024A       const varying
 D                                               options(*NoPass:*omit)
 D   argHost                         1024A       const varying
 D                                               options(*NoPass:*omit)
 D   argProtocol                     1024A       const varying
 D                                               options(*NoPass:*omit)
 D*
 D svDefaultHost        C                        CONST('smtp.example.com')
 D svDefaultProto       C                        CONST('smtp')
 D svSession            S                        like(Session)
 D                                               inz(*NULL)
 D svProp               S                        like(Properties)
 D                                               inz(*NULL)
 D svAuth               S                        like(Authenticator)
 D                                               inz(*NULL)
 D svMsg                S                        like(MimeMessage)
 D                                               inz(*NULL)
 D svPropKey            S                        like(jString)
 D svPropValue          S                        like(jString)
 D                                               inz(*NULL)
 D svDebug              S              1N
 D svHost               S           1024A
 D svUser               S           1024A
 D svPassword           S           1024A
 D svProtocol           S           1024A
  /free
    if %parms < 4;
```

```
    svProtocol = svDefaultProto;
  else;
    svProtocol = argProtocol;
  endif;
  if %parms < 3;
    svHost = svDefaultHost;
  else;
    svHost = argHost;
  endif;
  if %parms < 2;
    svPassword = *BLANKS;
  else;
    svPassword = argPassword;
  endif;
  if %parms < 1;
    svUser = *BLANKS;
  else;
    svUser = argUser;
  endif;
  svDebug = *ON;
```

Figure 13.23: Custom procedure to create a JavaMail MimeMessage (part 1 of 4)

Up to this point in the procedure, we have performed validation on the parameters that are being used. All the parameters are optional, ensuring that the expected values will be initialized, either to the incoming values or to the default settings.

The procedure also defines an **svDebug** variable used to turn on the debugging feature for the JavaMail **Session** object. This option makes it easy to turn the extra debugging information on or off within your service program. The **svDebug** value is typically used only for development or troubleshooting.

The next section of the procedure (Figure 13.24) conditionally sets the **mail.user** and **mail.password** properties to support relays that don't want to use the user name or password.

```
    svProp = new_Properties();
    //-------------------------------------------------------------
    // User
    if (svUser = *BLANKS);
    else;
      svPropKey = new_String('mail.user');
```

```
      svPropValue = new_String(%Trim(svUser));
      Properties_setProperty(svProp: svPropKey: svPropValue);
   endif;
   // Password
   if (svPassword = *BLANKS);
   else;
      svPropKey = new_String('mail.password');
      svPropValue = new_String(%Trim(svPassword));
      Properties_setProperty(svProp: svPropKey: svPropValue);
   endif;
```

Figure 13.24: Custom procedure to create a JavaMail MimeMessage (part 2 of 4)

I once needed to use an internal e-mail server relay without authentication and it would not work if I specified a user name or password. And if I set the values to blanks, that would not work either. So, I used the optional user name and password variables to determine whether the properties would be used or not. The host and protocol are not optional parameters for the e-mail server, so you must always specify these values.

Once all the parameters have been verified and all the applicable defaults have been assigned, our procedure uses these values to set the properties that will be used with the JavaMail **Session** we'll be using (Figure 13.25).

```
// Transport Protocol
svPropKey = new_String('mail.transport.protocol');
svPropValue = new_String(%trim(svProtocol));
Properties_setProperty(svProp: svPropKey: svPropValue);
// Host: URL Location of the SMTP server
svPropKey = new_String('mail.host');
svPropValue = new_String(%trim(svHost));
Properties_setProperty(svProp: svPropKey: svPropValue);
// LocalHost: Required or HELO will fail
svPropKey = new_String('mail.smtp.localhost');
svPropValue = new_String('mail.example.com');
Properties_setProperty(svProp: svPropKey: svPropValue);
// Create the Session with the Properties
svSession = Session_getDefaultInstance(svProp);
Session_setDebug(svSession:svDebug);
```

Figure 13.25: Custom procedure to create a JavaMail MimeMessage (part 3 of 4)

Next, we create the **MimeMessage** object that will be returned from the procedure (Figure 13.26). The **MimeMessage** is created using the **Session** object as the parameter to its constructor.

```
          // Create the Message with the Session
          svMsg = new_MimeMessage(svSession);
          AirEmail_setFrom(svMsg:'AS400@MCPressOnline.com');
          // Clean Up
          freeLocalRef(svPropKey);
          freeLocalRef(svPropValue);
          freeLocalRef(svProp);
          //
          return svMsg;
        /end-free
     P                       E
```

Figure 13.26: Custom procedure to create a JavaMail MimeMessage (part 4 of 4)

The **from** attribute of the message is set within the **AirEmail_newMessage** procedure as a hard-coded value. Because the message object is available within the application, you could change the default after the main e-mail object is constructed.

To support the possibility of future changes to your e-mail server, you may want to consider putting the default property values into an external file for easy changes that would not required a recompile.

The **MimeMessage** object and its constructor are defined in **SPAIREMAIL** (Figure 13.27).

```
     D MimeMessage...
     D                  S              O    CLASS(*JAVA
     D                                      :'javax.mail.internet-
     D                                      .MimeMessage')
```

Figure 13.27: MimeMessage RPG object reference in SPAIREMAIL

The constructor we'll use for the **MimeMessage** object accepts the **Session** as the parameter (Figure 13.28).

```
D new_MimeMessage...
D                   PR                    Like(MimeMessage)
D                                         ExtProc(*JAVA:
D                                         'javax.mail.internet-
D                                         .MimeMessage':
D                                         *CONSTRUCTOR)
D   argSession                            Like(Session)
```

Figure 13.28: Prototype for constructor method of MimeMessage class

We'll set the from address, subject, and text of the e-mail message using the methods available from the **MimeMessage** class (Figure 13.29).

Method Summary	
void	**setFrom**(<u>Address</u> address) Set the RFC 822 "From" header field.
void	**setSubject**(<u>String</u> subject) Set the "Subject" header field.
void	**setText**(<u>String</u> text) Convenience method that sets the given String as this part's content, with a MIME type of "text/plain".

Figure 13.29: Partial JavaDoc for MimeMessage methods

The **setFrom** method of the **MimeMessage** class accepts an object of type **Address** (Figure 13.30).

```
D MimeMessage_setFrom...
D                   PR                    extproc(*JAVA:
D                                         'javax.mail.internet-
D                                         .MimeMessage':
D                                         'setFrom')
D   argAddress                            Like(Address)
```

Figure 13.30: Prototype for setFrom method of MimeMessage class

The **AirEmail_setFrom** procedure (Figure 13.31) takes the character bytes and converts them to the **Address** objects required by the **MimeMessage** method. We can use the **InternetAddress** class here because it is a subclass of the **Address** class.

```
P AirEmail_setFrom...
P                  B                 EXPORT
D AirEmail_setFrom...
D                  PI
D   argMsg                           like(MimeMessage)
D   argFromEmail          1024A      const varying
D                                    options(*varsize)
D*
D svString       S                   like(jString)
D svAddress      S                   like(InternetAddress)
 /free
   svAddress = AirEmail_newInternetAddress(%trim(argFromEmail));
   MimeMessage_setFrom(argMsg:svAddress);
 /end-free
P                  E
```

Figure 13.31: Custom procedure to set the from value in MimeMessage

The subject is set using the **setSubject** method of the **MimeMessage** class with a **String** argument (Figure 13.32).

```
D MimeMessage_setSubject...
D                  PR                extproc(*JAVA:
D                                    'javax.mail.internet-
D                                    .MimeMessage':
D                                    'setSubject')
D   argString                        Like(jstring)
```

Figure 13.32: Prototype for setSubject method of MimeMessage class

The **AirEmail_setSubject** procedure (Figure 13.33) handles the bytes-to-string conversion.

```
P AirEmail_setSubject...
P                  B                 EXPORT
D AirEmail_setSubject...
D                  PI
D   argMsg                           like(MimeMessage)
D   argSubject            1024A      const varying
D                                    options(*varsize)
D*
D svString       s                   like(jString)
```

```
 /free
   svString = new_String(%trim(argSubject));
   MimeMessage_setSubject(argMsg:svString);
   freeLocalRef(svString);
 /end-free
P                     E
```

Figure 13.33: Custom procedure to set the subject value in MimeMessage

The text portion of the message is set using the **setText** method of the **MimeMessage** class with a **String** argument (Figure 13.34).

```
D MimeMessage_setText...
D                     PR              extproc(*JAVA:
D                                     'javax.mail.internet-
D                                     .MimeMessage':
D                                     'setText')
D   argString                         Like(jstring)
```

Figure 13.34: Prototype for setText method of MimeMessage class

The **AirEmail_setText** method (Figure 13.35) is where you set the text message content of the e-mail. If desired, you could automatically append corporate-specific legal information to the end of the message here. Because we are using the same user name, password, and from address on the e-mails, we'll identify the date, time, and user of the RPG program and place that information into the footer information of the message.

```
P AirEmail_setText...
P                     B               EXPORT
D AirEmail_setText...
D                     PI
D   argMsg                            like(MimeMessage)
D   argText                   65535A  const varying
D                                     options(*varsize)
D*
D svString            S               like(jString)
D svDate              S       8S 0
D svTime              S       6S 0
 /free
   // Create a standard footer to identify user sending e-mail
   // and concatenate it onto the end of the message automatically.
   svDate = %Dec(%Date():*ISO);
   svTime = %Dec(%Time():*ISO);
```

```
svString = new_String(%trim(argText)
            + X'0D25'
            + 'This Email may contain confidential '
            + 'information. '
            + X'0D25'
            + 'Yadda, Yadda, Yadda...'
            + X'0D25'
            + 'Please do not reply to this email. '
            + X'0D25'
            + 'Email sent by: '
            + %trim(QCUSER)
            + ' on ' + %editw(svDate:'   /  / ')
            + ' ' + %editw(svTime:'  :  :  '));
   MimeMessage_setText(argMsg:svString);
   freeLocalRef(svString);
  /end-free
P                    E
```

Figure 13.35: Custom procedure to set the text value in MimeMessage

Sending the Message

The JavaMail **Transport** class (Figure 13.36) sends the e-mail message we have created.

```
D Transport...
D                 S           O    CLASS(*JAVA
D                                  :'javax.mail-
D                                  .Transport')
```

Figure 13.36: Properties RPG object reference in SPAIREMAIL

The **send** method of the **Transport** class (Figure 13.37) sends the message — makes sense.

Method Summary	
Static void	**send**(Message msg, Address[] addresses) Send the message to the specified addresses, ignoring any recipients specified in the message itself.

Figure 13.37: Partial JavaDoc for send method of Transport class

The message is passed to the **send** method, along with the list of recipients, in an array of **Address** objects (Figure 13.38).

```
D Transport_send...
D                   PR                      extproc(*JAVA:
D                                           'javax.mail-
D                                           .Transport':
D                                           'send')
D                                           static
D  argMsg                                   like(Message)
D  argRecipients                            like(jobjectArray)
```

Figure 13.38: Prototype for send method of Transport class

Calling a Static Method Using JNI

In Chapter 6, we deferred the discussion of using class methods within the Java Native Interface until now. We will use JNI for the **send** method of the **Transport** class. The static **send** method will be identified in JNI using the **GetStaticMethodID** procedure provided in the **QSYSINC/QRPGLESRC,JNI** file (Figure 13.39).

```
D*--------------------------------------------------------------------
D*   jmethodID (*GetStaticMethodID)
D*     (JNIEnv *env, jclass clazz, const char *name, const char *sig);
D*--------------------------------------------------------------------
D GetStaticMethodID...
D                   PR                      LIKE(jmethodID)
D                                           EXTPROC(*CWIDEN
D                                           : JNINativeInterface.
D                                              GetStaticMethodID_P)
D env                                       LIKE(JNIEnv_P) VALUE
D clazz                                     LIKE(jclass) VALUE
D name                            *         OPTIONS(*STRING) VALUE
D sig                             *         OPTIONS(*STRING) VALUE
```

Figure 13.39: GetStaticMethodID function prototype in QSYSINC/QRPGLESRC,JNI

Once we have the static method identifier, we can use it with the **CallStaticVoid-Method** capabilities of JNI. The **CallStaticVoidMethod_P** pointer will qualify the method as a static method that returns a void value.

We'll name our procedure to reflect the class and method we'll be using. The signature of the method will be used to retrieve the method identifier from the **GetStaticMethodID** prototype. That method identifier will be used in our prototype, followed by the arguments that we'll use for the **send** method of the **Transport** class.

When you use the **CallStaticVoidMethod** JNI function, you are required to provide at least one optional parameter. To satisfy this requirement, we'll create a dummy parameter that will be added after our parameters (Figure 13.40).

```
D CallTransportSendMethod...
D                     PR                ExtProc(*CWIDEN:
D                                        JNINativeInterface.
D                                        CallStaticVoidMethod_P)
D   argEnv                              Like(JNIEnv_P) value
D   argClass                            Like(jclass) value
D   argMethodId                         Like(jmethodID) value
D   argMsg                              Like(MimeMessage) value
D   argRecipients                       Like(jobjectArray) value
D   argDummy                      1A    Options(*NoPass)
```

Figure 13.40: Prototype for CallTransportSendMethod in SPAIREMAIL

We'll be using JNI in our send procedure, so this prototype will be used for the **send** method of the **Transport** class.

MimeMessage

The **MimeMessage** is a subclass of the **Message** class that is the specified parameter for the **send** method. Even though we will be passing a **MimeMessage** object as the argument to the procedure, we need to define the prototype with the correct class for the signature match.

Figure 13.41 shows the object reference that is placed into **SPAIREMAIL** for the **Message** class.

```
D Message...
D                     S              O    CLASS(*JAVA
D                                          :'javax.mail-
D                                          .Message')
```

Figure 13.41: Message RPG object reference in SPAIREMAIL

I would say if there ever was logic that needed to be tucked away inside a procedure, it would be the logic needed to send an e-mail, so here we go. Figure 13.42 shows the first section of **AirEmail_send**, our custom procedure to send an e-mail.

```
P AirEmail_send...
P                       B                    EXPORT
D AirEmail_send...
D                       PI
D   argMsg                                   like(MimeMessage)
D   argRecipients                  1024A     dim(100) const
D                                            varying
D*
D sendClass             S                    like(jclass)
D sendId                S                    like(jMethodId)
D cd                    DS                   likeDs(iconv_t)
D string                S         1024A
D ebcdicString          S         1024A
D asciiTransport        S         1024A
D asciiSend             S         1024A
D asciiSignature        S         1024A
D displayString         S           52A
D toCCSID               S          10I 0
D i                     S          10I 0
D size                  S          10I 0
D elementCount          S          10I 0
D recipients            S                    like(jobjectArray)
 /free
   if (JNIEnv_P = *NULL);
     JNIEnv_P = getJNIEnv();
   else;
   endif;
   // Before sending the e-mail, push the addresses into
   // an InternetAddress Array that is the same size as the number
   // of elements. Otherwise, you will be sending NULL elements,
   // which will cause an error.
   elementCount = %elem(argRecipients);
   size = *ZEROS;
   for i = 1 to elementCount;
     if (argRecipients(i) = *BLANKS);
     else;
       size = size + 1;
     endif;
   endfor;
```

Figure 13.42: Custom procedure to send an e-mail (part 1 of 3)

The comment above the loop pretty much says it all, but it is an important note. When we send the array of objects into the **send** method of the **Transport** class, the array must be the correct size or it will give us an error. So, we need to make sure we know the number of elements that will be added.

I contemplated just using an **ArrayList** within the main program and then using the **toArray** method when passing the array to the **send** method, but I wanted to keep things as simple as possible for other RPG programmers in the shop who were unfamiliar with Java, so they could use the e-mail functionalities of the service program. So, I decided to support the use of an array of bytes within the main program to build the recipient list and then convert the array of bytes to objects when the e-mail was sent.

Once we know the number of recipients, we can create the **InternetAddress** array to be the correct size using the **AirEmail_newInternetAddressArray** procedure. Then, add the object elements to the array using the **AirEmail_addInternetAddress** procedure that we created earlier. The procedure code shown in Figure 13.43 performs these steps.

```
if (size = *ZEROS);
  return;
else;
  recipients = AirEmail_newInternetAddressArray(size);
  for i = 1 to elementCount;
    if (argRecipients(i) = *BLANKS);
    else;
      AirEmail_addInternetAddress(recipients:argRecipients(i));
    endif;
  endfor;
endif;
```

Figure 13.43: Custom procedure to send an e-mail (part 2 of 3)

With the **InternetAddress** object array built, we can now call the **send** method of the **Transport** class (Figure 13.44). I know that the JNI code may not be the prettiest, but once you have it coded and working, the service program will keep you away from the ugliness of it.

```
// Create Conversion Descriptor for CCSID conversions
// EBCDIC->ASCII conversion
toCCSID = 1208;
cd = Air_openConverter(toCCSID);
ebcdicString = 'javax/mail/Transport';
asciiTransport = Air_convert(cd: %trim(ebcdicString));
ebcdicString = 'send';
asciiSend = Air_convert(cd: %trim(ebcdicString));
ebcdicString = '(Ljavax/mail/Message;'
            + '[Ljavax/mail/Address;)V';
asciiSignature = Air_convert(cd: %trim(ebcdicString));
// Get the Transport_send Method and call it.
sendClass = FindClass(JNIEnv_P:%trim(asciiTransport));
if (Air_isJVMError());
  displayString = 'FindClass Error';
  DSPLY displayString;
else;
endif;
// Get the STATIC send Method ID using the CLASS
sendID = GetStaticMethodID(JNIENV_p:sendClass
                          :%trim(asciiSend)
                          :%trim(asciiSignature));
if (Air_isJVMError());
  displayString = 'GetStaticMethodID Error';
  DSPLY displayString;
else;
endif;
//-----------------------------------------------------------------
// SEND THE E-MAIL!
//-----------------------------------------------------------------
CallTransportSendMethod(JNIEnv_P:sendClass:
                        sendID:argMsg:recipients);
if (Air_isJVMError());
  displayString = 'TransportSend Error';
  DSPLY displayString;
else;
endif;
// Clean Up
Air_closeConverter(cd);
freeLocalRef(sendClass);
freeLocalRef(sendID);
/end-free
 P                      E
```

Figure 13.44: Custom procedure to send an e-mail (part 3 of 3)

You may notice that I looped through the entire array looking for elements that are not blank. I did this to support the worst case, where an application may insert blanks between valid elements; I didn't want to truncate valid e-mail addresses from the list. I also didn't want to sort the array because there could be political reasons for the specified order of recipients. For example, you might want the chief technical officer to be the first recipient listed in your e-mail when it is sent.

You could specify the recipients by adding them to the message, but I chose to use the **Transport.send** method instead. This is because adding recipients directly to the message requires access to **Message.RecipientType.TO**, which is a static inner class of the **Message** object. The **Message.RecipientType.TO** approach would have been difficult to work within JNI, so I decided to specify the recipients using **Transport.send** instead. When you specify the recipients in the **Transport.send** method, it overrides any recipients specified on the message.

The **Transport.send** method requires an array of Internet addresses to be sent as the second parameter. In the RPG program, we will create an array of **1024A** fields for the recipients for RPG programmer-friendliness. This array has 100 elements, but you could change this number to whatever size you find acceptable.

For this example, the **MimeMessage** object is created with the **AirEmail_newMessage** procedure. The **MimeMessage** is then modified to set the subject, message, and recipients. Then the message is sent.

Figure 13.45 shows the complete code needed to send a text e-mail using the methods we've discussed so far.

```
     .
     . <Insert common header code here (Figure 13.3)>
     .
 D  msg            S                        like(MimeMessage)
 D  recipients     S              1024A     dim(100)
  /free
   CallP JavaServiceProgram();
   msg = AirEmail_newMessage();
   AirEmail_setSubject(msg:'AS400 Email');
   AirEmail_setText(msg:'Hello World! '
                    + 'This is an Email from the 400!');
```

```
recipients = *BLANKS;
recipients(1) = 'ThomasSnyder@example.com';
recipients(2) = 'ThomasJSnyder@FrontierNet.net';
AirEmail_send(msg:recipients);
// Clean Up
freeLocalRef(msg);
*inlr = *ON;
/end-free
```

Figure 13.45: RPG program sending a text e-mail

It's funny. After all the code that was involved to create the procedures to send the e-mail, this is what we are left with to send the e-mail from an RPG application. I love service programs!

When you execute this code, you will receive some output because we activated debug on the session. You can review the output to troubleshoot any problems you may encounter when you are setting things up. After you have thoroughly tested your programs, you can turn off this feature by changing the hard-coded value in the **AirEmail_newMessage** procedure.

This Java code sample is very customized to show how you can use JavaMail to create a text e-mail client. You could replace the host, user, and password and run it yourself to see whether it works.

This is a minimal e-mail, but it will let you test out your JavaMail installation and configuration. Upon successful execution of this class, you'll be able to verify that your external Jar files are visible to the application. You will also know that your SMTP server is accessible from the IBM i system on the network, that your user ID and password are valid on the e-mail server, and that your service program is working properly.

14

JavaMail Formatting and Attachments

In the preceding chapter, we covered quite a bit of material that was focused on getting the core components of our e-mail service program established. Now, let's step back a bit to talk about e-mail standards as a foundation for the topics in this chapter, which focus on formatting and attachments.

The Simple Mail Transfer Protocol is a widely used standard for sending e-mail on the Internet. When SMTP was first created, it was intended to support only ASCII text data to be contained within the e-mails. The Multipurpose Internet Mail Extensions (MIME) standards were developed later to support binary files through SMTP.

SMTP is used only for the delivery of e-mails, which is all that we discuss in this book. The MIME extension of SMTP lets us specify the content of a message and lets us include the binary information we'll be discussing in the form of images and attachments.

Sending an E-Mail with HTML Content

We will use Hypertext Markup Language to handle the formatting in our e-mails. Using MIME, we can specify that the contents of the message are in HTML format.

Figure 14.1 shows a sample e-mail that contains HTML content.

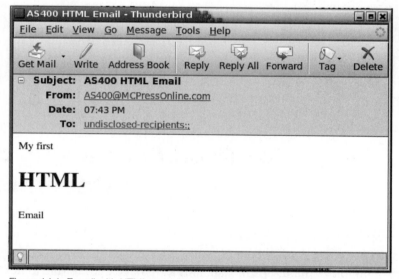

Figure 14.1: E-mail with HTML content viewed in recipient e-mail client

If you have experience with HTML, you will easily be able to format your e-mails to look very appealing to your users. If you don't have experience with HTML, you can further expand your relationships with the Internet department to put together some reusable templates for you. HTML is not a difficult language to understand, and we'll be using it only for some basic formatting, so even if you don't know HTML, you shouldn't have a problem understanding the provided examples.

In Chapter 13, we created our e-mails to contain simple text. To support HTML in our e-mail, we will create a multipart MIME message that sets the content type to HTML. Figure 14.2 shows the **MimeMultipart** RPG object reference in **SPAIREMAIL**.

```
D MimeMultipart...
D                    S              0     CLASS(*JAVA
D                                         :'javax.mail.internet-
D                                         .MimeMultipart')
```

Figure 14.2: MimeMultipart RPG object reference in SPAIREMAIL

The multipart message will be made up of one or more body parts (Figure 14.3).

```
D new_MimeBodyPart...
D                    PR                   Like(MimeBodyPart)
D                                         ExtProc(*JAVA:
D                                         'javax.mail.internet-
D                                         .MimeBodyPart':
D                                         *CONSTRUCTOR)
```

Figure 14.3: Prototype for default constructor method of MimeBodyPart class

We'll use the **setContent** method of the **MimeBodyPart** class (Figure 14.4) to indicate the content type of each particular body part.

Method Summary	
void	setContent(Object o, String type) A convenience method for setting this body part's content.

Figure 14.4: Partial JavaDoc for setContent method of MimeBodyPart class

Figure 14.5 shows the prototype for the **setContent** method of the **MimeBodyPart** class.

```
D MimeBodyPart_setContent...
D                    PR                   extproc(*JAVA:
D                                         'javax.mail.internet-
D                                         .MimeBodyPart':
D                                         'setContent')
D   argObject                             Like(jObject) const
D   argType                               Like(jString) const
```

Figure 14.5: Prototype for setContent method of MimeBodyPart class

You specify the content type in the second parameter of the **setContent** method. RFC2045 and RFC2046 define the content types that can be used, and you can find a list of available values on the Internet Assigned Numbers Authority (IANA) Web site, *http://www.iana.org/assignments/media-types*.

When we pass in the string value, we'll use a forward slash (/) to separate the content type and subtype. Because we're working with HTML, we'll use the **text/html** value to indicate that the content for the body part will be in HTML. If you wanted to specify plain text, you would use the **text/plain** value.

When we have completed the creation of the body part, we can add it to the multipart message using the **addBodyPart** method of the **MimeMultipart** class (Figure 14.6).

Method Summary	
void	**addBodyPart**(BodyPart part) Adds a Part to the multipart.

Figure 14.6: Partial JavaDoc for addBodyPart method of MimeMultipart class

The **addBodyPart** method, whose prototype is shown in Figure 14.7, accepts a **BodyPart** object parameter. We'll be passing a **MimeBodyPart** object, which is a subclass of **BodyPart**.

```
D MimeMultipart_addBodyPart...
D                   PR              extproc(*JAVA:
D                                   'javax.mail.internet-
D                                   .MimeMultipart':
D                                   'addBodyPart')
D   argBodyPart                     Like(BodyPart)
```

Figure 14.7: Prototype for addBodyPart method of MimeMultipart class

When creating e-mails that are being sent from the IBM i system, I like to include some disclaimer information. So, in addition to the typical string conversion and body part details in our typical custom procedure, we'll provide a selectable option to concatenate the disclaimer information at the end of the message content. Figure 14.8 shows the first section of the procedure to add HTML content.

```
P AirEmail_addHTML...
P                       B                EXPORT
D AirEmail_addHTML...
D                       PI
D   argMultipart                        like(MimeMultipart)
D   argHTML                   65535A    const varying
D                                       options(*varsize)
D   argFooter                     1N    const options(*nopass)
D*
D svString        S                     like(jString)
D svDate          S           8S 0
D svTime          S           6S 0
D svFooter        S           1N
D svBodyPart      S                     like(MimeBodyPart)
 /free
   // Create a standard footer to identify user sending email
   // and concatenate it onto the end of the message automatically.
   if %parms > 2;
     eval svFooter = argFooter;
   else;
     eval svFooter = *OFF;
   endif;
   if svFooter;
     svDate = %Dec(%Date():*ISO);
     svTime = %Dec(%Time():*ISO);
     svString = new_String(%trim(argHTML)
                      + '<br>'
                      + 'This Email may contain confidential '
                      + ' information.<br>'
                      + 'Yadda, Yadda, Yadda...<br>'
                      + 'Please do not reply to this
email.<br>'
                      + 'Email sent by: '
                      + %trim(QCUSER)
                      + ' on ' + %editw(svDate:'   /  / ')
                      + ' ' + %editw(svTime:'  :  : '));
   else;
     svString = new_String(%trim(argHTML));
   endif;
```

Figure 14.8: Procedure to add HTML content to a MimeMultipart object (part 1 of 2)

After the message string is created (with or without the optional disclaimer footer), the procedure constructs the **MimeBodyPart** object (Figure 14.9). The content of the body part is set to contain the message string, and the content type is set to **text/html**.

```
svBodyPart = new_MimeBodyPart();
MimeBodyPart_setContent(svBodyPart: svString:
                        new_String('text/html'));
MimeMultipart_addBodyPart(argMultipart: svBodyPart);
// Clean Up
freeLocalRef(svBodyPart);
freeLocalRef(svString);
/end-free
P                        E
```

Figure 14.9: Procedure to add HTML content to a MimeMultipart object (part 2 of 2)

Even though the examples we're using here assign a generic from address to the outgoing e-mails, you still will be able to identify the user who sent the e-mail by referring to the user information that is included in the e-mail. The user information is retrieved from a program status data structure that is defined in the service program to identify the user profile of the person who sent the e-mail.

After all the body parts have been added to the multipart message, the content will be added to the message using the **setContent** method of the **MimeMessage** class (Figure 14.10).

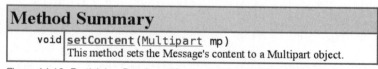

Method Summary	
void	`setContent(Multipart mp)` This method sets the Message's content to a Multipart object.

Figure 14.10: Partial JavaDoc for setContentMethod of MimeMessage class

Figure 14.11 shows the prototype for the **setContent** method.

```
D MimeMessage_setContent...
D                     PR                      extproc(*JAVA:
D                                             'javax.mail.internet-
D                                             .MimeMessage':
D                                             'setContent')
D   argMultipart                              Like(Multipart)
```

Figure 14.11: Prototype for setContent method of MimeMessage class

With the **MimeMessage** content assigned, we can now send the e-mail. Figure 14.12 shows the main RPG program that generates the HTML e-mail shown earlier.

```
    .
    . <Insert common header code here (Figure 13.3)>
    .
D   airMessage    S               like(MimeMessage)
D   airMultipart  S               like(MimeMultipart)
D   recipients    S       1024A   dim(100)
D   htmlString    S       65535A  varying
 /free
  CallP JavaServiceProgram();
  // Create the message
  airMessage = AirEmail_newMessage();
  AirEmail_setSubject(airMessage:'AS400 HTML Email');
  recipients = *BLANKS;
  recipients(1) = 'TomSnyder@MCPressOnline.com';
  recipients(2) = 'TomSnyder@Example.com';
  // Create the Multipart content
  htmlString = 'My first <h1>HTML</h1> Email';
  airMultipart = new_MimeMultipart(new_string('related'));
  AirEmail_addHTML(airMultipart: htmlString);
  // Add the Multipart content to the Message and send it.
  MimeMessage_setContent(airMessage: airMultipart);
  AirEmail_send(airMessage:recipients);
  // Clean Up
    .
    . <Insert cleanup code here>
    .
 /end-free
```

Figure 14.12: RPG program to create an e-mail with HTML content

For the sample HTML e-mail, we formatted the word "HTML" to be larger than the rest of the text by using the **<h1>** HTML keyword to indicate the beginning of the formatting and the **</h1>** keyword to indicate the end of the formatting.

Sending an HTML E-Mail with Images in RPG

Sending an image by using HTML code to refer to an image available through a URL is a simple matter of pointing to the image's location on the Internet. Figure 14.13 shows a sample e-mail that contains an image specified this way.

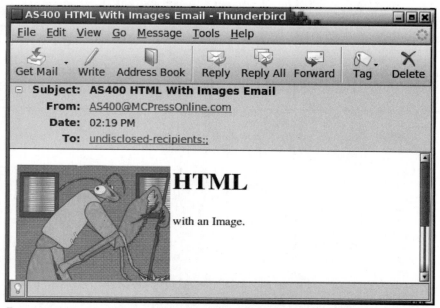

Figure 14.13: E-mail with image viewed in recipient e-mail client

The praying mantis picture is available on the Internet, so we'll create a reference to the image, just as you would for a Web page (Figure 14.14).

```
   .
   . <Insert common header code here (Figure 13.3)>
   .
 D  airMessage      S                    like(MimeMessage)
 D  airMultipart    S                    like(MimeMultipart)
 D  recipients      S           1024A    dim(100)
 D  htmlString      S          65535A    varying
  /free
   CallP JavaServiceProgram();
   airMessage = AirEmail_newMessage();
   AirEmail_setSubject(airMessage: 'AS400 HTML With Images Email');
   recipients = *BLANKS;
```

```
    recipients(1) = 'ThomasSnyder@example.com';
    recipients(2) = 'ThomasJSnyder@FrontierNet.net';
    // Create the Multipart content
    htmlString = '<img src="'
               + 'http://www.2wolvesout.com/graphics/mantis.jpg" '
               + 'align=left>'
               + '<h1>HTML</h1>'
               + ' with an Image.';
    airMultipart = new_MimeMultipart(new_string('related'));
    AirEmail_addHTML(airMultipart: htmlString);
    // Add the Multipart content to the Message and send it.
    MimeMessage_setContent(airMessage: airMultipart);
    AirEmail_send(airMessage: recipients);
    // Clean Up
    .
    . <Insert cleanup code here>
    .
    *inlr = *ON;
    /end-free
```

Figure 14.14: RPG program to create an e-mail with an image

No additional Java or RPG capabilities are being added here. We're doing all the work with HTML. The image source is being pointed to an image that is available on the Internet using HTML keywords:

```
<img src="http://www.2wolvesout.com/graphics/mantis.jpg" align=left>
```

When the e-mail client displays the e-mail message, the HTML code will present the image in the e-mail. Aligning the image to the left not only aligns the image but also allows the text to be displayed alongside the image.

One benefit of using this method to display images is that it minimizes the e-mail size. That's because the image is not physically contained in the e-mail but is displayed by referring to an image that is accessible via the Internet.

Another benefit (or disadvantage, depending on your perspective) is that the displayed image can change if the image at the location being pointed to changes. If you want to ensure that the contents of the e-mail do not change, you may not want to use this method.

Providing images this way is simple enough, but most e-mail clients normally won't display images unless you select the option to do so. Later, we'll discuss how to embed images so that the images are typically displayed without further action by the recipients.

Sending an E-mail with Attachments

In the next example, we will send an e-mail, attaching to it an Excel spreadsheet and a PDF file that we created in previous chapters. Figure 14.15 shows the e-mail message produced by this example.

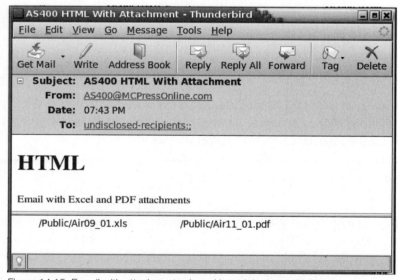

Figure 14.15: E-mail with attachments viewed in recipient e-mail client

The JAF supports the MIME types we will use for binary file attachments. In preparation for the inclusion of the JAF in Java 6, we'll put the activation references into the **SPAIRJAVA** prototype file instead of the **SPAIREMAIL** file.

The JAF contains the **DataSource** class, which is an interface that will provide the data we'll use for the attachments, along with the type of data. We will be using the **FileDataSource** class, but the **DataHandler** object, to be discussed shortly, needs the **DataSource** class defined for the method signature. Figure 14.16 shows the RPG object reference variable for the **DataSource** object.

```
D DataSource...
D                   S              O   CLASS(*JAVA
D                                      :'javax.activation.DataSource')
```

Figure 14.16: RPG object variable for DataSource object in SPAIRJAVA

The **FileDataSource** class provided with JAF (Figure 14.17) will contain the physical binary data of the attachments along with the MIME type we'll use for our e-mail.

```
D FileDataSource...
D                   S              O   CLASS(*JAVA
D                                      :'javax.activation.FileDataSource')
```

Figure 14.17: RPG object variable for FileDataSource object in SPAIRJAVA

The constructor method for the **FileDataSource** class (Figure 14.18) accepts a **String** parameter that will contain the file location of the attachment.

```
D new_FileDataSource...
D                   PR             O   EXTPROC(*JAVA
D                                      :'javax.activation.FileDataSource'
D                                      :*CONSTRUCTOR)
D   argFileName                        like(jstring) const
```

Figure 14.18: Prototype for constructor of javax.activation.FileDataSource class

The **DataHandler** class (Figure 14.19) is used to provide an interface to file commands that can be used with the data.

```
D DataHandler...
D                   S              O   CLASS(*JAVA
D                                      :'javax.activation.DataHandler')
```

Figure 14.19: RPG object variable for reference to DataHandler object in SPAIRJAVA

We'll create our data handler using a data source in the constructor (Figure 14.20).

```
D new_DataHandler...
D                   PR              O  EXTPROC(*JAVA
D                                      :'javax.activation.DataHandler'
D                                      :*CONSTRUCTOR)
D   argDataSource                      like(DataSource)
```

Figure 14.20: Prototype for constructor method of javax.activation.DataHandler class

Switching away from the **SPAIRJAVA** file, we'll define the **MimeBodyPart** methods using the JAF classes in the **SPAIREMAIL** prototype file. Figure 14.21 shows the method summary for the four methods of interest here.

Method Summary	
void	**setDataHandler**(DataHandler dh) This method provides the mechanism to set this body part's content.
void	**setDisposition**(String disposition) Set the "Content-Disposition" header field of this body part.
void	**setFileName**(String filename) Set the filename associated with this body part, if possible.
void	**setHeader**(String name, String value) Set the value for this header_name.

Figure 14.21: Partial JavaDoc for setContentMethod of MimeMessage class

The **setDataHandler** method of the **MimeBodyPart** class (Figure 14.22) sets the **DataHandler** object as the content of the body part.

```
D MimeBodyPart_setDataHandler...
D                   PR              extproc(*JAVA:
D                                   'javax.mail.internet-
D                                   .MimeBodyPart':
D                                   'setDataHandler')
D   argHandler                      like(DataHandler)
```

Figure 14.22: Prototype for setDataHandler method of MimeBodyPart class

The **setHeader** method (Figure 14.23) assigns the content type of the attachment in the body part. We will also use this method to assign a content ID, which can be used to identify the attachment.

```
D MimeBodyPart_setHeader...
D                     PR              extproc(*JAVA:
D                                     'javax.mail.internet-
D                                     .MimeBodyPart':
D                                     'setHeader')
D   argName                          like(jString) const
D   argValue                         like(jString) const
```

Figure 14.23: Prototype for setHeader method of MimeBodyPart class

We'll be using the **setDisposition** method of the **MimeBodyPart** class (Figure 14.24) to identify the body part as an attachment.

```
D MimeBodyPart_setDisposition...
D                     PR              extproc(*JAVA:
D                                     'javax.mail.internet-
D                                     .MimeBodyPart':
D                                     'setDisposition')
D   argDisp                          like(jString) const
```

Figure 14.24: Prototype for setDisposition method of MimeBodyPart class

The **setFileName** method (Figure 14.25) sets the name of the attachment that will be seen by the recipient.

```
D MimeBodyPart_setFileName...
D                     PR              extproc(*JAVA:
D                                     'javax.mail.internet-
D                                     .MimeBodyPart':
D                                     'setFileName')
D   argFileName                      like(jString) const
```

Figure 14.25: Prototype for setFileName method of MimeBodyPart class

To simplify the process of adding an attachment to an e-mail, we will create a new procedure called **AirEmail_addAttachment** that accepts the file name and content type to attach the file to a body part. Figure 14.26 shows this custom procedure.

```
P AirEmail_addAttachment...
P                     B                    EXPORT
D AirEmail_addAttachment...
D                     PI
D   argMultipart                          like(MimeMultipart)
D   argFileName                  65535A   const varying
D                                         options(*varsize)
D   argType                      512A     const varying
D                                         options(*varsize)
D   argCid                       256A     const varying
D                                         options(*varsize)
D*
D svBodyPart          S                   like(MimeBodyPart)
D svDataSource        S                   like(FileDataSource)
D svDataHandler       S                   like(DataHandler)
D svDate              S         8S 0
D svTime              S         6S 0
D svCid               S         256A
 /free
  svCid = '<' + %trim(argCid) + '>';
  svBodyPart = new_MimeBodyPart();
  svDataSource = new_FileDataSource(new_String(%trim(argFileName)));
  svDataHandler = new_DataHandler(svDataSource);
  MimeBodyPart_setDataHandler(svBodyPart: svDataHandler);
  MimeBodyPart_setHeader(svBodyPart
                   :new_String('Content-Type')
                   :new_String(%trim(argType)));
  MimeBodyPart_setDisposition(svBodyPart: new_String('attachment'));
  MimeBodyPart_setHeader(svBodyPart
                   :new_String('Content-ID')
                   :new_String(%trim(svCid)));
  MimeBodyPart_setFileName(svBodyPart
                     :new_String(%trim(argFileName)));
  MimeMultipart_addBodyPart(argMultipart: svBodyPart);
  freeLocalRef(svBodyPart);
  freeLocalRef(svDataHandler);
  freeLocalRef(svDataSource);
 /end-free
P                     E
```

Figure 14.26: Custom procedure AirEmail_addAttachment

That should do it for the steps involved to assign an attachment to a body part. Figure 14.27 shows the RPG program to attach an Excel spreadsheet and a PDF to an e-mail and send it.

```
   .
   . <Insert common header code here (Figure 13.3)>
   .
D  airMessage      S                    like(MimeMessage)
D  airMultipart    S                    like(MimeMultipart)
D  recipients      S           1024A    dim(100)
D  htmlString      S          65535A    varying
 /free
  CallP JavaServiceProgram();
  airMessage = AirEmail_newMessage();
  AirEmail_setSubject(airMessage:'AS400 HTML With Attachment');
  recipients = *BLANKS;
  recipients(1) = 'TomSnyder@MCPressOnline.com';
  recipients(2) = 'TomSnyder@Example.com';
  // Create the Multipart content
  airMultipart = new_MimeMultipart(new_string('related'));
  htmlString = '<h1>HTML</h1>'
             + ' Email with Excel and PDF attachments';
  AirEmail_addHTML(airMultipart:htmlString);
  // Add an Excel Attachment
  AirEmail_addAttachment(airMultipart
                    :'/Public/Air09_01.xls'
                    :'application/vnd.ms-excel'
                    :'attach1');
  // Add a PDF Attachment
  AirEmail_addAttachment(airMultipart
                    :'/Public/Air11_01.pdf'
                    :'application/pdf'
                    :'attach2');
  // Add the Multipart content to the Message and send it.
  MimeMessage_setContent(airMessage: airMultipart);
  AirEmail_send(airMessage:recipients);
  // Clean Up
   .
   . <Insert cleanup code here>
   .
  *inlr = *ON;
 /end-free
```

Figure 14.27: RPG program adding attachments to an e-mail

Sending an E-Mail with Embedded Images in Java

In our final e-mail example, we'll work with images again. This time, we'll embed the image right into the e-mail, as shown in Figure 14.28.

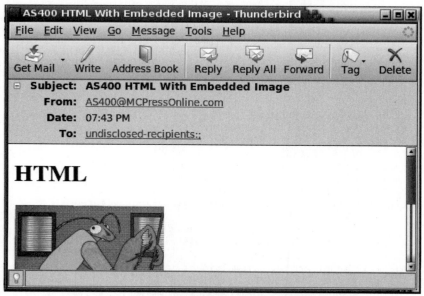

Figure 14.28: E-mail with an embedded image viewed in recipient e-mail client

We will embed the image into the e-mail by adding the image to the e-mail message as an attachment. Then, we'll reference the content ID that is assigned to the header of the body part.

Figure 14.29 shows the RPG program to add the embedded image to an e-mail. The HTML code in this example does not refer to an image source on the Internet. Instead, it uses the content id (**cid**) that was assigned to the attachment of the e-mail and displays it.

```
   .
   .  <Insert common header code here (Figure 13.3)>
   .
D  airMessage      S                    like(MimeMessage)
D  airMultipart    S                    like(MimeMultipart)
D  recipients      S           1024A    dim(100)
D  htmlString      S          65535A    varying
 /free
   CallP JavaServiceProgram();
   airMessage = AirEmail_newMessage();
   AirEmail_setSubject(airMessage:'AS400 HTML With Embedded Image');
   recipients = *BLANKS;
   recipients(1) = 'TomSnyder@MCPressOnline.com';
   recipients(2) = 'TomSnyder@Example.com';
   // Create the Multipart content
   airMultipart = new_MimeMultipart(new_string('related'));
   htmlString = '<h1>HTML</h1>'
              + '<img src="'
              + 'cid:attach1">'
              + ' with an Embedded Image.';
   AirEmail_addHTML(airMultipart:htmlString);
   // Add the Attachment
   AirEmail_addAttachment(airMultipart
                         :'/Public/mantis.jpg'
                         :'image/jpg'
                         :'attach1');
   // Add the Multipart content to the Message and send it.
   MimeMessage_setContent(airMessage: airMultipart);
   AirEmail_send(airMessage:recipients);
   // Clean Up
   .
   .  <Insert cleanup code here>
   .
   *inlr = *ON;
 /end-free
```

Figure 14.29: RPG program adding an embedded image to an e-mail

That's a Wrap

Well, that was our final example. I hope you have enjoyed the book and were able to find a lot of useful examples that you can start implementing right away. In addition to using the provided prototypes and procedures, I hope you have gained an understanding of how to use the JavaDocs to enhance your service programs to keep growing. Have fun!

EBCDIC/ASCII/Hexadecimal Translation Table

The following tables represent the most commonly used subset of available characters.

Lowercase characters	Hexadecimal EBCDIC	Hexadecimal ASCII	Uppercase characters	Hexadecimal EBCDIC	Hexadecimal ASCII
a	81	61	A	C1	41
b	82	62	B	C2	42
c	83	63	C	C3	43
d	84	64	D	C4	44
e	85	65	E	C5	45
f	86	66	F	C6	46
g	87	67	G	C7	47
h	88	68	H	C8	48
i	89	69	I	C9	49
j	91	6A	J	D1	4A
k	92	6B	K	D2	4B

Lowercase characters	Hexadecimal EBCDIC	Hexadecimal ASCII	Uppercase characters	Hexadecimal EBCDIC	Hexadecimal ASCII
l	93	6C	L	D3	4C
m	94	6D	M	D4	4D
n	95	6E	N	D5	4E
o	96	6F	O	D6	4F
p	97	70	P	D7	50
q	98	71	Q	D8	51
r	99	72	R	D9	52
s	A2	73	S	E2	53
t	A3	74	T	E3	54
u	A4	75	U	E4	55
v	A5	76	V	E5	56
w	A6	77	W	E6	57
x	A7	78	X	E7	58
y	A8	79	Y	E8	59
z	A9	7A	Z	E9	5A

Other characters	Hexadecimal EBCDIC	Hexadecimal ASCII	Control characters	Hexadecimal EBCDIC	Hexadecimal ASCII
Space	40	20	NUL	00	00
.	4B	2E	SOH	01	01
<	4C	3C	STX	02	02
(	4D	28	ETX	03	03
+	4E	2B	HT	05	09
|	4F	7C	DEL	07	7F
&	50	26	VT	0B	0B
!	5A	21	FF	0C	0C
$	5B	24	CR	0D	0D
*	5C	2A	SO	0E	0E
)	5D	29	SI	0F	A9
;	5E	3B	DLE	10	10
-	60	2D	DC1	11	11

Other characters	Hexadecimal EBCDIC	Hexadecimal ASCII	Control characters	Hexadecimal EBCDIC	Hexadecimal ASCII
/	61	2F	DC2	12	12
,	6B	2C	BS	16	08
%	6C	25	CAN	18	18
_	6D	5F	EM	19	19
>	6E	3E	FS	22	1C
?	6F	3F	LF	25	0A
:	7A	3A	ESC	27	1B
#	7B	23	ACK	2E	06
@	7C	40	BEL	2F	07
'	7D	27	SYN	32	16
{	C0	7B	RS	35	1E
}	D0	7D	EOT	37	04
\	E0	5C	DC4	3C	14
			NAK	3D	15
			SUB	3F	1A

Numeric characters	Hexadecimal EBCDIC	Hexadecimal ASCII
0	F0	30
1	F1	31
2	F2	32
3	F3	33
4	F4	34
5	F5	35
6	F6	36
7	F7	37
8	F8	38
9	F9	39

B

Data Formats for Use with HSSFDataFormat

The following table lists the format indexes and strings for the built-in formats used with the **HSSFDataFormat** class.

Index	Format string
0	"General"
1	"0"
2	"0.00"
3	"#,##0"
4	"#,##0.00"
5	"($#,##0_);($#,##0)"
6	"($#,##0_);[Red]($#,##0)"
7	"($#,##0.00);($#,##0.00)"
8	"($#,##0.00_);[Red]($#,##0.00)"
9	"0%"
0xa	"0.00%"
0xb	"0.00E+00"

0xc	"# ?/?"
0xd	"# ??/??"
0xe	"m/d/yy"
0xf	"d-mmm-yy"
0x10	"d-mmm"
0x11	"mmm-yy"
0x12	"h:mm AM/PM"
0x13	"h:mm:ss AM/PM"
0x14	"h:mm"
0x15	"h:mm:ss"
0x16	"m/d/yy h:mm"
0x17–0x24	*Reserved for international and undocumented.*
0x25	"(#,##0_);(#,##0)"
0x26	"(#,##0_);[Red](#,##0)"
0x27	"(#,##0.00_);(#,##0.00)"
0x28	"(#,##0.00_);[Red](#,##0.00)"
0x29	"_(*#,##0_);_(*(#,##0);_(* \"-\"_);_(@_)"
0x2a	"_($*#,##0_);_($*(#,##0);_($* \"-\"_);_(@_)"
0x2b	"_(*#,##0.00_);_(*(#,##0.00);_(*\"-\"??_);_(@_)"
0x2c	"_($*#,##0.00_);_($*(#,##0.00);_($*\"-\"??_);_(@_)"
0x2d	"mm:ss"
0x2e	"[h]:mm:ss"
0x2f	"mm:ss.0"
0x30	"##0.0E+0"
0x31	"@" – *This is text format.*
0x31	"text" – *Alias for "@".*

C

References and Resources

RPG

ILE RPG Language Reference (SC09-2508-04).

ILE RPG Programmer's Guide (SC09-2507-06).

ILE RPG/400 Reference (SC09-2077-00).

Moving to Integrated Language Environment for RPG IV. IBM Redbook (GG24-4358-00).

Who Knew You Could Do That with RPG IV? A Sorcerer's Guide to System Access and More. IBM Redbook (SG24-5402-00).

"Additional RPG Coding for Using Java"
WebSphere Development Studio Client Information Center

http://publib.boulder.ibm.com/infocenter/iadthelp/v7r0/index.jsp?topic=/com. ibm.etools.iseries.pgmgd.doc/c0925076177.htm

"Free-Form Syntax"

IBM i Information Center

http://publib.boulder.ibm.com/infocenter/iseries/v6r1m0/topic/rzasd/ sc092508682.htm

Free-Format RPG IV: How to Bring Your RPG Programs Into the 21st Century. By Jim Martin. Lewisville, TX: MC Press Online, 2005.

Java

Java 2 Platform Standard Edition v1.4.2 JavaDocs

http://java.sun.com/j2se/1.4.2/docs/api

Java Native Interface (JNI) 1.4.2 Specification

http://java.sun.com/j2se/1.4.2/docs/guide/jni

Building Java Applications for the iSeries Server with VisualAge for Java 3.5. IBM Redbook (SG24-6245-00).

POI

The Apache POI Project

http://poi.apache.org

POI API Documentation

http://poi.apache.org/apidocs/index.html

iText

iText Home Page

http://www.lowagie.com/iText

iText JavaDocs

http://www.1t3xt.info/api

iText in Action: Creating and Manipulating PDF. By Bruno Lowagie. New York: Manning Publications, 2007.

JavaMail

JavaMail Home Page

http://java.sun.com/products/javamail

JavaMail API Design Specification Version 1.4

http://java.sun.com/products/javamail/JavaMail-1.4.pdf

JavaMail API Documentation

http://java.sun.com/products/javamail/javadocs/index.html

JavaBeans Activation Framework (JAF)

http://java.sun.com/javase/technologies/desktop/javabeans/jaf

JavaBeans Activation Framework JavaDocs

http://java.sun.com/javase/technologies/desktop/javabeans/glasgow/javadocs/index.html

Other Topics

Modernizing IBM eServer iSeries Application Data Access – A Roadmap Cornerstone. IBM Redbook (SG24-6393-00).

OS/400 National Language Support APIs (SC41-5863-03).

Index

A

access control, Java and JNI, private vs. public, 83–85
activation groups, 26–29, 34–36, **35**, 39–40, **40**
    *CALLER option in, 27, 40
    *ELIGIBLE option and, 29
    identifying, on open files, 39–40, **40**
    named, 27–28
    *NEW option in, 27
    reclaiming, with Reclaim Activation Group (RCLACTGRP), 28–29
    separate, use of, 28
adding elements to PDF document, 254, **254**
addresses for e-mail, 321–327, **321–327**. *See also* e-mail
    multiple, 322–327, **323–327**, 343
    order of, 343
Adobe, 1. *See also* PDF
Advanced Integrated RPG. *See* AIR
advanced RPG, 47–76
    APIs and, 67–76
    built-in functions and, 56–67. *See also* built-in functions (BIFs)
    free-format syntax and, 47–48, 47*t*
    opcodes in, free-format, 47–48, 47*t*
AIR, 5
AIR service program, 6–8, 7*t*

AirExcel_setCellValueXxx, 188–189, **188–189**
AIRLIB, 8
AIRSRC, 8
alignment of Cell contents, 181–182, **181**, **182**
alignment of image, 293, **293–294**
anchors, for hyperlinks, 280–285, **280–285**
Apache POI, 155–156, 156*t*. *See also* Excel spreadsheets; POI
APIs, 16, 67–76
    bit operations and, 61
    built-in functions (BIFs) vs., 68
    Code Conversion Allocation (QtqlconvOpen()), 69–71, **70**, 72–76, **72**, 73–**74**, **75**
    Code Conversion Deallocation (iconv_close()), 71, 74
    conversion descriptor for CCSID conversion, 71
    Convert Data (QDCXLATE), 69, 130
    custom procedure creation using, 72–76, **72**, 73–**74**, **75**
    EBCDIC and ASCII conversion using Code Conversion (iconv()), 68–69
    exception handling, 55–56
    Execute Command (QCMDEXC) API in, 25, 53–54, **54–55**
    finding, API finder website for, 68
    Java Invocation, 106

NOTE: Boldface numbers indicate code and illustrations; *t* indicates a table.

APIs, *continued*
  opcodes vs., 68
  open, for Java file descriptors, 117–118,
    117, 118*t*
  Register a User Written Condition Handler
    (CEEHDLR) API in, 55
application programming interface. *See* APIs
arrays of objects, 144–148, **144–148**
ASCII, 12–13, 130
  EBCDIC/Hex translations tables for, 363*t*,
    364*t*, 365*t*
  Code Conversion Allocation
    (QtqlconvOpen()) API for, 69–71, **70**,
    72–76, **72**, 73–**74**, **75**
  Code Conversion Deallocation
    (iconv_close()) API for, 71, 74
  coded character set identifiers (CCSIDs) and,
    69, 69*t*
  Convert Data (QDCXLATE) API for, 69, 130
  EBCDIC conversion to/from, 68–69, 130,
    140–141, **140–141**
  string manipulation BIFs to clean, 57–61,
    58–59
attachments to e-mail, 354–359, **354–359**
authentication, e-mail and, 332

B

bar codes, 310–313, **302**
  characters above/below, 304, **305**
  guard bars in, 306–307, **306–307**, 311–312,
    311–312
  image creation from, 307–309, **307–309**
  object references for, 309–310, **309–310**
  supplemental digits in, 303–304, **303–304**
  types of, EAN, UPC, etc., 302, 305–306,
    305–306
Barozzi, Nicola Ken, 4
batch processing, Java standard streams and, 117
BEGSR, 50–51, **50–51**
binding, modules and, 19–20
bit operation BIFs, 61–63, 62*t*, **62–63**
  integer bytes and ranges in, 62, 62*t*
  unsigned integer bytes and ranges, 62, **62**
%BITAND, 61
%BITNOT, 61

%BITOR, 61
%BITXOR, 61
borders around images, 291–297, **291**, **292–297**
built-in data formats, Excel/HSSFDataFormat,
    191–192, **191**, **192**, **193**, 192*t*, 367*t*, 368*t*
built-in functions (BIFs), 20, 56–67
  APIs and vs., 68
  bit operation, 61–63, 62*t*, **62–63**
  learning more about, references for, 67
  quantification, 63–67, **64–67**
  string manipulation, 56–61

C

*CALLER option, 40
  activation groups and, 27
calling programs, RPG, 78
CALLP, free-format syntax and, 49
camel case in Java names, 83
CEEHDLR (Register a User Written Condition
    Handler) API, 55
CEEHDLU (Unregister a User Written
    Condition Handler) API, 55
Cells, in Excel spreadsheets, 166–169, **166–169**,
    175, 227–229, **227**, **228**, **229**
  alignment of contents in, 181–182, **181**, **182**
  blank cells in, 231, **231–232**
  boolean, 232, **232**
  constructors for font and cell styles for,
    183–184, **184**
  data types in, getCellType, 228, **228** 233, **233**
  fill pattern in, 182–183, **182–183**
  font assigned to, 183, **183**
  formulas in, 232, **232**
  formulas in, getCellFormula, 229, **229**
  formulas in, setCellFormula method for,
    218–219, **218**, **219**
  null, Iterator class for, 222–223, **222**, **223**
  number of, getCellNum, 229, **229**
  numeric value assigned to, 170–171, **171**,
    188–189, **188–189**
  numeric value of, getNumericCellValue, 229,
    229, 232, **232–233**
  string value assigned to, 169–170, **169**, **170**,
    188–189, **188–189**

string value of, getStringCellValue, 229, **229**, 233, **233**
styles for, 181–183, **181–183**
unknown numbers of, Iterator class for, 222–223, **222**, **223**
values in, getBooleanCellValue, 228–229, **228**
working with, within Rows, 226–227, **226**, **227**
cells, in PDF tables, 275–276, **275**, **276**
CHAIN, free-format syntax and, 50, 53
%check string manipulation BIF, 57, 60
%checkR string manipulation BI, 60
%checkR string manipulation BIF, 57
Chunk text object, PDF/iText, 250–251, **250–251**
CL, naming conventions for, 6
class path, Java, 82
classes, 15, 77, 129–133
    bit operations with, 61
    constructor methods for, 78, **79**
    creating, 79, **79**
    fields within, accessing, 129–130
    finding, 131, **131**
    get and set field routines in, 134, 134*t*, 143–144, **143**
    identifying fields in, 131–132, **131–132**
    identifying methods of, 132–133
    importing, 81
    inheritance in, 88–90, **88–89**
    interface in, 96–100, **96–100**
    naming, 79
    Object class and, 91
    packaging, 80
    path for, 82
    polymorphism in, 90–91, **90–91**
Code Conversion (iconv()) API, 68–69
Code Conversion Allocation (QtqlconvOpen()) API, 69–71, **70**, 72–76, **72**, **73–74**, **75**
Code Conversion Deallocation (iconv_close()) API, 71, 74
coded character set identifiers (CCSIDs), 69, 69*t*, 69
    conversion descriptor APIs and, 71
cohesion, 39
colors, in Excel spreadsheets, **177**, 178–181, **178**, **179**, **180–181**, 184–188, **185–188**
colors, in PDF docs, 268–271, **268–271**

for font, 272, **272**
    hexadecimal codes for, 268–271, **268–271**
column width, Excel, 199–203, **199–203**
comments, Java and JavaDoc, 51, 101–104, **101**, **102**, **103**, 104*t*. *See also* JavaDoc
common code for e-mail/JavaMail, 318, **318–319**
common code for Excel spreadsheets, 158–159
common code for PDF document, 245–246, **245**
compatibility issues, Java, 106
compiler directives, 43–46, 44*t*
    errors and, 46
    free-format syntax and, 46, 48
    specs for, 46
    variables and, 46
compiling
    compiler directives for (ILE), 43–46, 44*t*
    Create Bound RPG Program (CRTBNDRPG) and, 9
    Create Program (CRTPGM) and, 9
    Create RPG Module (CRTRPGMOD) and, 9
    examples from book, 8–9, **9**
    ILE source into PGM objects, 21–22
compliance, 5
constants, in Excel project, 159–161, **160–161**
constructor methods, 78, **79**
constructors, 109, **109**
Convert RPG Source (CVTRPGSRC), 21
COPY files
    embedded SQL and, 4
    ILE and, 35–36
    naming conventions for, 6
    OPM to ILE source conversion and, 21
    service programs and, 8
/COPY compiler directive, 43
/COPY statement, procedures and, 23
Create Bound RPG Program (CRTBNDRPG), 9, 21–22
Create Program (CRTPGM), 9, 22
Create RPG Module (CRTRPGMOD), 9, 22
Create RPG Program (CRTRPGPGM), 21–22
Create Service Program (CRTSRVPGM), 30
Create Source Physical File (CRTSRCPF), 20
CRTBNDRPG (Create Bound RPG Program), 9, 21–22
CRTPGM (Create Program), 9, 22

CRTRPGMOD (Create RPG Module), 9, 22
CRTRPGPGM (Create RPG Program), 21–22
CRTSRCPF (Create Source Physical File), 20
CRTSRVPGM (Create Service Program), 30
currency formatting, in Excel spreadsheets, 194–195, **194**
custom procedure creation with APIs, 72–76, **72**, 73–**74**, **75**
CVTRPGSRC (Convert RPG Source), 21

D

D spec, in service program, 50–51, **50–51**
data formatting, Excel, 189–195, **190–195**
data types, 14
date and time formatting, in Excel spreadsheets, 190–191, **190**, **191**, 194, 196–198, **196–198**
default access, 84
/DEFINE compiler directive, 43
development skills, 14–15
display property setting, Excel, 203–207, **203–207**
document and Document class, in PDF, 246–248, **246–248**
downloading source code, 8
downloads for examples, websites for, 4

E

EAN bar codes. *See* bar codes
EBCDIC. *See also* ASCII
    ASCII conversion to/from using Code Conversion (iconv()), 68–69, 130, 140–141, **140–141**
    ASCII/Hex translation tables for, 363*t*, 364*t*, 365*t*
    Code Conversion Allocation (QtqlconvOpen()) API for, 69–71, **70**, 72–76, **72**, 73–**74**, **75**
    Code Conversion Deallocation (iconv_close()) API for, 71, 74
    coded character set identifiers (CCSIDs) and, 69, 69*t*
    Convert Data (QDCXLATE) API for, 69, 130
Eclipse IDE, 100
electronic document creation, 17
%ELEM, 64

*ELIGIBLE option, activation groups and, 29
/ELSEIF compiler directive, 43–44, 44*t*, 46
/ELSE compiler directive, 43–44, 44*t*
e-mail, 13, 17–18, 315–361. *See also* JavaMail
    addresses for, 321–327, **321–327**
    addresses in
        multiple, 322–327, **323–327**, 343
        order of, 343
    attachments to, 354–359, **354–359**
    authentication in, 332
    common code for, 318, **318–319**
    distributing documents using, 17–18
    formatting for, 345–361
    From line in, 334–335, **334**, **335**
    HTML content in, 346–351, **346**, **347–351**
    images in, Java, 360–361, **360**, **361**
    images in, RPG, 352–354, **352**, **352–353**
    JavaDocs for, 319
    JavaMail for, 18, 316–319
    JavaMail implementation requirements for, 317
    JavaMail installation for, 317–318, **317–318**
    MIME messages in, 330–337, **330–337**
    MimeMessage subclass in, 339–344, **339–344**
    Multipurpose Internet Mail Extension (MIME) for, 345
    Send method for, 338–339, **338**, **339**
    sending a message using, 319–320, **320**
    session creation for, 327–329, **327–329**, 329*t*
    Simple Mail Transfer Protocol (SMTP) for, 345
    SPAIRE-MAIL and, 319
    storing and managing on IFS, 315–316
    Subject line in, 335–336, **335–336**
    SVAIREMAIL service program for, 7, 319
    Text portion of, 336, **336–337**
    Transport class to send message in, 337–338, **337**, **338**
    user name and passwords for, 320–321, 332
embedded SQL, 5
    pre-V6R1 support for, 4
encapsulation, 20, 84–87, **85–86**, **87**
/END-EXEC compiler directive, 44
/END-FREE compiler directive, 44, 46, 48
/ENDIF compiler directive, 43–44, 44*t*, 46
ENDSR, 50–51, **50–51**
%eof, 49–50

error handling. *See* exception handling
%ERROR, 55
European Article Number (EAN) bar code. *See*
    bar codes
EVAL, free-format syntax and, 50
Excel spreadsheets, 1–2, 12, 13, 17, 155–241, **177**
    AirExcel_setCellValueXxx, 188–189, **188–189**
    built-in data formats for, 191–193, **191**, **192**,
        193, 192*t*, 367*t*, 368*t*, 367
    Cell in, 166–169, **166–169**, 175, 226–229,
        226–229, 231–233, **231–233**
        constructors for font and cell styles for,
            183–184, **184**
        styles for, 181–183, **181–183**
    column width in, 199–203, **199–203**
    constants in, 159–161, **160–161**
    constructors for font and cell styles for,
        183–184, **184**
    currency formatting in, 194–195, **194**
    data formatting in, 189–195, **190–195**
    date and time formatting in, 190–191, **190**,
        191, 194, 196–198, **196–198**
    FileOutputStream for, 172–173, **173**
    font and cell style constructors in, 183–184, **184**
    fonts and colors in, **177**, 178–181, **178**, **179**,
        180–181, 184–188, **185–188**
    formatting and properties in, 177–215
    formulas in, 217–222, **218**
        MAX and maximum values, 221–222, **221**
        program example using, 219–222, **219–222**
        setCellFormula method for, 218–219,
            218, **219**
        Total and SUM, 220–221, **221**
    graphs and charts in, 235–241, **236**, **239**
    headers and footers in, 207–215, **208–215**
    Hello World application using RPG and,
        174–175, **174**
    hierarchy of spreadsheet items in, 175
    Horrible Spreadsheet Format (HSSF) in POI
        and, 155
    HSSFDataFormat in, 367*t*, 368*t*
    images in, 235–241, **236**, **239**
    Iterator class and, 222–223, **222**, **223**,
        230–231, **230**, **231**
    landscape page orientation for, 204–205, **205**,
        206–207, **206**
    loops in, 230–231
    numeric value assigned to cell in, 170–171,
        171, 188–189, **188–189**
    POI and,
        creating spreadsheets with, 155–156, 156*t*
        installing, 156–157, **157**
        version compatibility in, 157–158
    print and display property setting for,
        203–207, **203–207**
    reading an existing spreadsheet in, 230–235,
        230–235
    recalculation in, forcing, 240–241
    Row in, 164–166, **164–166**, 175, 224–226,
        226–227, **226**, **227**
    RPG common code for, 158–159
    Sheet in, 162–164, **162–164**, 175
    sheet indexes in, 223–224, **224**
    SPAIREXCEL and, 159
    spreadsheet creation, with POI, 155–156, 156*t*
    string value assigned to cell in, 169–170, **169**,
        170, 188–189, **188–189**
    SVAIREXCEL service program for, 7, 159
    templates for, 235–237, **236**, **237**
    text wrap in, 199–203, **199–203**
    updating existing, 238–239, **238**, **239**
    Visual Basic for Applications (VBA) and,
        240–241
    Workbook in, 161–162, **161–162**, 171–173,
        171–173, 175
    zoom in, 204, 206–207
exception handling, 149–153, **149–153**
    compiler directives and, 46
    %ERROR in, 55
    Java, 149–153, **149–153**
    MONITOR in, 55–56
    %OPEN in, 55
    PERCOLATE and, 55
    PROMOTE and, 55
    Register a User Written Condition Handler
        (CEEHDLR) API in, 55
    RESUME and, 55
    %STATUS in, 55
    STDERR in, 116–118

exception handling, *continued*
    subroutines and, 56
    try/catch in, 55–56
    Unregister a User Written Condition Handler
        (CEEHDLU) API in, 55
/EXEC SQL compiler directive, 44
Execute Command (QCMDEXC) API, 25,
    53–54, **54–55**
exporting procedures in service program, 30–31
extends keyword, 88–90, **88–89**
external file processing, string manipulation
    BIFs and, 57–61, **58–59**

F

F spec, in service program, 50–51, **50–51**
fields, 129–130
    accessing, 129–130
    get and set routines for, 134, 134*t*, 143–144, **143**
    identifying, 131–132, **131–132**
    ILE and, length of, 20
file definitions, 82
file descriptors, opening, open API, 117–118,
    117, 118*t*
file names, naming conventions for, 6
file operation status, free-format syntax and,
    determining, 49–50
File Transfer Protocol (FTP), 12–13
FileOutputStream, 172–173, **173**
fill pattern in Cell, 182–183, **182–183**
fixed-format programs
    free-format syntax and vs., 49
    RPG, in ILE, 34–36, **35**
    RPG, in OPM, 32–34, **32, 33, 34**
fonts, in Excel spreadsheets and, **177**, 178–188,
    178, 179, 180–181, 183 185–188
fonts, in PDF docs, 271–274, **271–274**
    color of, 272, **272**
footer. *See* headers and footers, Excel
formatting
    in e-mail, 345–361. *See also* e-mail
    in Excel, 177–215. *See also* Excel
    in PDF documents, 267–289, **267**
formulas in Excel, 217–222, **218**, 229, 232, **232**
    forcing spreadsheet recalculation and, 240–241
    MAX and maximum values, 221–222, **221**

    program example using, 219–222, **219–222**
    setCellFormula method for, 218–219, **218, 219**
    Total and SUM, 220–221, **221**
    Visual Basic for Applications (VBA) and,
        240–241
Free-Format RPG IV, 67
free-format syntax, 48–56, 47*t*
    CALLP in, 49
    compiler directives and, 46, 48
    converting to, 48–56
    %eof and, 49–50
    EVAL in, 50
    exception monitoring, 55–56
    file operation status in, 49–50
    fixed-format vs., 49
    opcodes in, RPG, 47–48, 47*t*
    prototyping and, 53–54, **54–55**
    specs in service programs and, F and D,
        51–53, **52–53**
    subroutines in, 50–51, **50–51**
/FREE compiler directive, 44, 46, 48

G

garbage collection, 123–125, **123–125**
global variables, 84
graphs and charts, 235–241, **235, 239**
    Excel spreadsheets and, 235–241, **235, 239**
    recalculating the spreadsheet for, forcing,
        240–241
    templates for, 235–237, **236, 237**
    updating existing spreadsheet with, 238–239,
        238, 239
    Visual Basic for Applications (VBA) and,
        240–241
guard bars in bar codes 306–307, **306–307**,
    311–312, **311–312**

H

headers and footers, Excel, 207–215, **208–215**
heap, 109
Hello World in Excel–RPG application,
    174–175, **174**
Hello World in Java/RPG, 126–127, **126**
Hello World in PDF, 260–261, **260–261**

hexadecimal codes
    ASCII/EBCDIC translation tables for, 363*t*, 364*t*, 365*t*
    color codes, 268–271, **268–271**
Horrible Spreadsheet Format (HSSF), 17, 155
HTML, 254, 257, 346–351, **346**, **347–351**. *See also* e-mail
    e-mail containing, 346–351, **346**, **347–351**
hyperlinks, PDF docs, 279–285, **279**, **280–285**
    TAG statement in RPG and, 282
Hypertext Markup Language. *See* HTML

I

IBM, 16
    naming conventions for, 6
IBM i operating system, version, 3
iconv() (Code Conversion API), 68–69
iconv_close() (Code Conversion Deallocation) API, 71, 74
/IF compiler directive, 43–44, 44*t*, 46
ILE, 11, 14, 19–46
    activation groups and, 26–29, 34–36, **35**, 39–40, **40**
    advanced RPG in. *See* advanced RPG
    built-in functions (BIFs) in, 20
    cohesion and, 39
    compiler directives in, 43–46, 44*t*
    compiling ILE source into a PGM object in, 21–22
    concepts of programming in, 31–42
    Convert RPG Source (CVTRPGSRC) and, 21
    converting existing OPM source code to, 20–21
    COPY files and, 35–36
    COPY files and, in OPM to ILE conversion, 21
    Create Bound RPG Program (CRTBNDRPG) and, 21–22
    Create Program (CRTPGM) and, 22
    Create RPG Module (CRTRPGMOD) and, 22
    Create RPG Program (CRTRPGPGM) and, 21–22
    Create Source Physical File (CRTSRCPF) and, 20
    encapsulation and, 20
    field size/length in, 20
    fixed-format programs in, ILE/RPG, 34–36, **35**

fixed-format programs in, OPM/RPG, 32–34, **32**, **33**, **34**
    modules and modular programming in, 19, 23
    OPM programming vs., 31–42
    parameter passing in, keywords for, 24–25
    performance benefits of, 19
    procedure interface in, 25–26
    procedures in, 20, 23, 37–39, **37–38**
    prototyping in, 23–24, **24**
    record size/length in, 20
    reusability of code created in, 19
    service programs in, 29–31, 41–42, **41–42**
    /COPY statement and, 23
    subroutine converted to procedure in, 36–37, **36**
    subroutines and, 23
    variables and scope in, 20
ILE RPG Language Reference, 5
ILE RPG Programmer's Guide, 5
ILE RPG Reference, 67
images, 235–241, **235**, **239**
    adding into document, 296–297, **296–297**
    align, 293, **293–294**
    border properties for, 294–295, **294–295**
    borders around, 291–297, **291**, **292–297**
    create, 292, **292–293**
    in e-mail, Java, 360–361, **360**, **361**
    in e-mail, RPG, 352–354, **352**, **352–353**
    in Excel spreadsheets and, 235–241, **235**, **239**
    in PDF docs, 291–301, **291**, **292–301**
    text wrapped around, 297–301, **298**, **299–301**
importing Java classes, 81
importing packages, * to indicate, 80–81
INCLUDE statement, service programs and, 8
/INCLUDE compiler directive, 43
indexes, Sheet, 223–224, **224**
inheritance, 88–90, **88–89**
    extends keyword for, 88–90, **88–89**
    overriding, 92–94, **92–93**
    polymorphism and, 90–91, **90–91**
instance variables, RPG code sample to access Java, 137–144, **137–144**
instances, 82
integrated development environment (IDE), Java, 100
Integrated Language Environment. *See* ILE

---

interface, Java, 96–100, **96–100**
Internet Assigned Numbers Authority (IANA), 348
ISO-8859 character set, 69
Iterator class, 222–223, **222**, **223**, 230–231,
   230, **231**
iText, 17. *See also* PDF
   Chunk text object in, 250–251, **250–251**
   components of, 246–253
   document and Document class in, 246–248,
     246–248
   download website for, 4
   hyperlinks and anchors in, 280–285, **280–285**
   Hypertext Markup Language (HTML) and,
     254, 257
   installing, 243–244, **244**
   JavaDocs for, 104*t*, 246
   naming conventions for, 6
   Paragraph text object in, 252–253, **252**, **253**
   Phrase text object in, 251–252, **251–252**
   rectangles and Rectangle class in, 247,
     248–250, **247**, **248–250**, 258, **258**
   references and resources for, 371
   Rich Text Format (RTF) and, 254, 257
   text components in, 250–253
   version compatibility for, 245

J

Jar files, 81
   external, installing on the IFS, 113–116,
     114–115
   external, referring to, 111–113
Java and JNI, 2–3, 14, 77–104, 129–153
   access control in, 83–84
   arrays of objects in, 144–148, **144–148**
   ASCII-to-EBCDIC conversion in, 130,
     140–141, **140–141**
   batch processing and, standard streams and, 117
   bit operations with classes in, 61
   character sets used in, Unicode, 130
   class path in, 82
   classes in, 77, 129–133. *See also* classes
   comments in, 51, 101–104, **101**, **102**, **103**,
     104*t*. *See also* JavaDocs
   compatibility of, backward and forward, 106
   constants in, 159–161, **160–161**

constructor methods in, 78, **79**
default access in, 84
destroying JVM in, 118, 120, **120–121**
downloading resources for, 4
encapsulation in, 84–87, **85–86**, **87**
exception handling in, 149–153, **149–153**
fields in classes, accessing, 129–130
file descriptors in, opening, open API,
   117–118, **117**, 118*t*
garbage collection in, 123–125, **123–125**
get and set field routines in, 134, 134*t*,
   143–144, **143**
heap allocation in, 109
Hello World program using, 126–127, **126**
images in e-mails and, 360–361, **360**, **361**
importing classes to programs in, 81
inheritance in, 88–90, **88–89**
integrated development environment (IDE)
   and, 100
interface in, 96–100, **96–100**
Invocation API, 106
Iterator class for, 222–223, **222**, **223**,
   230–231, **230**, **231**
Jar files in, 81, 111–116, **114–115**
Java Native Interface (JNI) in, 129–153
JavaBeans Naming Standards in, 84–87,
   85–86, **87**
JavaDoc commenting tool and, 51, 101–104,
   101, **102**, **103**, 104*t*, 159
JNI file for, 110
main method in, 83
methods in, 14, 78
methods, accessing from within RPG, 108, **108**
naming conventions for, 5–6, 79–80, 83
Object class in, 91
object constructors in, 109, **109**
objects in, 78–79
objects in, accessing from within RPG, 107, **107**
overloading in, 94–95, **94**, **95**
overriding in, 92–94, **92–93**
packages in, 79–81
POI version compatibility and, 157–158
polymorphism in, 90–91, **90–91**
pop a frame, 125, **125**
primitive types in, 110–111, 110–111*t*, **111**

private vs. public access in, 83–85
protected access in, 84
QJVAJNI in, JNI service program for, 121
QSYSINC/QRPGLESRC,JNI file in, 110
reference variables in, 78, 109
references and resources for, 370
reusable code and, 15
RPG and, 105–127
    code sample to access instance variables
      in, 137–144, **137–144**
    example of concepts used by, 135–137,
      135–136
    integration with, 15–16
Send method, in e-mail, 338–339, **338**, **339**
serialization in, 121–123, **122**
standard streams in, STDIN, STDOUT,
    STDERR, 116–118
starting JVM in, 118, 119–120, **119–120**
static methods in, 82
subpackages in, 80–81
SVAIRJAVA service program for, 7, 113
synchronization in, 122
this keyword in, 87
thread-safe RPG with
    THREAD(*SERIALIZE) in, 121–123, **122**
try/catch exception monitoring in, 55–56
type signatures in, 133, 133*t*
variables in, 84–87, **85–86**, **87**
version of, determining, 105–106, **106**
Java Archive. *See* Jar files
Java Native Interface (JNI), 129–153. *See also*
    Java and JNI
Java Software Development Kit (SDK), 3
Java Virtual Machine, 16
JavaBeans Naming Standards in, 84–87, **85–86**,
    87, 84
JavaDoc commenting tool, 51, 101–104, **101**,
    102, **103**, 104*t*
    iText and, 246
    JavaMail and, 319
    POI and, 159
JavaMail, 18, 316–319. *See also* e-mail
    download website for, 4
    implementation requirements for, 317
    installation for, 317–318, **317–318**

JavaDocs for, 104*t*, 319
    references and resources for, 371
JNI file, QSYSINC/QRPGLESRC,JNI file in, 110
JNI service program QJVAJNI, 121
JNI type signatures, 133, 133*t*
Johnson, Marc, 4

L
landscape orientation
    for Excel spreadsheet, 204–205, **205**,
      206–207, **206**
    for PDF doc, 273
%LEN, 64
libraries
    AIRLIB, 8
    RPG, vs. Java packages, 80
lists, in PDF doc, 286–289, **286**, **286–289**
loops, 230–231

M
main method, 83
Martin, Jim, 67
MAX and maximum values, 221–222, **221**
memory allocation,
    Java heaps in, 109
    RPG, 78
metadata (author, dates, etc.), in PDF, 262–266,
    262–266
methods, 14, 78
    accessing through RPG, 108, **108**
    conversion in, 108
    defining, 108
    identifying, in Java class, 132–133
    interface in, 96–100, **96–100**
    JavaBeans naming standards in, 86–87, **87**
    main, 83
    naming, 108
    overloading in, 94–95, **94**, **95**
    overriding in, 92–94, **92–93**
    private vs. public attribute in, 83–85
    prototyping, 108
    static, in Java, 82
    this keyword in, 87
    type signatures for, 133, 133*t*

Microsoft Excel. *See* Excel spreadsheets

Microsoft Office, Apache POI project and, 155–156, 156*t*

MIME format, 13

MIME messages, e-mail, 330–337, **339–337**

MimeMessage subclass, e-mail and, 339–344, **339–344**

minimum requirements for book's programming, 3–4

modern solutions, 11–18

modernization and the IBM i series, 1–2

modules and modular programming, 19, 23
    binding of, 19–20
    performance issues and, 19

MONITOR, 55–56

MOVE, free-format syntax and, 51

Multipurpose Internet Mail Extension (MIME), 345

N

naming conventions, 5–6, 36, 108
    activation groups and, 27–28
    camel case in Java and, 83
    Java, Java classes, 79, 83
    JavaBeans Naming Standards in, 84–87, **85–86, 87**
    packages, 79–80

*NEW option, activation groups and, 27

numbered lists. *See* lists, in PDF docs

O

Object class, 91

object constructors, 109, **109**

objects, 14, 78–79
    arrays of, 144–148, **144–148**

Office, Microsoft, Apache POI project and, 155–156, 156*t*

Oliver, Andrew, 4

opcodes
    APIs and vs., 68
    free-format RPG, 47–48, 47*t*

OPEN, free-format syntax and, 50

open source, 5–6, 16, 17

%OPEN, 55

operating system version, IBM i, 3

OPM, 11, 14
    converting existing code to ILE from, 20–21
    fixed-format programs in, 32–34, **32, 33, 34**
    ILE programming concepts vs., 31–42

ordered lists. *See* lists, in PDF docs

Original Program Model. *See* OPM

Outlook, Microsoft, Apache POI project and, 155–156, 156*t*

overloading, 94–95, **94, 95**

overriding, 92–94, **92–93**

P

packages, 79–81
    adding classes to, 80
    asterisk (*) and importing, 80–81
    naming, 79–80
    referencing, 80

Paragraph text object, PDF/iText, 252–253, **252, 253**

parameter passing, keywords for, 24–25

%PARMS, 64

password, e-mail, 320–321, 332

PDF docs, 1–2, 12, 13, 17, 243–313
    add new page to, 279, **279**
    adding elements to document in, 254, **254**
    anchors, for hyperlinks, 280–285, **280–285**
    bar codes in, 301–313, **302**
        characters above/below, 304, **305**
        guard bars in, 306–307, **306–307**, 311–312, **311–312**
        image creation from, 307–309, **307–309**
        object references for, 309–310, **309–310**
        supplemental digits in, 303–304, **303–304**
        types of, EAN, UPC, etc., 302, 305–306, **305–306**
    Chunk text object in, 250–251, **250–251**
    colors in, 268–271, **268–271**
    common code for, 245–246, **245**
    document and Document class in, 246–248, **246–248**
    fonts for, 271–274, **271–274**
    formatting for, 267–289, **267**
    Hello World application using, 260–261, **260–261**
    hyperlinks in, 279–285, **279, 280–285**

Hypertext Markup Language (HTML) and, 254, 257
images in, 291–301, **291**, **292–301**
    adding into document, 296–297, **296–297**
    align, 293, **293–294**
    border properties for, 294–295, **294–295**
    borders around, 291–297, **291**, **292–297**
    create, 292, **292–293**
    text wrapped around, 297–301, **298**, **299–301**
iText components for, 246–253
iText installation for, 243–244, **244**
JavaDocs for iText and, 246
landscape orientation for, 273
lists in, 286–289, **286**, **286–289**
metadata (author, dates, etc.) for, 262–266, **262–266**
open and close document in, 259–260, **259**, **260**
Paragraph text object in, 252–253, **252**, **253**
Phrase text object in, 251–252, **251–252**
rectangles and Rectangle class in, 247, 248–250, **247**, **248–250**, 258, **258**
Rich Text Format (RTF) and, 254, 257
saving file in, 254–260, **255–260**
SPAIRPDF for, 7, 245–246
tables in, 274–278, **274**, **275–278**
    cells added to, 275, **275**, 276, **276**, 278
    column number in, 277
    column widths in, 275–276, **276**, 278, **278**
    create, 275, **275**
text components in, 250–253
PERCOLATE, 55
performance issues, ILE, 19
PGM objects, compiling ILE source code into, 21–22
Phrase text object, PDF/iText, 251–252, **251–252**
POI, 17
    download website for, 4
    Excel spreadsheet creation using, 155–156, 156*t*. *See also* Excel
    installing, 156–157, **157**
    JavaDocs for, 104*t*, 159
    naming conventions for, 6
    references and resources for, 370
    version compatibility in, 157–158
pointers, 109

polymorphism, 90–91, **90–91**
Poor Obfuscation Implementation. *See* POI
popping a frame, 125, **125**
portability issues, 12–13
Portable Document File. *See* PDF
Postal Alpha Numeric Encoding Technique (PLANET). *See* bar codes
Postal Numeric Encoding Technique (POSTNET). *See* bar codes
PowerPoint, Microsoft, Apache POI project and, 155–156, 156*t*
primitive types, Java, 110–111, 110–111*t*, **111**
print and display property setting, Excel, 203–207, **203–207**
private attribute, 83–85
procedure interface, ILE, 25–26
procedures, 20, 23, 37–39, **37–38**
    APIs to create custom, 72–76, **72**, 73–**74**, **75**
    cohesion of, 39
    /COPY statement and, 23
    exporting, in service program, 30–31
    global variables in, 84
    interface for, 25–26
    Java methods vs., 78
    methods vs., 84
    parameter passing in, keywords for, 24–25
    subroutine converted to, 36–37, **36**
    syntax of, 25–26, **25**
Programming Development Manager (PDM), 100
PROMOTE, 55
protected access, 84
prototyping, 108
    Execute Command (QCMDEXC) API in, 25, 53–54, **54–55**
    free-format syntax and, 53–54, **54–55**
    ILE and, 23–24, **24**
PTF vs. manual updating, 112
public attribute, 83–85
Publisher, Microsoft, Apache POI project and, 155–156, 156*t*

Q

QCMDEXC (Execute Command) API, 25, 53–54, **54–55**
QDCXLATE (Convert Data) API, 69, 130

QJVAJNI service program, 106, 121
QJVAJNI64 service program, 106
QSYSINC/QRPGLESRC,JNI file in, 110
QtqlconvOpen() (Code Conversion Allocation)
   API, 69–71, **70**, 72–76, **72**, 73–**74**, **75**
quantification BIFs, 63–67, **64–67**

R

radixes, 269–270
Rational Developer for System i (RDi), 100
RCLACTGRP (Reclaim Activation Group), 28–29
READ, free-format syntax and, 49–50
READC, free-format syntax and, 50
READE, free-format syntax and, 50
reading an existing spreadsheet in, 230–235,
   230–235
READP, free-format syntax and, 50
READPE, free-format syntax and, 50
recalculating spreadsheet, forcing, 240–241
Reclaim Activation Group (RCLACTGRP), 28–29
records, 82
   ILE and, length/size of, 20
rectangles and Rectangle class, in PDF, 247,
   248–250, **247**, **248–250**, 258, **258**
reference variables, 78, 109
references and resources, 369–372
referencing
   accessing Java objects from within RPG,
      107, **107**
   external Jar files, 111–113
   pointers and, 109
Register a User Written Condition Handler
   (CEEHDLR) API in, 55
RESUME, 55
reusability of code, 5, 15
   cohesion and, 39
   ILE and, 19
Rich Text Format (RTF), 254, 257
Row, in Excel, 164–166, **164–166**, 175
   cells in, working with, 226–227, **226**, **227**
   working with, within Sheets, 224–226, **225**, **226**
RPG, 1–2, 5, 100
   accessing Java methods from within, 108, **108**
   accessing Java objects from within, 107, **107**
   advanced topics in. *See* advanced RPG

calling programs in, 78
class paths and, 82
classes in Java vs., 78
common code for e-mail/JavaMail in, 318,
   318–319
common code for Excel spreadsheets in,
   158–159
common code for PDF in, 245–246, **245**
developmental skills for, 14–15
end of file indicator and Java Iterator class
   with, 223
file definition in, 82
fixed-format programs of, in ILE, 34–36, **35**
fixed-format programs of, in OPM, 32–34,
   32, **33**, **34**
font and color program for Excel in,
   184–188, **185–188**
garbage collection in, 123–125, **123–125**
Hello World program, Java/RPG, 126–127, **126**
hyperlinks and TAG statement in, 282
images in e-mails and, 352–354, **352**, **352–353**
instances in, 82
Java and, 15–16, 105–127
Java instance variable access, code sample
   showing, 137–144, **137–144**
JNI concepts used by, example of, 135–137,
   135–136
libraries vs. Java packages, 80
memory allocation in, 78
naming conventions for, 6
primitive types in, 110–111, 110–111*t*, **111**
records and, 82
references and resources for, 369–370
reusable code, 15
serialization in, 121–123, **122**
synchronization in, vs. Java, 122
thread-safe, with THREAD(*SERIALIZE)
   in, 121–123, **122**

S

saving PDF file, 254–260, **255–260**
scope of variables in ILE, 20
Send method, e-mail and, 338–339, **338**, **339**
serialization, 121–123, **122**
service programs, 14, 29–31, 41–42, **41–42**, 84

AIR, 6–8, 7*t*
  combining, 8
  COPY files and, 8
  Create Service Program (CRTSRVPGM)
    and, 30
  downloading source code for, 8
  exporting procedures in, 30–31
  files used in, 41–42, **41–42**
  ILE and, 29–31
  INCLUDE statement and, 8
  naming conventions for, 6
  QJVAJNI in, JNI service program for, 121
  specs in, F and D, 50–51, **50–51**
  SVAIREMAIL, 7, 319
  SVAIREXCEL, 7, 159
  SVAIRFUNC, 7
  SVAIRJAVA, 7, 113
  SVAIRPDF, 7, 245–246
session creation for e-mail, 327–329, **327–329**, 329*t*
setCellFormula method for, 218–219, **218**, **219**
SETGT, free-format syntax and, 50
SETL, free-format syntax and, 50
SETLL, free-format syntax and, 49
Sheet, in Excel, 162–164, **162–164**, 175
  indexes for, 223–224, **224**
  rows within, working with, 224–226, **225**, **226**
Simple Mail Transfer Protocol (SMTP), 345
%SIZE, 64
source code
  AIRSRC for, 8
  compiling examples from book, 8–9, **9**
  downloads for, 8
  naming conventions for, 6
  OPM to ILE conversion, 20–21
SPAIREMAIL, 319
SPAIREXCEL, 158, 159
SPAIRFUNC, 158
SPAIRJAVA, 158
SPAIRPDF, 245–246
specs
  compiler directives and, 46
  service program use of, F and D, 50–51, **50–51**
spreadsheets. *See* Excel spreadsheets
SQL, 5
  compiler directives and, 43–46, 44*t*

COPY files and, 4
  embedded, pre-V6R1 support for, 4
Stampoultzis, Len, 4
standard extensions, 111
standardization, 5, 13
static methods, 82
%STATUS, 55
STDERR, 116–118
STDIN, 116–118
STDOUT, 116–118
string manipulation BIFs, 56–61
  external file processing with, 57–61, **58–59**
subpackages, Java, 80–81
subroutines, 14
  BEGSR and, 50–51, **50–51**
  copy/COPY statement and, 23
  ENDSR and, 50–51, **50–51**
  exception handling and, 56
  free-format syntax and, 50–51, **50–51**
  MOVE in, 51
  procedures and, converting to, 36–37, **36**
  variables in, 84
%substr string manipulation BIF, 57, 60
SUM, 220–221, **221**
Sun Microsystems, 16
  naming conventions for, 6
SVAIREMAIL, 7, 319
SVAIREXCEL, 7, 159
SVAIRFUNC, 7
SVAIRJAVA, 7, 113
SVAIRPDF, 7, 245–246
synchronization, 122
syntax of procedures in ILE, 25–26, **25**
System Openness Includes (QSYSINC) library, 3

T

tables, in PDF doc, 274–278, **274**, **275–278**
  cells added to, 275, **275**, 276, **276**, 278
  column number in, 277
  column widths in, 275–276, **276**, 278, **278**
  create, 275, **275**
TAG statement, vs. anchors for hyperlinks, 282
templates, for Excel spreadsheets, 235–237, **236**, **237**
text components in PDF/iText, 250–253, 250

NOTE: Boldface numbers indicate code and illustrations; *t* indicates a table.

text wrap, 199–203, **199–203**, 297–301, **298,
298,
299–301**
this keyword, 87
THREAD(*SERIALIZE) in, 121–123, **122**
thread-safe RPG, THREAD(*SERIALIZE) in,
121–123, **122**
throwing exceptions, 149–153, **149–153**
totals and SUM, 220–221, **221**
translation tables, ASCII/EBCDIC/Hex, 363*t*,
364*t*, 365*t*
Transport class, e-mail and, 337–338, **337, 338**
%trimL string manipulation BIF, 56, 60
%trim string manipulation BIF, 56, 60
%trimR string manipulation BIF, 56, 60
try/catch exception monitoring, 55–56
type signatures, JNI, 133, 133*t*

U
/UNDEFINE compiler directive, 43
Unicode character set, 130
Universal Product Code (UPC) bar code. *See*
bar codes
Unix, bit operations and, 61
unordered lists. *See* lists, in PDF docs
Unregister a User Written Condition Handler
(CEEHDLU) API in, 55
unsigned integer bytes and ranges, bit
operations, 62, **62**
UPC bar code. *See* bar codes
updating, manual vs. PTF, 112
usability of solutions, 13
user name, e-mail, 320–321, 332
UTF-8/16/32 character sets, 69

V
variables, 14, 20

accessing Java objects from within RPG,
107, **107**
compiler directives and, 46
global, 84
ILE and, 20
Java and, 84–87, **85–86, 87**
primitive types as, 110–111, 110–111*t*, **111**
private vs. public, 83–85
reference, 78, 109
RPG code sample to access Java instance,
137–144, **137–144**
scope of, 20
serialization and, 121–123, **122**
version
IBM i operating systems, 3
Java, 105–106, **106**
Visio, Microsoft, Apache POI project and,
155–156, 156*t*
Visual Basic for Applications (VBA), 240–241

W
websites for downloads, 4
WebSphere Development Studio (WDSC), 100
Word, Microsoft, Apache POI project and,
155–156, 156*t*
Workbooks, in Excel, 161–162, **161–162**, 175
FileOutputStream for, 172–173, **173**
saving, 171–173, **171–173**
sheet indexes for, 223–224, **224**
WRITE, free-format syntax and, 50

X
%xlate string manipulation BIF, 57, 60, 61

Z
zoom, Excel, 204, 206–207